Rowsher Nevzoee (signature)

International Human Rights

Dilemmas in World Politics

Dilemmas in World Politics offers teachers and students in international relations a series of quality books on critical issues, trends, and regions in international politics. Each text examines a "real world" dilemma and is structured to cover the historical, theoretical, practical, and projected dimensions of its subject.

BOOKS IN THIS SERIES

International Human Rights, Third Edition
Jack Donnelly

The United Nations in the Twenty-first Century, Third Edition
Karen A. Mingst and Margaret P. Karns

Global Environmental Politics, Fourth Edition
Pamela S. Chasek, David L. Downie, and Janet Welsh Brown

Southern Africa in World Politics
Janice Love

Ethnic Conflict in World Politics, Second Edition
Barbara Harff and Ted Robert Gurr

Dilemmas of International Trade, Second Edition
Bruce E. Moon

Humanitarian Challenges and Intervention, Second Edition
Thomas G. Weiss and Cindy Collins

The European Union: Dilemmas of Regional Integration
James A. Caporaso

Global Gender Issues, Second Edition
Spike Peterson and Anne Sisson Runyon

Democracy and Democratization in a Changing World, Second Edition
Georg Sørensen

Revolution and Transition in East-Central Europe, Second Edition
David S. Mason

One Land, Two Peoples, Second Edition
Deborah Gerner

Dilemmas of Development Assistance
Sarah J. Tisch and Michael B. Wallace

East Asian Dynamism, Second Edition
Steven Chan

International Human Rights

THIRD EDITION

JACK DONNELLY
University of Denver

A Member of the Perseus Books Group

Dilemmas in World Politics

Find us on the World Wide Web at www.westviewpress.com.

Westview Press books are available at special discounts for bulk purchases in the United States by corporations, institutions, and other organizations. For more information, please contact the Special Markets Department at the Perseus Books Group, 11 Cambridge Center, Cambridge MA 02142, or call (617) 252-5298 or (800) 255-1514, or e-mail special.markets@perseusbooks.com.

Library of Congress Cataloging-in-Publication Data

Donnelly, Jack.
International human rights / Jack Donnelly.—3rd ed.
    p. cm.—(Dilemmas in world politics)
Includes bibliographical references and index.

ISBN-13: 978-0-8133-4326-6 (paperback : alk. paper)
ISBN-10: 0-8133-4326-7 (paperback : alk. paper)

1. Human rights. I. Title. II. Series.

JC571.D753 2007
341.4'8—dc22

                                                                    2006015002

    09 / 10 9 8 7

Contents

Tables, Figures, and Boxes

Acknowledgments

I began working on the first edition of this book fifteen years ago. Over that time, I have had the help of literally dozens of friends, colleagues, students, research assistants, and editors. Any list would be both too long, losing the individuals in a stream of names, and too short, for I am sure that I would neglect mentioning at least a few people who contributed to the book. Thus, let me simply say: Thanks to all of you. (You know who you are.)

I cannot, however, skip mentioning one special debt. My wife Katy has caused this third edition to be done at least a year or two later than it should have been. For that, and so much else, I thank her.

Denver, Colorado
February 2006

Acronyms

AI	Amnesty International
ANC	African National Congress
AOHR	Arab Organization for Human Rights
APDH	Permanent Assembly for Human Rights
ARENA	National Republican Alliance
ASEAN	Association of Southeast Asian Nations
CADHU	Argentine Human Rights Commission
CAT	Committee Against Torture
CCP	Chinese Communist Party
CEDAW	Committee on the Elimination of Discrimination Against Women
CELS	Center for Legal and Social Studies
CESCR	Committee on Economic, Social, and Cultural Rights
COMADRES	Committee of Mothers of Political Prisoners, Disappeared, and Assassinated in El Salvador
CONADEP	Argentine National Commission on Disappeared Persons, the Sabato Commission
COPACHI	Committee of Cooperation for Peace
CRC	Committee on the Rights of the Child
CSCE	Conference on Security and Co-operation in Europe
CVR	Commission for Truth and Reconciliation, the Rettig Commission
ECOSOC	Economic and Social Council
ERP	Revolutionary Army of the People
ESMA	Navy Mechanics School
EU	European Union
EUFOR	European Union Force
FEDEFAM	Federation of Families of Disappeared Persons and Political Prisoners

FSLN	Sandinista National Liberation Front
G7	Group of Seven
GA	UN General Assembly
HRC	Human Rights Committee
IACHR	Inter-American Commission of Human Rights
IFOR	Implementation Force
INTERFET	International Force for East Timor
MNCs	Multinational Corporations
NAACP	National Association for the Advancement of Colored People
NGOs	Non-governmental Organizations
NSM 39	National Security Memorandum 39
OAU	Organization of African Unity
OECD	Organisation for Economic Co-operation and Development
OSCE	Organization for Security and Co-operation in Europe
SERPAJ	Service for Peace and Justice
SFOR	Stabilization Force
UNAMIR	United Nations Assistance Mission in Rwanda
UNPAs	United Nations Protected Areas
UNTAET	United Nations Transitional Administration in East Timor

International Human Rights

Introduction

A Note to the Reader

This is a book about the international relations of human rights since the end of World War II; that is, the ways in which states and other international actors have addressed human rights. Although the topic is broad in scope, it is narrower than some readers might expect.

Life, liberty, security, subsistence, and other things to which we have human rights may be denied by an extensive array of individuals and organizations. "Human rights," however, are usually taken to have a special reference to the ways in which states treat their own citizens. For example, domestically, we distinguish muggings and private assaults, which are not typically considered human rights violations, from police brutality and torture, which are. Internationally, we distinguish terrorism, war, and war crimes from human rights abuses, even though they both lead to denials of life and security. Although the boundaries are not always entirely clear— for example, disappearances became an important form of human rights abuse in the 1970s (see Chapter 4) when perpetrators attempted to obscure the nature of their actions by operating at the boundary between private violence (murder) and state terrorism—the distinction is part of our ordinary language and focuses our attention on an important set of political problems.

No single book can cover all aspects of the politics of human rights. My concern is international human rights policies, a vital and now well-established area of policy and inquiry. This does not imply that international action is the principal determinant of whether human rights are respected or violated. In fact, much of the book demonstrates the limits of international action.

Nonetheless, one of this book's distinctive features, as opposed to most other discussions of international human rights, is its substantial attention to the domestic politics of human rights. Chapter 4 provides a relatively detailed look at human rights violations in the Southern Cone of South America. In addition, briefer domestic case studies of South Africa, Central America, China, and the former Yugoslavia appear in later chapters.

Another distinctive feature of this book, along with the other volumes in the Dilemmas in World Politics series, is a relatively extensive emphasis on theory. Chapter 2 addresses philosophical issues of the nature, substance, and source of human rights; the place of human rights in the contemporary international society of states; and the theoretical challenges posed to the very enterprise of international human rights policy by arguments of radical cultural relativism and political realism (Realpolitik, or "power politics"). Chapter 3 explores the important theoretical issue of the universality (and relativity) of human rights. Like the domestic case studies, this discussion may appear to be more than is strictly necessary in a book on international human rights. Both the case studies and the theory, however, provide important background, context, and insights. I encourage readers at least to look them over, even—perhaps especially—if at the outset those issues do not seem central to their own concerns.

I have tried to write a book that assumes little or no background knowledge. Most readers with an interest in the topic, regardless of age or experience, should find this book accessible. However, I have tried not to write a textbook, a term that has justly acquired pejorative overtones. I have also taken care not to write "down," either in style or in substance. Furthermore, although I have made an effort to retain some balance in the discussion, I have not expunged my own views and interpretations.

Textbook presentations of controversial issues—when they are not entirely avoided—tend to involve bland and noncommittal presentations of "the two sides" to an argument. By contrast, I often lay out and defend one interpretation and give less (or even scant) attention to alternative views. I have made great efforts to be accurate and fair, but there is no false pretense of "objectivity."

I thus draw the reader's attention to the Discussion Questions for each chapter. There is almost a short chapter's worth of material in these questions, which often frame alternative interpretations and highlight controversial claims in the main body of the text. These are an integral part of the book and provide at least a partial corrective to any "imbalance" in the main text.

Unlike many authors of introductory books, I have not set out with the principal goal of providing information—although there is a lot of straightforward factual information for the reader to absorb. Neither do I aim to convey the received wisdom on the subject—although this book does provide an overview of the kinds of issues typically addressed, and some important perspectives that have been commonly adopted, in the study of international human rights. Rather, I hope to get you to think about why and how human rights are violated, what can (and cannot) be done about such violations through international action, why human rights remain such a small part of international relations, and what might be done about that. These are pressing political issues that merit, even demand, thought and attention.

1

Human Rights as an Issue in World Politics

Before World War II, human rights were systematically violated but rarely discussed in international politics. Racial discrimination permeated the United States. The Soviet Union was a totalitarian secret-police state. Britain, France, the Netherlands, Portugal, Belgium, the United States, and Spain maintained colonial empires in Africa, Asia, and the Caribbean. The political history of most Central and South American countries was largely a succession of military dictatorships and civilian oligarchies. Although such phenomena troubled many people, they were not considered a legitimate subject for international action. Rather, human rights were viewed as an internal (domestic) political matter, an internationally protected exercise of the sovereign rights of states. Even genocidal massacres, such as Russian pogroms against the Jews or the Turkish slaughter of Armenians, drew little more than anguished statements of disapproval.

As we will see in more detail in Chapter 2, international relations have for the past three centuries been organized around the principle of sovereignty. States, the principal actors in international relations, are seen as **sovereign**, that is, subject to no higher political authority. The principal duty correlative to the right of sovereignty is **nonintervention**, the obligation not to interfere in matters essentially within the domestic jurisdiction of sovereign states. Human rights, which typically involve a state's treatment of its own citizens in its own territory, were traditionally seen as such a matter of protected domestic jurisdiction. One purpose of this book is to chronicle a fundamental change in this dominant international understanding of the range of state sovereignty over the past sixty years.

In the nineteenth and early twentieth centuries, the European Great Powers and the United States did occasionally intervene in the Ottoman and Chinese empires to rescue nationals caught in situations of civil strife and to establish or protect special rights and privileges for Christians, Europeans, and Americans. Virtually never did they intervene to protect foreign nationals from their own government.

3

In fact, human rights were seldom even a topic of diplomatic discussion. Likewise, the "humanitarian law" of war, expressed in documents such as the 1907 Hague Conventions, limited only what a state could do to foreign nationals, not what it could do to its own nationals (or peoples over whom it exercised colonial rule).

The principal exception was the international campaign against slavery. The major powers at the Congress of Vienna in 1815 recognized an obligation to abolish the slave trade, which was finally banned by treaty in 1890. But a treaty to abolish slavery, not just the international trade in slaves, was not even drafted until 1926.

Other exceptions came after World War I. The International Labor Organization (ILO) dealt with some workers' rights issues, and the League of Nations had limited powers to protect ethnic minorities in selected areas.[1] Generally, though, prior to World War II, human rights were not an accepted subject of international relations. In assessing current international human rights activity, we must keep in mind this starting point.

1. THE EMERGENCE OF INTERNATIONAL HUMAN RIGHTS NORMS

A dramatic event that crystallizes awareness often is crucial to making a problem an active subject of international concern and action. For example, the discovery of the Antarctic ozone hole in 1985 contributed significantly to the development of international environmental action in general and led to the 1987 Montreal Protocol on Substances that Deplete the Ozone Layer. The catalyst that made human rights an issue in world politics was the Holocaust, the systematic mass murder of millions of innocent civilians by Germany during World War II.

The response of the Allies was shameful. Before the war, little was done to aid Jews trying to flee Germany and the surrounding countries. Some who escaped were even denied refuge by Allied governments, including the United States. During the war, no effort was made to impede the functioning of the death camps. The Allies did not even target the railway lines that brought hundreds of thousands to the slaughter at Auschwitz and other death camps. The world watched—or, rather, turned a blind eye to—the genocidal massacre of six million Jews, half a million Gypsies (Roma), and tens of thousands of communists, social democrats, homosexuals, church activists, and just ordinary decent people who refused complicity in the new politics and technology of barbarism.

As the war came to an end, Allied leaders and citizens, previously preoccupied with military victory, began to confront this horror. However, as the world faced the Holocaust, it found itself armed only with moral outrage. Shocking as the Nazi atrocities were, the international community lacked the legal and political language to condemn them.

Massacring one's own citizens simply was not an established international legal offense. The German government may have been liable under the laws of war for its treatment of citizens in occupied territories, but in killing German nationals it was merely exercising its sovereign rights. Traditional "**realist**" diplomacy, which defined

---

BOX 1.1   Treaties as a Source of International Law

Lawmaking treaties such as the 1948 Genocide Convention and the 1966 International Human Rights Covenants typically are drafted by an international organization or conference and then presented to states for their consideration—or, as international lawyers put it, they are "opened for signature and ratification." Neither the drafting of a treaty nor its approval by the United Nations or another international organization gives it legal effect. For a treaty to be binding, it must be accepted by sovereign states. And it is binding only on those states that have formally and voluntarily accepted it.

Signing a treaty is a declaration by a state that it intends to be bound by the treaty. That obligation, however, only becomes effective after the treaty has been *ratified* or acceded to according to the constitutional procedures of that country. (In the United States, the president signs a treaty and then transmits it to the Senate for ratification, for which a two-thirds vote is required.) States that have ratified or acceded to a treaty are said to be *parties* to the treaty. Typically a specified number of states must become parties before the treaty becomes binding. When sufficient ratifications have been filed, the treaty is said to enter into force.

---

the national interest in terms of state power (see also §2.8), could find no national interest that was threatened by the barbarous treatment of foreign civilians.

The Nuremberg War Crimes Trials (1945–1946) introduced the novel charge of crimes against humanity. For the first time, officials were held legally accountable to the international community for offenses against individual citizens, not states, and individuals who in many cases were nationals, not foreigners.

Human rights really emerged as a subject of international relations, though, in the United Nations (UN), created in 1945. The Covenant of the League of Nations, the predecessor of the UN, had not even mentioned human rights. In sharp contrast, the Preamble of the UN Charter includes a determination "to reaffirm faith in fundamental human rights" and Article 1 lists "encouraging respect for human rights and for fundamental freedoms for all" as one of the organization's principal purposes.

The United Nations moved quickly to elaborate international human rights standards. On December 9, 1948, the Convention on the Prevention and Punishment of the Crime of Genocide was opened for signature (see Box 1.1). The following day, the UN General Assembly (GA) adopted without dissent the **Universal Declaration of Human Rights,**[2] which even today provides the most authoritative statement of international human rights norms. This vital document is reprinted in the Appendix. Its main provisions are summarized in Table 1.1.

2. FROM COLD WAR TO COVENANTS

Although human rights continued to be discussed at the United Nations after the adoption of the Universal Declaration, the rise of the **cold war**, the ideological and geopolitical struggle between the United States and the Soviet Union, brought this initial progress to a halt. After the Iron Curtain descended in Central and Eastern Europe in 1948 and the victory of the communists in China in 1949, human rights increasingly became just another arena of superpower struggle. For example, in the late 1950s the Commission on Human Rights, under Western control, extensively discussed freedom of information (a right that the Soviets systematically violated) but ignored not only all economic and social rights but most other civil and political rights as well. Conversely, the Soviets tried to focus attention on racial discrimination and unemployment in the capitalist West. Although each side pointed to real abuses, charges of human rights violations were largely tactical maneuvers in a broader political and ideological struggle.

The foreign policies of both superpowers regularly and flagrantly disregarded human rights. The United States was willing to accept the most vicious human rights practices in "friendly" anticommunist regimes. For example, in Guatemala in 1954 the United States overthrew the freely elected government of Jacobo Arbenz Guzmán, in part because of its redistributive policies that aimed to better implement economic and social rights. This ushered in thirty years of military rule that culminated in the systematic massacre of tens of thousands in the early 1980s. Elsewhere as well, the United States not only tolerated gross and systematic violations of human rights in "friendly" (anticommunist) countries but warmly embraced the responsible regimes. The Soviet Union likewise was ready to use force when necessary to sustain "friendly" totalitarian regimes in its sphere of influence. For example, Soviet tanks rolled into Hungary in 1956 to put an end to liberal political reforms and reimpose totalitarian dictatorship.

The cold war also derailed further elaboration of international human rights standards. The Universal Declaration of Human Rights is a resolution of the UN General Assembly, not a treaty. Thus it is not, per se, legally binding (see Box 1.2). A draft covenant to give human rights binding force in international law was largely completed by 1953 but was tabled for more than a decade, a hostage to East-West ideological rivalry.

Progress again began to be made in the early 1960s, in part as a result of effective UN human rights activity on behalf of self-determination and decolonization. When the United Nations was founded in 1945, most of Africa and Asia were under Western colonial rule. The process of decolonization that began in 1947 with the independence of Indonesia and India accelerated dramatically in Africa in the late 1950s—in 1956, the Gold Coast became the first black African country to gain independence, as Ghana—and the 1960s. UN membership doubled in less than a decade, and by the mid-1960s, Afro-Asian states formed the largest voting bloc in the UN.

These newly independent countries had a special interest in human rights. They found a sympathetic hearing from some Western European and Latin American countries. The UN thus began to reemphasize human rights. In 1965, the International Convention on the Elimination of All Forms of Racial Discrimination was opened for signature and ratification. In December 1966, the **International Human Rights Covenants** were finally completed. (The single treaty envisioned in 1948

TABLE 1.1   Internationally Recognized Human Rights
_____

The International Bill of Human Rights recognizes the rights to:
  Equality of rights without discrimination (D1, D2, E2, E3, C2, C3)
  Life (D3, C6)
  Liberty and security of person (D3, C9)
  Protection against slavery (D4, C8)
  Protection against torture and cruel and inhuman punishment (D5, C7)
  Recognition as a person before the law (D6, C16)
  Equal protection of the law (D7, C14, C26)
  Access to legal remedies for rights violations (D8, C2)
  Protection against arbitrary arrest or detention (D9, C9)
  Hearing before an independent and impartial judiciary (D10, C14)
  Presumption of innocence (D11, C14)
  Protection against ex post facto laws (D11, C15)
  Protection of privacy, family, and home (D12, C17)
  Freedom of movement and residence (D13, C12)
  Seek asylum from persecution (D14)
  Nationality (D15)
  Marry and found a family (D16, E10, C23)
  Own property (D17)
  Freedom of thought, conscience, and religion (D18, C18)
  Freedom of opinion, expression, and the press (D19, C19)
  Freedom of assembly and association (D20, C21, C22)
  Political participation (D21, C25)
  Social security (D22, E9)
  Work, under favorable conditions (D23, E6, E7)
  Free trade unions (D23, E8, C22)
  Rest and leisure (D24, E7)
  Food, clothing, and housing (D25, E11)
  Health care and social services (D25, E12)
  Special protections for children (D25, E10, C24)
  Education (D26, E13, E14)
  Participation in cultural life (D27, E15)
  A social and international order needed to realize rights (D28)
  Self-determination (E1, C1)
  Humane treatment when detained or imprisoned (C10)
  Protection against debtor's prison (C11)
  Protection against arbitrary expulsion of aliens (C13)
  Protection against advocacy of racial or religious hatred (C20)
  Protection of minority culture (C27)
_____

Note: This list includes all rights that are enumerated in two of the three documents of the International Bill of Human Rights or have a full article in one document. The source of each right is indicated in parentheses, by document and article number. D = Universal Declaration of Human Rights. E = International Covenant on Economic, Social, and Cultural Rights. C = International Covenant on Civil and Political Rights.

evolved into two: the International Covenant on Economic, Social, and Cultural Rights and the International Covenant on Civil and Political Rights.)

The Covenants, together with the Universal Declaration, represent an authoritative statement of international human rights norms. These three documents, which (along with the human rights provisions of the UN Charter) are often referred to collectively as the International Bill of Human Rights, present a summary statement of the minimum social and political guarantees recognized by the international community as necessary for a life of dignity in the contemporary world. They are summarized in Table 1.1.

3. THE 1970S: FROM STANDARD SETTING TO MONITORING

The very comprehensiveness of the International Human Rights Covenants, however, meant that further progress on international human rights would now depend primarily on implementing these standards—an area in which the United Nations had been, and still is, far less successful. The existence of international norms does not in itself give the United Nations, or anyone else, the authority to implement them, or even to inquire into how states implement (or do not implement) them. By ratifying the covenants, states agree to follow international human rights standards. As we will see in more detail in Chapter 5, however, they do not authorize international enforcement of these standards.

The late 1960s saw a flurry of international monitoring initiatives. In 1967, Economic and Social Council Resolution 1235 authorized the Commission on Human Rights to discuss human rights violations in particular countries. In 1968, a Special Committee of Investigation was created to consider human rights in the territories occupied by Israel after the 1967 war. In the same year, the UN Security Council imposed a mandatory blockade on the white minority regime in Southern Rhodesia. The 1965 racial discrimination convention, which requires parties to file periodic reports on implementation, came into force in 1969. In 1970, Economic and Social Council Resolution 1503 authorized the Commission on Human Rights to conduct confidential investigations of complaints that suggested "a consistent pattern of gross and reliably attested violations of human rights and fundamental freedoms." Although all of these efforts were limited and largely symbolic, the UN was at last beginning to move, however tentatively, from merely setting standards to examining how those standards were implemented by states.

The United Nations operates under severe structural constraints. It is an **intergovernmental organization**, established by a multilateral treaty (the UN Charter) among sovereign states. Its members are sovereign states, and delegates to the United Nations represent states, not the international community, let alone individuals whose rights are violated. Like other intergovernmental organizations, the UN has only those powers that states—which are also the principal violators of human rights—give it. Thus, perhaps more surprising than the limits on its human rights monitoring powers is the fact that the UN actually acquired even these limited pow-

BOX 1.2   Sources of International Law

The two main sources of international law are treaties and custom. Other sources—for example, the writings of publicists, general principles of law recognized in the domestic law of most states, national and international judicial decisions, or *jus cogens* (overriding international norms, very much like the classical idea of the natural law)—are either of lesser importance or their status is a matter of controversy.

Treaties are essentially contractual agreements of states to accept certain specified obligations. The process by which treaties become binding is briefly discussed in Box 1.1.

Customary rules of international law are well-established state practices to which a sense of obligation has come to be attached. One classic example often used in teaching international law in the United States is the case of *The Scotia*. The U.S. Supreme Court decided in 1871 that it had become a binding customary practice of the international law of the sea that ships show colored running lights in a pattern originally specified by Great Britain, and the Court awarded damages on the basis of this unwritten, customary law. In the area of human rights, a U.S. District Court held in the 1980 case of *Filartiga v. Peña-Irala,* brought by the family of a Paraguayan torture victim, that torture was a violation of customary international law.

Some lawyers have argued that the Universal Declaration of Human Rights has, over time, become a part of customary international law, or at least strong evidence of custom. Even if this is true, the Universal Declaration per se does not establish international legal obligations. That task was reserved by its drafters for a later treaty, which was ultimately adopted by the UN General Assembly in 1966, and entered into force in 1976.

ers. Although it is little comfort to victims, a balanced assessment of the human rights achievements of the UN and other intergovernmental organizations cannot ignore the limits imposed by state sovereignty.

Modest monitoring progress continued in the 1970s. In response to the 1973 military coup in Chile (see Chapter 4), the UN created an Ad Hoc Working Group on the Situation of Human Rights in Chile. In 1976, the International Human Rights Covenants entered into force, leading to the creation of the **Human Rights Committee** (HRC), which is charged with monitoring implementation of the International Covenant on Civil and Political Rights (see §5.3.A).

Human rights were explicitly introduced into the bilateral foreign policies of individual countries in the 1970s, beginning in the United States. In 1973, Congress recommended, and in 1975 required, U.S. foreign aid policy to take into account (although not be determined by) the human rights practices of recipient countries. Such legislation was both nationally and internationally unprecedented. When

Jimmy Carter became president in 1977, the executive branch also became generally supportive of pursuing human rights in foreign policy. Although practice regularly fell short of rhetoric, these American initiatives helped to open space for new ways of thinking about and acting on international human rights concerns (see Chapter 5).

The 1970s also saw substantial growth in the number and range of activities of human rights **nongovernmental organizations** (NGOs), private associations that engage in political activity. Such groups act as advocates for victims of human rights violations by publicizing violations and lobbying to alter the practices of states and international organizations.

Best known is Amnesty International (AI), which was founded in 1961, received the Nobel Peace Prize in 1977, and has an international membership of more than a million people. AI's best-known activity is writing letters on behalf of individual prisoners of conscience, incarcerated for their beliefs or nonviolent political activities. In its first thirty years, it investigated and publicized the cases of more than 42,000 prisoners. Amnesty International also publishes an annual report, special reports on individual countries, and occasional reports on torture and other general issues of concern. In addition, its representatives testify before national legislatures and intergovernmental organizations and publicize human rights issues through public statements and appearances in the media (see also §6.10).

4. THE 1980S: FURTHER GROWTH AND INSTITUTIONALIZATION

Multilateral, bilateral, and nongovernmental human rights activity continued to increase, more or less steadily, through the 1980s. Particularly impressive was the substantial further development of international human rights norms. In December 1979, the Convention on the Elimination of Discrimination Against Women was opened for signature and ratification. The Convention Against Torture and Other Cruel, Inhuman, or Degrading Treatment or Punishment was completed in 1984. The General Assembly adopted the Declaration on the Right to Development in 1986. The decade came to a close with the Convention on the Rights of the Child in November 1989.

In the area of monitoring, the Human Rights Committee began to review periodic reports submitted under the International Covenant on Civil and Political Rights. The Committee on Economic, Social, and Cultural Rights was established in 1985 to improve reporting and monitoring in this important area (see §5.3.A). The Commission on Human Rights undertook "thematic" initiatives on disappearances, torture, and summary or arbitrary executions. Furthermore, a larger and more diverse group of countries came under commission scrutiny (see §5.1).

The process of incorporating human rights into bilateral foreign policy also accelerated in the 1980s. The Netherlands and Norway have had particularly prominent international human rights policies (see §6.5). Both the Council of Europe and the European Community (EC; now the European Union [EU]) introduced human rights concerns into their external relations. A few Third World countries, such as Costa Rica, have also emphasized human rights in their foreign policies.

Perhaps more surprising was the persistence of the issue of human rights in U.S. foreign policy. Ronald Reagan campaigned for the presidency in 1980 against President Carter's human rights policy. His revival of the cold war against the Soviet "evil empire" led many people to fear (or hope) that human rights would again be forced to the sidelines. Although U.S. international human rights policy did become less evenhanded in the 1980s, when George H. W. Bush took office in 1989 human rights had a secure (although hardly uncontroversial) and well-institutionalized place in American foreign policy. Regular, continuing action on behalf of international human rights had bipartisan support in Congress, and the Bureau of Human Rights and Humanitarian Affairs was increasingly seen as an integral part of the State Department rather than as an unwanted intrusion.

The 1980s also saw a dramatic decline in the fortunes of repressive dictatorships. Throughout Latin America, military regimes that had appeared unshakable in the 1970s crumbled in the 1980s (see §4.5). By 1990, elected governments held office in every continental country in the Western Hemisphere (although the democratic credentials of some, such as Paraguay, were extremely suspect). In addition, there were peaceful transfers of power after elections in several countries in 1989, including Argentina, Brazil, El Salvador, and Uruguay.

In Asia, the personalist dictatorship of Ferdinand Marcos was overthrown in the Philippines in 1986. South Korea's military dictatorship was replaced by an elected government in 1988. Taiwan ended four decades of imposed single-party rule. In Pakistan, Benazir Bhutto was elected president in December 1988, ending a dozen years of military rule. Asia, however, also presented the most dramatic human rights setback of the decade—the June 1989 massacre in Beijing's Tiananmen Square (see Chapter 7).

The changes with the greatest international impact, however, occurred in Central and Eastern Europe. Soviet-imposed regimes in East Germany and Czechoslovakia crumbled in the fall of 1989 in the face of peaceful mass protests. In Hungary and Poland, where liberalization had begun earlier in the decade, Communist Party dictatorships also peacefully withdrew from power. Even Romania and Bulgaria ousted their old communist governments (although their new governments included numerous former communists with tenuous democratic credentials). In the USSR, where *glasnost* (openness) and *perestroika* (restructuring) had created the international political space for these changes, the Communist Party fell from power after the abortive military coup of August 1991, and the Soviet Union was dissolved four months later.

5. THE 1990S (I): CONSOLIDATING PROGRESS

With the collapse of the Soviet empire, the cold war international order crumbled. Although this certainly altered the context for international human rights, the "new world order" triumphantly proclaimed by American President George H. W. Bush has proved not entirely new and often rather disorderly. Although the 1990s saw gradual, but generally positive, change in most regions, there were also striking examples of the most retrograde barbarism (see Chapter 8).

In Latin America and Central and Eastern Europe, the progress of the 1980s was largely maintained. In many cases, such as El Salvador and Hungary, liberalization has substantially deepened. In a few countries, such as the Czech Republic, Argentina, and Mexico, something close to full democratization seems to have been achieved. In most of the former Soviet republics, however, the commitment to and understanding of both democracy and human rights of the countries' elected leaders (and most of their opponents) even today is hardly inspiring. In several Latin American countries as well, such as Guatemala and Paraguay, elected governments provide a sort of liberalized, semiauthoritarian rule.

In Sub-Saharan Africa, where one-party and no-party states remained the norm throughout the 1980s, political liberalization was widespread in the 1990s. Progress has been less consistent, and usually less deep, than in much of Latin America. Nonetheless, relatively open multiparty elections became common and by the end of the millennium even standard. In March 1991, Benin's Nicéphore Soglo became the first candidate in the history of mainland Africa to defeat an incumbent president in a democratic election. Even more dramatic was the November 1991 defeat of Kenneth Kaunda, Zambia's president for the first twenty-five years of its independence. The end of apartheid in South Africa, which held its first elections under the principle of universal suffrage in 1994, was a dramatic change indeed.

But in Nigeria, Africa's most populous country, the military annulled the results of elections in 1992 and 1993, and General Sani Abacha exercised particularly harsh military rule over the country from 1993 until his death in 1998. And the regime of Olusegun Obasanjo, although (more or less freely) elected in 1999 and 2003, remains incredibly corrupt. Zaire emerged from four decades of suffering under the personalist dictatorship of Mobutu Sese Seko only to collapse into chaotic violence. Liberia's fourteen-year civil war killed more than 200,000 out of a population of about 3 million and turned a full third of the population into refugees. Genocide in Rwanda killed over three-quarters of a million. More generally, most African countries had mediocre or worse records on internationally recognized civil and political rights and experienced a second decade of stagnation or decline in the enjoyment of economic, social, and cultural rights.

In Asia, the picture in the 1990s was also mixed but more generally positive. South Korea and Taiwan consolidated democratic, rights-protective regimes. Cambodia, with a substantial assist from the United Nations, cast off Vietnamese occupation and freely elected a government that was by far the most liberal it had seen in decades. Tentative and partial liberalization has occurred in Vietnam. Indonesia saw limited political reform with the expulsion of the Suharto regime in 1998. And India, for all its problems, remained the world's largest multiparty electoral democracy.

China, however, despite its substantial economic opening and political reform, remained a highly repressive, Stalinist party state. Burma continued to repress its internal democracy movement and rebuff international pressures for liberalization. Pakistan and Afghanistan were racked by ethnic and religious violence, and Afghanistan suffered under the theocratic brutality of Taliban rule from 1996 to 2001. North Korea consolidated its position as the world's most closed and politically backward state. And many Asian governments and elites began to argue that international human rights standards did not apply in their entirety in Asia (see §7.5).

The mixed pictures in Africa and Asia are, sadly, far more encouraging than those in the Middle East. Hafiz al-Assad, Saddam Hussein, and Muammar Qaddafi sustained their personalist dictatorships in Syria, Iraq, and Libya. Religious intolerance and the suppression of all dissent remained the norm in Iran, although some modest social liberalization occurred at the end of the decade. The Gulf States remained as closed and undemocratic as ever. Increasingly violent Islamic fundamentalist movements led to growing repression in Egypt and plunged Algeria into shockingly brutal civil war. The new Palestinian entity, run by Yasir Arafat's Palestine Liberation Organization (PLO), showed little more concern for human rights than the former Israeli occupiers. Modest liberalization in the monarchies of Jordan, Morocco, and Kuwait are about the only examples of substantial progress in the region during the 1990s.

A similar pattern of solidifying past gains coupled with modest progress in selected areas is apparent at the international level. Perhaps most striking was the decisive rebuff of arguments by China and other countries at the World Human Rights Conference in Vienna in 1993 against the full implementation of internationally recognized human rights in the short and medium term. The very decision to hold the World Conference indicates the growing force of the idea of international human rights. Such events, particularly when coupled with the changes in national practices already noted, signify a deepening penetration of the international consensus on human rights norms, which was often shallow in the 1970s and 1980s (see also §§3.5–7).

This deepening penetration of international norms can be seen in the United States as well. Although probably the most vocal proponent of international human rights in the 1970s and 1980s, the United States steadfastly refused to be bound by international human rights treaties in its own practice. In 1992, however, the Senate finally ratified the International Covenant on Civil and Political Rights (but not the International Covenant on Economic, Social, and Cultural Rights). And in 1994, the United States also became a party to the torture convention and signed the women's rights convention. As we will see in §6.1, the United States has had an awkward and ambivalent relationship with the global human rights regime. In the 1990s, however, especially under President Bill Clinton, it no longer held itself to be completely unique and entirely aloof from international human rights norms.

At the United Nations, there was a noticeable decline in political partisanship in the early 1990s. The creation, at the end of 1993, of a High Commissioner for Human Rights, proved to be an important step in expanding both the scope and depth of multilateral monitoring (see §5.2). Although politics has crept back in, especially in the early years of the new millennium, the global human rights regime remains stronger and more nonpartisan than at any point in the cold war.

In bilateral relations as well, human rights became a more deeply entrenched and less controversial foreign policy concern. In addition, national nongovernmental human rights organizations and advocates became a significant part of the political landscape in a growing number of countries in the Third World and former Soviet bloc, and transnational human rights NGOs increased their prestige and influence in a growing number of countries.

6. THE 1990S (II): RESPONDING TO GENOCIDE

The incremental consolidation of national and international progress discussed in the preceding section is probably the most important and enduring contribution of the 1990s. The most dramatic, however, was the development of a practice of legitimate military humanitarian intervention against genocide (see Chapter 8).

The 1948 Genocide Convention, building on the Nuremberg charge of crimes against humanity, had made genocide an international crime. International practice during the cold war era, however, failed to turn that theory into practice. In places such as Burundi, East Pakistan (Bangladesh), Cambodia, and Uganda, **genocide** (killing people because of their race, religion, ethnicity, or culture, with the aim of exterminating the group) and politicide (mass killing for other political purposes) were met by verbal expressions of concern but little concrete action—except by neighboring states such as India, Vietnam, and Tanzania with a strong selfish interest in intervening.

The international tribunals for the former Yugoslavia and Rwanda, created in 1991 and 1994, revived the Nuremberg precedent—or perhaps more accurately, began a process that transformed Nuremberg from an isolated exception into a precedent. The adoption of the Rome Statute in 1998 and the creation of the International Criminal Court in 2002 mark an even deeper normative transformation. And the interventions in Kosovo and East Timor in 1999 consolidated an international practice of humanitarian intervention against genocide that had been fitfully emerging during the preceding decade (see §§8.4–7).

The roots of this transformation lie in significant changes in multilateral **peacekeeping**. During most of the cold war, peacekeeping operations scrupulously avoided direct reference to human rights. This reflected the politicized nature of UN human rights discussions and the desire of most states to avoid creating precedents for UN field action on behalf of human rights. In the late 1980s and 1990s, however, the link between human rights and international peace and security, which has been a central part of United Nations rhetoric since the drafting of the UN Charter, finally became part of UN practice.

In the 1990s, UN operations in Bosnia, Cambodia, Central African Republic, Croatia, Democratic Republic of the Congo, East Timor, El Salvador, Guatemala, Haiti, Kosovo, Liberia, Mozambique, Namibia, Northern Iraq, Rwanda, Sierra Leone, and Somalia had significant human rights mandates. Peacekeepers have monitored the activities of the police and security forces, verified the discharge of human rights undertakings in agreements ending civil wars, supervised elections, encouraged authorities to adopt and comply with international human rights treaties, and provided human rights education. In El Salvador, Haiti, Guatemala, and Rwanda, peacekeepers even had explicit mandates to investigate human rights violations.

Peacekeeping, however, proved inadequate in the context of genocidal political conflict in Rwanda and Bosnia (see §§8.1–3). In Rwanda, the peacekeeping force present in the country was attacked by the *génocidaires* and was actually reduced to less than a thousand troops as three-quarters of a million people were massacred in barely a hundred days. The record in Bosnia was more mixed; UN action limited the scope of the genocide, but UN troops stood by during the massacre at Srebrenica.

Even such limited efforts would have been inconceivable during the cold war. Along with the operations in Somalia in 1992 and 1993, they represented the first serious efforts of post–cold war international society to confront the increasingly prominent problems of violent ethnic conflict, genocide, and what during the decade came to be called "failed states." But the tentative nature of these missions, and the dramatically tragic failure in Rwanda, provoked surprisingly serious and penetrating self-examination by both individual states and the broader international community that came to a head in 1999.

As "ethnic cleansing" in Kosovo, an ethnically Albanian province of Serbia, seemed to be approaching all-out genocide, the United States, chastened by its failure in Rwanda, convinced NATO to embark on a three-month bombing campaign that ultimately led to international administrative control over Kosovo (see §8.4). No less striking was the UN intervention in East Timor, a Portuguese colony that was illegally seized by Indonesia in 1974 and collapsed into genocide in 1999. Despite Indonesia's size, considerable oil wealth, strategic location, and record of Western support over the preceding decades, the United Nations intervened to stop the killing and supervise a transition to Timorese independence (see §8.6).

As we will see in §8.7, the international community has recognized only a right, not a duty, of humanitarian intervention. Furthermore, this right is limited to the case of genocide. Nonetheless, for the first time in history the international community has not merely pronounced genocide an international crime but developed a practical mechanism for enforcement and punishment (though it still lacks much of an ability to prevent genocide).

More generally, the post–cold war era brought national and international action on behalf of human rights to a new level of intensity and effectiveness. By the end of the millennium, human rights had achieved a firm, and modestly expanding, place in international relations.

7. INTERNATIONAL HUMAN RIGHTS AFTER 9/11

It is commonplace, especially in the United States, to claim that the attacks of September 11, 2001, "changed everything." This is, at best, a serious exaggeration. The human rights progress of the 1980s and 1990s has in most places been maintained.

In some countries, it has even been extended. The Arab world in particular has begun to take small but symbolically significant steps toward the international human rights mainstream. In 2004 and 2005, Georgia's Orange Revolution, Ukraine's Pink Revolution, and the violently repressed protests in Uzbekistan indicate significant change along the borders of Russia.

The "war on terrorism," however, has generally reduced international attention to human rights (see Chapter 10). Furthermore, in a number of countries it has provided a widely accepted excuse for increased repression. Less dramatically, the war on terrorism has led to modest but significant restrictions on civil liberties in a number of other countries, including the United States and, after the 2005 London underground bombings, the United Kingdom. And U.S. abuses of (often illegally held) prisoners in Iraq, Afghanistan, and Guantánamo, as well as the kidnapping and international transport ("extraneous rendition") of suspects, have provoked widespread national and international attention and criticism.

The limits of American tolerance for human rights abuses, however, seem to be much narrower than during the cold war. Consider the fairly strong criticism of the massacre of innocent civilians in friendly Uzbekistan in 2005 and the unwillingness of the United States to remain silent even when the Uzbek government retaliated by canceling its military basing agreement. It also suggests that American, and broader international, willingness to accept human rights abuses in the name of antiterrorism may be declining.

If this is true, as I think is likely, then when we look back on the early years of the twenty-first century, the biggest change may lie in the accelerating and deepening impact of globalization. States are the central mechanism for implementing and enforcing internationally recognized human rights (see §9.2). Even if the threat to states posed by globalization is overstated, the relative capabilities of states are declining, especially when it comes to being able to extract revenues to support social welfare programs that realize economic and social rights. But no alternative source of provision seems to be emerging to fill the resulting gap. Therefore, as I suggest in more detail in Chapter 9, global markets are likely to be a bigger threat to human rights in the coming decades than either terrorists or the war against them.

DISCUSSION QUESTIONS

1. Why should Americans be concerned with human rights practices abroad? Why should *states* or intergovernmental organizations be concerned?

   Anyone under thirty probably takes it for granted that states pursue human rights in their foreign policies. As we have seen, however, this is historically unusual. Whether you think the traditional practice of not pursuing international human rights objectives is good or bad, it is important to understand the logic underlying it. How can it be justified? Why do you think that people in the past were willing to treat human rights violations as a purely national concern?

2. Why have these traditional views changed over time? Consider the following possibilities:

    Changing moral sensibilities. *Are* our moral views all that much different from those of other generations? (If so, what does that suggest about the universality of human rights?) Or is it that we now feel freer to act on these values? If so, why? Can changes in ideas, by themselves, have a significant impact on policy?

    Changes in the character of international relations. Have peace and prosperity changed our views of human rights? Growing international interdependence? The end of the cold war? Decolonization? And then what about post-9/11 changes?

    Changes in *national* human rights practices. Or is it that we are now doing better at home and thus want to project that progress abroad? Are we still doing better at home after 9/11?

3. How deeply have these changing views toward international human rights penetrated? We often talk about international human rights, but action regularly falls far short of rhetoric. Why? Is it due to a lack of *real* interest? Constraints on our ability to achieve our objectives? Competing objectives?

4. Should international agencies like the United Nations be involved in enforcing internationally recognized human rights? Why? What would be sacrificed by a greater international role? What would be gained? Can international organizations be trusted to make the sensitive political choices involved in human rights issues? Can *states* be trusted?

5. If you think that there should be a larger international role, why do you think that this has not come about? What would be required to overcome the existing impediments? How costly—economically, politically, and in human terms—would this be? Would these costs be worthwhile? Do you think that change is likely in the next few years? The next few decades? What factors would lead one to expect continuity? What factors suggest change?

6. What kind of actor is best suited to pursue international human rights: individuals, NGOs, states, or intergovernmental organizations? What are the strengths and weaknesses of each?

SUGGESTED READINGS

There are a number of good introductory overviews of international human rights. The best, in my view, is David P. Forsythe, *Human Rights in International Relations* (Cambridge: Cambridge University Press, 2000). Forsythe gives considerable attention to NGOs, international humanitarian law, and the role of transnational actors, making it a good complement to this volume. Those with a somewhat more theoretical inclination might prefer Michael Freeman, *Human Rights: An Interdisciplinary Approach* (Cambridge: Polity Press, 2002). Micheline Ishay, *The History of Human*

Rights (Berkeley: University of California Press, 2004) is a good place to start for those with a historical bent. Anthony Woodiwiss, *Human Rights* (London: Routledge, 2005), and Brian Orend, *Human Rights: Concept and Context* (Peterborough, Canada: Broadview Press, 2002) may also be of interest.

There are also several good general readers. First on my list is Patrick Hayden, ed., *The Philosophy of Human Rights* (St. Paul, Minn.: Paragon House, 2001). This huge and very reasonably priced volume includes an excellent selection of international documents, extensive excerpts from important historical and contemporary theorists, and excellent essays on a wide range of contemporary human rights issues. Micheline Ishay, *The Human Rights Reader* (New York: Routledge, 1997), and Jon E. Lewis, ed., *A Documentary History of Human Rights: A Record of the Events, Documents and Speeches That Shaped Our World* (New York: Carroll & Graf, 2003) are complementary volumes that together provide good coverage of history and theory. Edward Lawson, ed., *Encyclopedia of Human Rights* (New York: Taylor and Francis, 1991) is comprehensive but becoming dated. A new encyclopedia of human rights, edited by David P. Forsythe and published by Routledge, should be available by 2008. Attention should also be drawn to *Human Rights Quarterly*. This interdisciplinary journal is generally considered to be the best scholarly journal in the field, but its articles are typically quite accessible to the average reader.

The Web sites of Amnesty International (www.amnesty.org), Human Rights Watch (www.hrw.org), Minorities Rights Group (www.minorityrights.org), and other NGOs have much useful current information on human rights situations in individual countries. The site of the High Commissioner for Human Rights, http://www.ohchr.org/english/, is a superb resource for international law and activities of the United Nations system.

There is a substantial literature on the Universal Declaration of Human Rights that merits attention given its centrality to the global human rights regime. Johannes Morsink, *The Universal Declaration of Human Rights: Origins, Drafting, and Intent* (Philadelphia: University of Pennsylvania Press, 1999) is the standard study, offering a theoretically informed history of the drafting of the Declaration and a thoughtful analysis of its content (although many readers will find the level of detail on drafting somewhat ponderous). Ashlid Samnoy's *Human Rights as International Consensus: The Making of the Universal Declaration of Human Rights, 1945–1948* (Bergen, Norway: Chr. Michelsen Institute, 1993) covers similar ground somewhat more briefly but is not widely available. (Her essay "The Origins of the Universal Declaration of Human Rights" in the Alfredsson and Eide volume cited in the next paragraph is a solid short introduction.) Mary Ann Glendon's *A World Made New: Eleanor Roosevelt and the Universal Declaration of Human Rights* (New York: Random House, 2001) is excellent and immensely readable, although, as its title indicates, it is somewhat more limited in its scope. John P. Humphrey, *Human Rights and the United Nations: A Great Adventure* (Dobbs Ferry, N.Y.: Transnational Publishers, 1984) is a memoir by the most senior human rights official in the Secretariat in the early years of the United Nations.

Two useful comprehensive surveys of the Universal Declaration are Gudmundur Alfredsson and Asbjørn Eide, eds., *The Universal Declaration of Human Rights:*

A Common Standard of Achievement (The Hague: Martinus Nijhoff, 1999), and Asbjørn Eide, Gudmundur Alfredsson, Göran Melander, Lars Adam Rehof, Allan Rosas, and Theresa Swinehart, eds., *The Universal Declaration of Human Rights: A Commentary* (Oslo, Norway: Scandinavian University Press, 1992). On the role of the smaller states in the drafting process, see Susan Waltz, "Universalizing Human Rights: The Role of Small States in the Construction of the Universal Declaration of Human Rights," *Human Rights Quarterly* 23 (February 2001): 44–72, and Mary Ann Glendon, "The Forgotten Crucible: The Latin American Influence on the Universal Declaration of Human Rights Idea," *Harvard Human Rights Journal* 16 (2003): 27–39.

For critical perspectives on international human rights that see the entire enterprise as, at best, seriously distorted by hegemonic American dominance, see two books and one edited collection by Tony Evans: *U.S. Hegemony and the Project of Universal Human Rights* (Houndmills, U.K.: Macmillan Press, 1996); *The Politics of Human Rights: A Global Perspective,* 2nd ed. (London: Pluto Press, 2005); and *Human Rights Fifty Years On: A Reappraisal* (Manchester, U.K.: Manchester University Press, 1998). See also David Chandler, ed., *Rethinking Human Rights: Critical Approaches to International Relations* (Houndmills, U.K.: Palgrave Macmillan, 2002).

2

◄○►

Theories of Human Rights

The preceding chapter reviewed major developments in the international politics of human rights over the past several decades. This chapter examines three sets of theoretical issues:

1. philosophical theories of human rights;
2. the place of human rights in international society; and
3. political realism, which challenges the very idea of international human rights policies.

1. THE NATURE OF HUMAN RIGHTS

The term **human rights** indicates both their nature and their source: They are the *rights* that one has simply because one is *human*. They are held by all human beings, irrespective of any rights or duties that individuals may (or may not) have as citizens, members of families, workers, or parts of any public or private organization or association.

If all human beings have human rights simply because they are human, then human rights are held equally by all.[1] Because being human cannot be renounced, lost, or forfeited, human rights are also inalienable. Even the cruelest torturer and the most debased victim are still human beings. In practice, not all people *enjoy* all their human rights, let alone enjoy them equally. Nonetheless, all human beings *have* the same human rights and hold them equally and inalienably.

What exactly does it mean to have a right? In English, "right" has two principal moral and political senses.

"Right" may refer to what is right, the right thing to do. For example, we say that it is right to help the needy and wrong (the opposite of right) to lie, cheat, or steal. The focus here is on the righteousness of the required action and on the duty-bearer's obligation to do "what is right."

21

"Right" may also refer to a special entitlement that one has to something. In this narrower sense, we speak of having, claiming, exercising, enforcing, and violating rights.[2] The focus is on the relationship between right-holder and duty-bearer. Many things to which people do not have a (human) right would nevertheless *be* right for every human being to have or enjoy: for example, to be treated with consideration and respect by strangers or to have a loving and supportive family.

Both rights, in the sense of entitlement, and considerations of righteousness create relations between those who have a duty and those who are owed or benefit from that duty. Rights, however, involve a special set of social institutions, rules, or practices. Rights place right-holders and duty-bearers in a relationship that is largely under the control of the right-holders, who may ordinarily exercise their rights as they see fit. Furthermore, claims of rights ordinarily take priority over ("trump") other kinds of demands, including righteousness.

If Anne has a right to x with respect to Bob, it is not simply desirable, good, or even merely right that Anne enjoy x. She is *entitled* to it. Should Bob fail to discharge his obligations, besides acting improperly and harming Anne, he violates her rights. This makes him subject to remedial claims and sanctions that she largely controls.

Anne does not merely benefit from Bob's obligation. She may assert her right to x. If he still does not discharge his duty, she may press further claims against Bob (or excuse him), largely at her discretion. She is in charge of the relationship, as suggested by the language of "exercising" rights. Rights empower, as well as benefit, their holders.

Although rights do not have absolute priority, they do typically have prima facie priority over competing claims. Likewise, although there are limits, discretionary exercise is a central and distinguishing feature of rights. The power and control of rights in ordinary circumstances are precisely what make them so valuable to right-holders.

Human rights are a special type of right. Most fundamentally, they are paramount moral rights. Human rights are also recognized in international law (see §3.5). Most countries recognize many of these rights in their national legal systems as well. The same "thing"—for example, food or protection against discrimination—thus is often guaranteed by several different types of rights.

One "needs" *human* rights principally when they are not effectively guaranteed by national law and practice. If one can secure food or equal treatment through national legal processes, one is unlikely to advance human rights claims. One still has those human rights, but they are not likely to be used (as human rights). For example, in the United States both constitutional and statutory law prohibit racial discrimination. Discrimination based on sexual preference, however, is not prohibited in most jurisdictions. Therefore, gay rights activists frequently claim a human right to nondiscrimination. Racial minorities, by contrast, usually claim legal and constitutional rights—"civil rights."

Human rights is the language of victims and the dispossessed. Human rights claims usually seek to alter legal or political practices. Claims of human rights thus aim to be self-liquidating. To assert one's human rights is to attempt to change political structures and practices so that it will no longer be necessary to claim those rights (as human rights). For example, the struggle against apartheid in South Africa was a struggle to change South African laws and practices so that average South Africans could turn to the legislature, courts, or bureaucracy should they be denied, for example, equal protection of the laws or political participation.

Human rights thus provide a moral standard of national political legitimacy. They are also emerging as an international political standard of legitimacy. Only when citizens no longer need to assert their human rights regularly against their government is that government likely to be considered fully legitimate in the contemporary world (see Chapter 3).

2. THE SOURCE OR JUSTIFICATION OF HUMAN RIGHTS

How does being human give rise to rights? To answer this question we need a theory of human nature. Although I am unable to offer one, I can point out some basic distinctions that provide useful insights.

Theories of human nature deal with what it means to be "human." A scientific approach to human nature involves an empirical investigation of the psychobiological makeup of human beings. A moral or philosophical approach focuses on what it means to be a person, a *human* being capable of reflective action and subject to the constraints of morality. Although moral theories may be constrained by science, they address different issues.

Those who seek to ground human rights in science usually speak of basic human needs. But any list of needs that can plausibly claim to be empirically established provides an obviously inadequate list of rights: life, food, protection against cruel or inhuman treatment, and perhaps companionship. Science simply is incapable of providing the appropriate theory of human nature. (As we will see in §3.3, an anthropological approach that seeks to ground human rights on cross-cultural consensus faces equally serious problems.)

We have human rights not to what we need for survival but to what we need for a life of dignity. The human nature that is the source of human rights rests on a moral account of human possibility. It is concerned with what human beings might become, not what they have been historically or "are" in some scientifically determinable sense.

Human rights rest on an account of a life of dignity to which human beings are "by nature" suited. If the rights specified by the underlying theory of human nature are implemented and enforced, they should help to bring into being the envisioned type of person, one who is worthy of such a life. The effective implementation of human rights thus resembles a self-fulfilling moral prophecy.

Unfortunately, no philosophical theory of human nature has widespread acceptance. Furthermore, many moral theories, and their underlying theories of human nature, deny human rights. For example, Marxism explains moral beliefs in terms of class structure and struggle, which are determined by the means and mode of production. Radical behaviorists see human personality as the result of conditioning. For adherents of either theory, the idea that humans have rights "simply because they are human" probably makes no sense and certainly has no substantive moral implications. Moral or political theories that emphasize differences among communities are also likely to be incompatible with the idea of human rights.

However, there are a variety of bases for justifying human rights. For example, human rights have often been held to be given by God. Alan Gewirth has argued that we have human rights to those things that are necessary to act as a moral agent.[3] Human rights might also be seen as a political specification of Immanuel Kant's **categorical imperative**, the supreme principle of morality, which requires that we treat people as ends, never as means only. A list of human rights can be seen as a political specification of what it means to treat all human beings as ends.

Thus, we have a variety of possible moral justifications, as well as an array of theories that deny or radically devalue human rights. In what follows I assume that there are human rights; that is, that we have accepted some sort of philosophical defense for the existence of human rights. This theoretical evasion is justified by the fact that almost all states acknowledge the existence of human rights. It is further supported by the fact that there is an emerging international consensus, based on overlapping moral and religious theories, on human rights (see Chapter 3). Therefore, the assumption that there are human rights is relatively unproblematic for our purposes here, namely, studying the international politics of human rights.

3. LISTS OF HUMAN RIGHTS

Despite the lack of philosophical consensus, there is, as we saw in Chapter 1, an international *legal and political* consensus on the list of rights in the Universal Declaration of Human Rights and the International Human Rights Covenants (see Table 1.1). This consensus draws theoretical support from the fact that it can be derived from a plausible and attractive philosophical account, namely, the requirement that the state treat each person with equal concern and respect. Consider the Universal Declaration.

One must be recognized as a person (Universal Declaration, Article 6) in order to be treated with any sort of concern or respect. Personal rights to nationality and to recognition before the law, along with rights to life and to protection against slavery, torture, and other inhuman or degrading practices, can be seen as legal and political prerequisites to recognition and thus respect (Articles 3–5, 15). Rights to equal protection of the laws and protection against racial, sexual, and other forms of discrimination are essential to *equal* respect (Articles 1, 2, 7).

Equal respect for all persons is at most a hollow formality without the freedom to choose and act on one's own ideas of the good life. Freedoms of speech, conscience, religion, and association, along with the right to privacy, guarantee a private sphere of personal autonomy (Articles 12, 18–20). The rights to education and to participate in the cultural life of the community provide a social dimension to personal autonomy (Articles 26, 27). The rights to vote and to freedom of speech, press, assembly, and association guarantee political autonomy (Articles 18–21).

Rights to food, health care, and social insurance (Article 25) make equal concern and respect a practical reality rather than a mere formal possibility. The right to work is a right to economic participation very similar to the right to political participation (Article 23). A (limited) right to property may be justified in such terms (Article 17).

Finally, the special threat to personal security and equality posed by the modern state requires legal rights to constrain the state and its functionaries. These include rights to be presumed innocent until proven guilty, due process, fair and public hearings before an independent tribunal, and protection from arbitrary arrest, detention, or exile (Articles 8–11). Anything less would allow the state to treat citizens with differential concern or respect.

The idea of equal concern and respect certainly is philosophically controversial. It does, however, have a certain inherent plausibility. It is closely related to the basic fact that human rights are equal and inalienable. It even offers an attractive interpretation of the claim in the International Human Rights Covenants that the rights recognized "derive from the inherent dignity of the human person."

There are also powerful practical reasons for adopting the list of human rights in the Universal Declaration and the Covenants. To act internationally on the basis of a different list would risk the charge of imposing one's own biased preferences instead of widely accepted international standards.

4. THE STATUS OF ECONOMIC, SOCIAL, AND CULTURAL RIGHTS

Although almost all states have explicitly endorsed the list provided by the Universal Declaration—whatever their actual practices may be—there have been two very prominent exceptions in recent years.[4] First, some Asian commentators have argued that some international human rights norms are fundamentally incompatible with Asian values, which ought to receive priority. These arguments are discussed in §7.5. Second, some American and British conservatives have challenged the status of economic, social, and cultural rights.

Such critics argue that **economic, social, and cultural rights**, entitlements to socially provided goods, services, and opportunities such as food, health care, social insurance, and education, are at best less important than **civil and political rights**, such as due process, freedom of speech, and the right to vote, and probably not human rights at all. The right to paid holidays (Universal Declaration, Article 24) is an often-cited example.

The full right recognized in the Universal Declaration, however, is the right to "rest, leisure, and reasonable limitation of working hours and periodic holidays with pay." This is a very important right indeed. Consider the horrors of sixty-hour workweeks, fifty-two weeks a year, in nineteenth-century factories or twentieth-century sweatshops. Furthermore, one can point to even more minor civil and political rights. For example, Article 10 of the International Covenant on Civil and Political Rights proclaims the right of juveniles to separate prison facilities. In every country of the world, far fewer people have suffered from penal confinement as juveniles in the company of adult criminals than from the denial of reasonable rest and leisure. In any case, the right to paid holidays is hardly the typical economic and social right. Consider, for example, the rights to food, housing, health care, work, and social security.

Arguments of practicality, which are often advanced against economic and social rights, are more complex. For example, Maurice Cranston argued that "there is nothing especially difficult about transforming political and civil rights into positive rights" but that in most countries it is "utterly impossible" to realize most economic and social rights.[5] In fact, though, the victims of repression in countries such as Nazi Germany, the Soviet Union, apartheid–era South Africa, and contemporary China and North Korea have found it extremely difficult to transform internationally recognized civil and political rights into effective rights in national law.

Conversely, many of the impediments to implementing economic and social rights are political. For example, there is already enough food in the world to feed every person. Universal implementation of the right to food would "only" require redistributing existing supplies. Of course, health care and social services at the level provided in much of Western Europe cannot be universally implemented. That level has yet to be reached even by the United States. Nonetheless, almost all countries can make major improvements, at relatively modest cost, in realizing most economic and social rights. Furthermore, much the same is true of the advanced legal safeguards common in North America and Western Europe.

It is also often argued that there is a qualitative difference between "negative" civil and political rights and "positive" economic and social rights. Negative rights require only the forbearance of others to be realized. Violating a negative right thus involves actively causing harm, a sin of commission. Positive rights require that others provide active support. Violating a positive right involves only failing to provide assistance, a (presumably lesser) sin of omission.

All human rights, however, require both positive action and restraint by the state if they are to be effectively implemented. Some rights, of course, are relatively positive. Others are relatively negative. But this distinction does not correspond to the division between civil and political rights and economic and social rights.

The right to vote requires extensive positive endeavors, not forbearance, on the part of the government. So do the rights to due process, trial by a jury of one's peers, and access to legal remedies for violations of basic rights. Even the right to nondiscrimination may require—beyond refraining from discriminating—extensive, difficult, and costly state intervention (for example, affirmative action) if individuals are to be effectively protected against discrimination. "Simply" refraining in practice usually means assuring that certain things are not done, which can require considerable work over an extended period of time. In fact, were it easy to abstain, the right in question probably would not be very important (in that context).

The (social) right to marry and found a family is no less negative than the right to freedom of religion. The rights to participate in the cultural life of the community and to share in the benefits of science and technology are as negative (or positive) as the right to nondiscrimination. In many countries, the right to food would be more widely realized if governments would simply refrain from encouraging the production of cash crops such as coffee, cocoa, flowers, and fruits for export.

The moral basis of the positive-negative distinction is also questionable. Does it really make a moral difference if one kills someone through neglect or by positive action? What if the neglect is knowing and willful? Consider, for example, leaving an injured man to die; refusing to implement relatively inexpensive health care or nutrition programs for needy and malnourished children; or the fact that a black infant in the United States is twice as likely to die as a white infant.

Another way to approach the question of the status of economic, social, and cultural rights is to ask what a life with only civil and political rights would look like. Without minimum economic and social guarantees, a life of dignity is clearly impossible, especially in modern market economies. Even the Reagan administration in the United States and the Thatcher government in Britain, the two most prominent official advocates of a "free market" economy in the West in the past half century, stressed the importance of a "safety net" of economic and social rights for the "deserving poor."

Finally, we should note that most critics of economic and social rights destroy their own arguments by defending a right to property. This is an *economic* right, not a civil and political right—and a rather extravagant economic right at that. Furthermore, standard defenses of a right to property support other economic and social rights. For example, the right to work no less than the right to property allows economic participation in society and provides personal economic security.

There are, of course, differences between economic and social rights and civil and political rights. But there are no less important differences within each broad class of rights, as well as important similarities across these classes. For example, the (civil and political) right to life and the (economic and social) right to food can be seen as different means to protect the same value. Categorical distinctions, let alone blanket denials, simply do not withstand scrutiny.

5. DUTY-BEARERS OF HUMAN RIGHTS

Henry Shue argues that most rights, and all human rights, entail three kinds of duties: not to deprive the right-holder of the enjoyment of her right; to protect against deprivation; and to aid those whose rights have been violated. These duties, however, may be held by different actors.[6]

In both national practice and international law, as we will see in Chapter 5, duties to protect and aid fall almost exclusively on the state of which one is a national. Even deprivations by private individuals and groups are not typically called human rights violations. If an irate neighbor blows up a house killing a dozen people, it is murder. If irate police officers do the same thing, it is a violation of human rights. If foreign soldiers do it during war, it may be a war crime.

One might imagine different allocations of duties. The rights of children in all societies are implemented primarily through families. Many countries have significantly privatized old-age pensions. In Singapore, children have certain legal obligations to support their aged parents. Claims asserting duties of business enterprises not to deprive are appearing with some frequency today. It does not strain credulity to imagine a world in which regional and international organizations acquire obligations to implement and enforce human rights.

In practice, however, virtually all human rights today are implemented and enforced by states operating within recognized territorial jurisdictions. Although human rights are held universally (by all human beings), implementation and enforcement lie with states, which have duties to protect and aid only their own citizens (and certain others under their territorial jurisdiction). Neither states nor any other actors have legal rights or obligations to protect or aid victims in other jurisdictions (with the limited exception of genocide, considered in Chapter 8). In other words, we have a system of national implementation of international human rights.

6. SOVEREIGNTY, ANARCHY, AND INTERNATIONAL SOCIETY

Having surmounted, or at least disposed of, some of the more pressing philosophical questions, we can now turn to the place of human rights in international relations theories. The modern international system is often dated to 1648, when the Treaty of Westphalia ended the Thirty Years' War. As we saw in Chapter 1, though, human rights have been an issue in international relations for barely sixty years. The absence of human rights from the first three centuries of modern international relations was the direct result of an international order based on sovereign states.

To be **sovereign** is to be subject to no higher power. In early modern Europe, sovereignty was a personal attribute of rulers. For example, Thomas Hobbes wrote of "princes and other persons of sovereign authority." In many other times and places, as in medieval Europe, no (earthly) power was considered to be sovereign. In contemporary international relations, sovereignty is seen as an attribute of states.[7]

International relations is structured around the legal fiction that states have exclusive jurisdiction over their territory, its occupants and resources, and the events that take place there. Practice typically falls far short of precept, as usually is the case with legal and political principles. Nonetheless, the basic norms, rules, and practices of contemporary international relations rest on state sovereignty and the formal equality of (sovereign) states.

Nonintervention is the duty correlative to the right of sovereignty. Other states are obliged not to interfere with the internal actions of a sovereign state. Because human rights principally regulate the ways states treat their own citizens within their own territory, international human rights policies would seem to involve unjustifiable intervention.

A principal function of international law, however, is to overcome the initial presumption of sovereignty. A **treaty** is a contract between states to accept mutual obligations—that is, restrictions on their sovereignty. For example, a treaty of alliance may oblige a state to aid an ally that is attacked. Such a state is no longer (legally) free to choose whether or not to go to war. Through the treaty, it has voluntarily relinquished some freedom of action. International law, including international human rights law, is the record of restrictions on sovereignty accepted by states.

The choice of sovereignty as an ordering principle is conditioned by the fact that the realm of international relations is anarchic, a political arena without formal hierarchical relations of authority and subordination. But **anarchy**, the absence of hierarchical political rule, does not necessarily imply chaos, the absence of order. In addition to international law, states regulate their interaction through institutionalized practices such as diplomacy, balance of power, and recognition of spheres of influence. Although there is no international government, there is rule-governed social order. International relations take place within an anarchical **society of states**.[8]

The international society of states of the eighteenth, nineteenth, and early twentieth centuries gave punctilious respect to the sovereign prerogative of each state to treat its own citizens as it saw fit. Today, however, as we have seen, there is a substantial body of international human rights law. States have become increasingly vocal in expressing, and sometimes even acting on, their international human rights concerns. In addition, human rights NGOs, which seek to constrain the freedom of action of rights-violating states, have become more numerous and more active.

This reflects (and has helped to create) a transformed understanding of the place of individuals in international relations. States have traditionally been the sole subjects of international law, the only actors with international legal standing (the right to bring actions in international tribunals). The rights and interests of individuals traditionally were protected in international law only by states acting on their behalf. Although the International Bill of Human Rights does not empower individuals (or even other states) to act against states, contemporary international human rights law has given individuals and their rights a place in international relations.

It has also introduced a new conception of international legitimacy. Traditionally, a government was considered legitimate if it exercised authority over its territory and accepted the international legal obligations that it and its predecessors had contracted. What it did at home was largely irrelevant. Today, human rights provide a standard of moral legitimacy that has been (very incompletely) incorporated into the rules of the international society of states.

Consider the almost universal negative reaction to the Tiananmen massacre in 1989, when Chinese troops fired on unarmed student demonstrators and brutally crushed China's emerging democracy movement. China's diplomatic isolation reflected this new, human rights–based understanding of legitimacy. But, as we shall see in Chapter 7, that isolation lasted only a year or two. Even the strongest supporters of sanctions were not willing to allow Chinese brutality to interfere with long-term economic and security interests.

This tension is characteristic of the current state of international human rights. The future of international human rights activity can be seen as a struggle over balancing the competing claims of sovereignty and international human rights and the competing conceptions of legitimacy that they imply.

7. THREE MODELS OF
INTERNATIONAL HUMAN RIGHTS

The universality of human rights fits uncomfortably with a political order structured around sovereign states. Universal moral rights seem better suited to a cosmopolitan conception of world politics, which sees individuals more as members of a global political community ("cosmopolis") than as citizens of states. Instead of thinking of international relations (the relations between nation-states), a cosmopolitan thinks of a global political process in which individuals and other nonstate actors are important direct participants. We thus have three competing theoretical models of the place of human rights in international relations, each with its own conception of the character of the international community.

The traditional **statist** model sees human rights as principally a matter of sovereign national jurisdiction. Statists readily admit that human rights are no longer the exclusive preserve of states and that the state is no longer the sole significant international actor (if it ever was). They nonetheless insist that human rights remain *primarily* a matter of sovereign national jurisdiction and (ought to continue to be) a largely peripheral concern of international (interstate) relations. For statists, there is no significant, independent international community, and certainly no international body with the right to act on behalf of human rights. We have an international system but not much of an international society.

A **cosmopolitan** model starts with individuals rather than states—which are often "the problem" for cosmopolitans. Cosmopolitans see the state challenged both from below, by individuals and NGOs, and from above, by the truly global community (not merely international organizations and other groupings of states). International action on behalf of human rights is relatively unproblematic in such a model. In fact, cosmopolitans largely reverse the burden of proof, requiring justification for nonintervention in the face of gross and persistent violations of human rights. International society, in other words, is seen as a global or world society.

The space toward the center of the continuum defined by statism and cosmopolitanism is occupied by what we can call **internationalist** models. "The international community," in an internationalist model, is essentially the **society of states** (supplemented by NGOs and individuals, to the extent that they have been formally or informally incorporated into international political processes). International human rights activity is permissible only to the extent authorized by the norms of the society of states. These norms, however, may vary considerably across particular international societies. Consider, for example, the difference noted earlier between the late nineteenth and late twentieth centuries. Therefore, we need to distinguish strong internationalism and weak internationalism, based on the distance from the statist end of the spectrum.

Each of these three models can be read as making descriptive claims about the place that human rights do have in international relations or prescriptive claims about the place they ought to have. For example, a statist might argue (descriptively) that human rights are in fact peripheral in international relations, or (prescriptively) that they ought to be peripheral, or both.

Cosmopolitanism, however, even in this era of globalization, has little descriptive power. States and their interests still dominate world politics. The international political power of individuals, NGOs, and other nonstate actors is real, and appears to be growing, but is still relatively small—and power is a relative notion. The global political community—world society as opposed to the international society of states—is at best rudimentary. The cosmopolitan model, if more than a prescription about what is desirable, rests on predictions of the direction of change in world politics.

If the world envisioned by cosmopolitans has yet to come into being, that envisioned by statists is at least in part a thing of the past. Although accurate even into the 1970s, the statist model of international human rights today is at best a crude first approximation. Furthermore, it misleadingly directs attention away from three decades of significant, cumulative change.

Some sort of internationalist model—or a very heavily hedged statism—provides the most accurate description of the place of human rights in contemporary international relations. I began to lay out the evidence for this claim in Chapter 1. The case studies discussed in Chapters 5 through 10 indicate that a relatively weak internationalist model, with modest international societal constraints on state sovereignty, describes the nature of the contemporary international politics of human rights and is likely to continue to do so for at least the next several years.

Current descriptive power, however, is no guarantee of future accuracy. And it does not mean that internationalism is the best, or even a good, way to treat human rights in international relations. Nonetheless, as later chapters show in some detail, the international human rights reality that we face today is one of considerable state sovereignty, with modest limits rooted principally in the international society of states.

8. REALISM AND HUMAN RIGHTS

Before leaving the discussion of theory, we need to consider two common theoretical challenges to even this limited concern with international human rights, namely, political **realism**, or **Realpolitik** (power politics), and cultural relativism. The first is the subject of this section. The second, and the broader question of the nature of the universality of human rights, is the subject of the next chapter.

The theory of Realpolitik is an old and well-established theory of international relations, typically traced back to figures such as Niccolo Machiavelli in the early sixteenth century and Thucydides, whose *History* chronicles the great wars between Athens and Sparta in the final decades of the fifth century BCE. Realism stresses "the primacy in all political life of power and security."[9] Because men are egoistic and evil and because international anarchy requires states to rely on their own resources even for defense, realists argue that "universal moral principles cannot be applied to the actions of states."[10] To pursue a moral foreign policy would be not only foolishly unsuccessful but would leave one's country vulnerable to the power of self-interested states.

Realists argue that only considerations of the national interest should guide foreign policy. And the national interest, for the realist, must be defined in terms of power and security. For example, George Kennan, one of the architects of postwar U.S. foreign policy and one of the most respected recent realist writers, argued that a government's "primary obligation is to the *interests* of the national society it represents . . . its military security, the integrity of its political life and the well-being of its people." "The process of government . . . is a practical exercise and not a moral one."[11] As for international human rights policies,

it is difficult to see any promise in an American policy which sets out to correct and improve the political habits of large parts of the world's population. Misgovernment . . . has been the common condition of most of mankind for centuries and millennia in the past. It is going to remain that condition for long into the future, no matter how valiantly Americans insist on tilting against the windmills.[12]

Such arguments do contain a kernel of truth. The demands of morality often do conflict with the national interest defined in terms of power. But *all* objectives of foreign policy, not just moral ones, may compete with the national interest thus defined. For example, arms races may contribute to the outbreak of war. Alliances may prove dangerously entangling. The European alliance system of the early twentieth century transformed a regional dispute between Austria-Hungary and Russia into a devastating world war. Realists, however, rightly refuse to conclude that we should eschew arms or allies. They should also abandon their categorical attacks on morality in foreign policy. A valuable caution against moralistic excess has been wildly exaggerated into a general principle of politics.

Realist arguments against morality in foreign policy also appeal to the special office of the statesman. For example, Herbert Butterfield argued that although a man may choose to sacrifice himself in the face of foreign invasion, he does not have a "right to offer the same sacrifice on behalf of all his fellow-citizens or to impose such self-abnegation on the rest of his society."[13] But non-moral objectives as well may be pursued by statesmen with excessive zeal, and equally deadly consequences. And most moral objectives can be pursued at a cost far less than national survival. This certainly is true of many international human rights goals.

In addition, there is no reason that a country cannot, if it wishes, include human rights or other moral concerns in its definition of the national interest. Security, independence, and prosperity may be unavoidable necessities of national political life, but governments need not limit themselves to these necessities. Even if the primary obligation of governments must be to the national interest defined in terms of power, this need not be their sole, or even ultimate, obligation.

Using the anarchic structure of international relations as a rationale will not rescue realist amoralism. For example, Robert Art and Kenneth Waltz claim that "states in anarchy cannot afford to be moral. The possibility of moral behavior rests upon the existence of an effective government that can deter and punish illegal actions."[14] However, even if we set aside their confusion of morality and law, their logic is clearly faulty. Just as individuals may behave morally without government to enforce moral rules, so moral behavior is possible in international relations.

The costs of moral behavior are typically greater in an anarchic system of self-help enforcement. Nonetheless, states can often act on moral concerns without harm, and sometimes with success. Although there may be good policy reasons to pursue amoral, or even immoral, policies in particular instances, there are no good theoretical reasons for requiring amoral policies, or even accepting them as the norm.

DISCUSSION QUESTIONS

1. *Are* there such things as human rights? Where do they come from? How would you go about trying to convince someone who answers these questions differently from you? Do you find my claim that human rights rest on a moral account of human possibility to be plausible? Persuasive? Satisfying? Why?

2. I emphasize differences between rights and other sorts of moral principles and practices. Do I overemphasize the differences? What are the ways in which rights are similar to considerations of righteousness?

3. Should we prefer to protect human rights when doing so conflicts with social utility? Should the rights of the individual or the few take priority over the happiness of the many? (Try thinking about different rights in answering this question.) In particular, should *governments* act on any principle other than social utility?

4. How do we determine what constitutes a justifiable list of human rights? How would you go about trying to convince someone who proposes a radically different list? Would it be easier or harder if the list were less radically different?

5. What is the status of the principle of equal concern and respect, which I draw on to justify the list of human rights in the International Bill of Human Rights? Should this principle be preferred to others? What are some other plausible grounds that might underlie this particular list?

6. I make the assumption that some sort of justification of human rights is possible. Does it really matter *why* people believe that there are human rights?

7. Are economic, social, and cultural rights human rights? Why? Why are many Americans reluctant to consider these rights as legitimate human rights? Are the reasons philosophical? A reflection of the generally poor performance of the United States on assuring these rights? How different are such arguments from the old Soviet claims that civil and political rights are really not as important as economic, social, and cultural rights?

8. Is there a moral dimension to the "positive-negative" distinction? Is there really no difference between killing someone and failing to help someone

who is dying? Is there a moral distinction between personal behavior and the activity of governments?

9. What is the relation between philosophical theory and international legal norms in the case of human rights? Can we legitimately evade philosophical difficulties by pointing to international consensus? What are the costs of such a strategy? What are the costs of not following the consensus?

10. *Should* human rights function as an international standard of legitimacy? If so, what else, if anything, is required for international legitimacy? If a government meets all the other criteria but violates human rights, why should it be seen as *internationally* (rather than morally or nationally) illegitimate?

11. Sovereignty issues have impeded the acceptance of international human rights policies. Is that really such a bad thing? Do you want other countries and international organizations inquiring into the human rights practices of your country? International anarchy has its obvious drawbacks, but do you *really* want a higher political authority telling your country how to behave?

12. Which of the three models of international human rights—statist, cosmopolitan, or internationalist—do you find most attractive (issues of their current descriptive accuracy notwithstanding)? Why? What are the greatest strengths of your preferred model? Why might others find it defective?

13. Even if realists overstate their case, don't they have a legitimate one? How often do states have the political space and resources to be successful in pursuing international human rights concerns? Have recent international changes (e.g., the end of the cold war, globalization, 9/11) made it harder or easier? (In answering this question, consider a range of different rights.)

14. How often do states use "realism" as an excuse for not doing what they know they ought to do but don't want to be bothered with? Imagine personal moral relations if "realist" arguments were allowed. Are the differences between interpersonal and international relations really so great that we can allow radically different standards to apply? Conversely, are the similarities so great that we can apply the same standards without major modifications across the two realms?

SUGGESTED READINGS

Henry Shue's *Basic Rights: Subsistence, Affluence, and U.S. Foreign Policy,* 2nd ed. (Princeton: Princeton University Press, 1996) provides a subtle and powerful argument for the equal and overriding priority of rights to security, subsistence, and liberty; an extended discussion of the duties that flow from these rights; and a sensitive (if now rather dated) application of these theoretical ideas to U.S. foreign policy. A shorter version of the core of the argument is available in Shue's essay "Rights in the Light of Duties," in *Human Rights and U.S. Foreign Policy: Principles and Applications,* Peter G. Brown and Douglas MacLean, ed. (Lexington, Mass.: Lexington

Books, 1979). For an alternative perspective on economic, social, and cultural rights, see Maurice Cranston, "Are There Any Human Rights?" *Daedalus* 112 (Fall 1983): 1–18, and Hugo Adam Bedau, "Human Rights and Foreign Assistance Programs," in *Human Rights and U.S. Foreign Policy: Principles and Applications* (Lexington, Mass.: Lexington Books, 1979).

The most ambitious effort to develop a philosophical theory of human rights is Alan Gewirth, *Human Rights: Essays on Justification and Applications* (Chicago: University of Chicago Press, 1982). Gewirth's main argument, however, is dense, technical, and unlikely to be of interest to most readers of this volume. The chapters in Part Three of Patrick Hayden, ed., *The Philosophy of Human Rights* (St. Paul, Minn.: Paragon House, 2001), however, are well worth consulting. I have found that students particularly enjoy Martha Nussbaum's account of a "capabilities approach." William A. Edmundson, *An Introduction to Rights* (Cambridge: Cambridge University Press, 2004) is a good historical-philosophical survey.

My own more extensive theoretical account is offered in *Universal Human Rights in Theory and Practice,* 2nd ed. (Ithaca: Cornell University Press, 2003). For an excellent book-length discussion that emphasizes the similarities between rights and other grounds of action (in contrast to my emphasis on the special features of rights), see James W. Nickel, *Making Sense of Human Rights: Philosophical Reflections on the Universal Declaration of Human Rights* (Berkeley: University of California Press, 1987, available online at http://homepages.law.asu.edu/~jnickel/msohr%20welcome.htm). Two good article-length introductions to the theory of human rights are Nickel's chapter in the online *Stanford Encyclopedia of Philosophy* (http://plato.stanford.edu/archives/sum2003/entries/rights-human/), and Jerome J. Shestack, "The Philosophical Foundations of Human Rights," *Human Rights Quarterly* 20 (May 1998): 200–234. Peter Jones, *Rights* (New York: St. Martin's, 1994) offers an excellent theoretical overview of rights in their varied forms.

A powerful but brief and readily accessible version of the realist argument against pursuing moral issues, including human rights, in foreign policy is presented in George F. Kennan, "Morality and Foreign Policy," *Foreign Affairs* 63 (Winter 1985/1986): 205–218. A rather more nuanced version of a similar argument is provided in Chapter 4 of Hedley Bull's *The Anarchical Society,* 3rd ed. (New York: Columbia University Press, 2002). For a counter-argument, see Chapter 6 of Jack Donnelly, *Realism and International Relations* (Cambridge: Cambridge University Press, 2000).

3

◄○►

The Relative Universality
of Human Rights

International human rights are usually presented as universal rights. The foundational international legal instrument is the *Universal* Declaration of Human Rights. The 1993 World Human Rights Conference, in the first operative paragraph of the Vienna Declaration and Programme of Action, insisted that "the universal nature of these rights and freedoms is beyond question." The universality of human rights is a central theme in diplomatic, popular, and academic discussions alike.

Attacks on the universality of human rights, however, are also regular, forceful, and widespread. Proponents of relativism regularly present their arguments not only with considerable political passion but genuine theoretical force.

In this chapter I suggest that moral relativism—the belief that moral values (and thus conceptions of human rights) are determined by history, culture, economics, or some other social force—is best seen as a matter of degree. At one extreme is radical **relativism**, which sees culture (or history, or economics) as the source of all values.[1] Such a position in effect denies the very idea of human rights, for it implies that there are no rights that everyone is entitled to equally, simply as a human being. Radical relativism can be ignored once we have decided, as we have above, that there are human rights, rights that all human beings have, independent of society (and thus irrespective of their particular history or culture).

At the other end of the spectrum lies radical **universalism**, the view that all values, including human rights, are entirely universal, in no way subject to modification in light of cultural or historical differences. In its pure form, radical universalism would hold that there is only one set of human rights that applies at all times and in all places. In §3.8 I argue that this position, which I call ontological universality, is theoretically implausible and practically dangerous.

Rejecting the two end points of the spectrum leaves us with a considerable variety of "relativist" positions, which can be roughly divided into two ranges. *Strong relativism* holds that human rights (and other values) are principally, but not entirely, determined by culture or other circumstances. "Universal" human rights serve as a

37

check on culturally specific values. The emphasis, however, is on variation and relativity. *Weak relativism* reverses the emphasis. Universal human rights are held to be
subject only to secondary cultural modifications.

I will defend a form of weak cultural relativism on both descriptive and prescriptive grounds. In doing so, I identify several different senses of universality. Some I
will argue are defensible and of great theoretical and practical importance. Others,
however, are indefensible. And all the defensible forms of universality, I will argue,
allow considerable space for cultural, regional, national, and other variations in implementing "universal" human rights. I describe this as the *relative* universality of internationally recognized human rights, an apparently paradoxical notion that I will
seek to explain and defend as this chapter progresses.

1. CONCEPTUAL AND
SUBSTANTIVE UNIVERSALITY

Let us begin with what I will call *conceptual universality*. This form of universality is
implied by the very idea of human rights.

As we saw in §2.1, human rights are ordinarily understood to be the rights that
one has simply as a human being. As such, they are equal rights, because we either
are or are not human beings, equally. Human rights are also inalienable rights, because being or not being a human being is an inalterable fact of nature, not something that can be earned or lost. Human rights are thus "universal" rights in the sense
that they are held "universally" by all human beings. Conceptual universality is in effect just another way of saying that human rights are, *by definition,* equal and
inalienable.

Although analytically and substantively important, conceptual universality establishes only that *if* there are any such rights, they are held equally and universally by
all. It does not show that there *are* any such rights. Conceptually universal rights may
be so few in number or specified at such a high level of abstraction that they are of
little practical significance. And conceptual universality says nothing about the central question in most contemporary discussions of universality, namely, whether the
rights recognized in international instruments such as the Universal Declaration of
Human Rights and the International Human Rights Covenants are universal. This is
a substantive, not a conceptual, question. It will be our focus here.

2. UNIVERSAL POSSESSION,
NOT UNIVERSAL ENFORCEMENT

Another possible sense of the universality of human rights is that they are universally
implemented across the globe or enforced by a single central body in a system of
universal jurisdiction. Such a claim is obviously false. In many countries, the universal moral and international legal obligations of human rights are not effectively implemented or enforced. By this I mean not simply that human rights are regularly

violated (*all* kinds of rights are regularly violated; consider the tiny percentage of thefts that are successfully prosecuted in any major American city), but that in many states, the national government refuses to effectively implement human rights and grossly and systematically violates those rights.

Defensible claims of universality are "theoretical." More precisely, they are claims about the rights that we all *have* as human beings. Whether everyone, or even anyone, is in fact able to *enjoy* these rights is another matter. The sad fact remains that in far too many countries most internationally recognized human rights are not effectively implemented. In such countries, most people are not able to enjoy their human rights.

A large part of the reason for this lies in the system of national implementation of internationally recognized human rights (see also §§2.5, 9.2). As we will see in more detail in Chapter 5, implementation of authoritative international human rights norms is left almost entirely to sovereign states. Except in the European regional regime, supranational supervisory bodies are largely restricted to monitoring how states implement their international human rights obligations. Transnational human rights NGOs and other advocates likewise engage in largely persuasive activity, seeking to use national and international publicity to encourage states to change their human rights practices. And although other states are free to raise human rights violations as an issue of concern, they lack any authority to implement or enforce human rights within the sovereign jurisdiction of another state.

The system of national implementation of internationally recognized human rights does not make these rights any less real. They are moral rights. They are international legal rights. These international legal obligations are at least formally incorporated into the national law of the vast majority of the world's states. In all of these (and other) ways, human rights are real rights that provide protections to rightholders and resources that they can use to seek to improve their lives. Nonetheless, there is no system of universal international jurisdiction over human rights.[2] Notwithstanding the (conceptual or substantive) theoretical universality of human rights—that is, even if everyone does have the same human rights—implementation and enforcement of those rights are dependent on sovereign states and thus are highly relative.

3. HISTORICAL OR ANTHROPOLOGICAL UNIVERSALITY

Human rights are often held to be universal in the sense that all or most societies and cultures have practiced human rights throughout all or most of their history.[3] For example, Adamantia Pollis and Peter Schwab argue that "all societies have human rights notions." Yougindra Khushalani goes so far as to argue that "the concept of human rights can be traced to the origin of the human race itself."[4] Such claims to *historical or anthropological universality* are empirically false. If by human rights we mean equal and inalienable rights that all people have simply because they are human, and that these rights provide individual entitlements that can be exercised against the society and polity of which one is a member, then no pre-modern society, Western or non-Western, has in fact recognized or practiced human rights.

We must distinguish clearly between *values* such as justice, fairness, and humanity and particular *practices* that aim to realize those values. Most discussions of so-called non-Western conceptions of human rights confuse values such as limited government or respect for personal dignity with the practice of equal and inalienable individual human rights to realize such values.

Rights—entitlements that ground claims with a special force—are one particular practice for realizing social and political values. Human rights—equal and inalienable entitlements held by all individuals that may be exercised against the state and society—are a very distinctive way to seek to realize social values such as justice and human flourishing. There may be considerable historical/anthropological universality of basic values across time and culture.[5] There is no evidence, however, to support claims that any society, civilization, or culture had a widely endorsed vision of equal and inalienable individual human rights prior to the seventeenth century. Consider three more or less arbitrarily chosen examples.

"In almost all contemporary Arab literature on this subject [human rights], we find a listing of the basic rights established by modern conventions and declarations, and then a serious attempt to trace them back to Koranic texts." This now extensive literature typically claims that "Islam has laid down some universal fundamental rights for humanity as a whole, which are to be observed and respects under all circumstances . . . fundamental rights for every man by virtue of his status as a human being."[6] When we consider the details, however, such claims prove to be baseless.

For example, the scriptural passages that Khalid M. Ishaque argues establish a "right to protection of life" are in fact divine injunctions not to kill and to consider life inviolable.[7] The "right to justice" proves to be instead a duty of rulers to establish justice. The "right to freedom" is a duty not to enslave unjustly (not even a general duty not to enslave). "Economic rights" turn out to be duties to help to provide for the needy. And the purported "right to freedom of expression" is actually an obligation to speak the truth—that is, not even an obligation of others but an obligation of the alleged right-holder.

Turning to Africa, Dunstan Wai argues that "it is not often remembered that traditional African societies supported and practiced human rights. Traditional African attitudes, beliefs, institutions, and experiences sustained the 'view that certain rights should be upheld against alleged necessities of state.'"[8] This confuses human rights with limited government. Timothy Fernyhough likewise argues that "many precolonial societies were distinguished by their respect for judicial and political procedure."[9] The same, unfortunately, was true of South African apartheid. The question, of course, is whether judicial and political procedures were based on and compatible with human rights. In traditional Africa they were not.

Government can be limited on a variety of grounds, including divine commandment, legal rights, and extralegal checks such as a balance of power or the threat of popular revolt. The personal rights of precolonial Africans against their governments were based not on humanity but on such criteria as age, sex, lineage, achievement, or community membership. Not all rights are human rights. Most in fact arise from a source other than common humanity.

It is also regularly argued that "the protection of human rights is an integral part" of the traditions of Asian societies. Radhika Coomaraswamy has declared that "all the countries of the region would agree that 'human rights' as a concept existed in their tradition." Hung-Chao Tai has asserted that "human rights under the traditional Chinese political culture were conceived to be part of a larger body of morally prescribed norms of collective human conduct."[10] Such arguments involve similar confusions.

"In a broad sense, the concept of human rights concerns the relationship between the individual and the state; it involves the status, claims, and duties of the former in the jurisdiction of the latter. As such, it is a subject as old as politics, and every nation has to grapple with it."[11] But not all political relationships are governed by, related to, or even consistent with human rights. What the state owes those it rules is indeed a perennial question of politics. Human rights provide one answer. Divine right monarchy, the dictatorship of the proletariat, the principle of utility, aristocracy, theocracy, democracy, and plutocracy, however, offer other answers.

Individuals in traditional China may have held rights as members of families, villages, and other groups. The purpose of these rights, however, "was not to protect the individual against the state but to enable the individual to function more effectively to strengthen the state."[12] Whatever the value or importance of such rights, they are not human rights as that term is ordinarily used.

It has been argued that "different civilizations or societies have different conceptions of human well-being. Hence, they have a different attitude toward human rights issues."[13] But even this is misleading. Other societies may have (similar or different) attitudes toward issues that we consider today to be matters of human rights. However, unless they possess a concept of human rights, they are unlikely to have *any* attitude toward human rights.

Many arguments of anthropological universality are rooted in an admirable desire to show cultural sensitivity, respect, or tolerance. In fact, though, they impose an alien analytical framework that misunderstands and misrepresents the foundations and functioning of the societies in question.

I am *not* claiming that Islam, Confucianism, or traditional African ideas cannot support internationally recognized human rights. Quite the contrary, I argue in §3.6 that they not only logically can but in practice increasingly do. My point here is that Islamic, Confucian, and African societies did not develop human rights ideas or practices prior to the twentieth century.

The next section offers an explanation for this fact. Before proceeding, however, it is important to note that *exactly the same thing can be said of the pre-modern West*. Just as traditional Asian and African societies lacked ideas and practices of human rights, so did traditional Western societies.

The ancient Greeks, for example, notoriously distinguished between Hellenes and barbarians, practiced slavery, denied basic rights to foreigners and noncitizen Greeks, and severely restricted the political and other rights of even free adult (male) citizens. The idea that all human beings had equal and inalienable basic rights was equally foreign to Athens and Sparta, Plato and Aristotle, and Homer, Hesiod, Aeschylus, Sophocles, Euripides, Aristophanes, Herodotus, and Thucydides. The same is true, although the details differ, for ancient Rome, in both its republican and imperial eras. In medieval Europe, the spiritual egalitarianism and universality of Christianity expressed itself in a hierarchical, inegalitarian politics. Had medieval Europeans given any serious thought to the idea of equal legal and political rights for all human beings, they would have seen them as a moral abomination, a horrid transgression against divinely ordained order.

In the pre-modern world, both Western and non-Western alike, the duty of rulers to further the common good arose not from the rights (entitlements) of all human beings to be ruled justly but from divine commandment, natural law, tradition, or contingent political arrangements. Although the people could expect to benefit from the obligations of their rulers, in neither theory nor practice did they have human rights that could be exercised against unjust rulers. The reigning idea was natural right (in the sense of righteousness or rectitude), not natural or human rights (in the sense of equal and inalienable individual entitlements). (See §2.1.)

4. FUNCTIONAL UNIVERSALITY

The reference in the preceding paragraph to the pre-modern world, I will argue, points to the explanation for both the absence and the presence of human rights in particular societies at particular times. Human rights ideas and practices are a product not of culture but of the social forces of modernity, particularly modern markets and modern states.

Natural or human rights ideas first developed in the modern West. Early inklings are clear in Britain by the 1640s. A full-fledged natural rights theory is evident in John Locke's *Second Treatise of Government,* published in 1689 in support of the so-called Glorious Revolution of 1688. The American and French revolutions used these ideas as the basis for constructing new political orders. The essential point, however, is the modernity, not the cultural "Westernness," of human rights ideas and practices.

Nothing in classical or medieval culture made the West unusually conducive to the development of human rights ideas. Quite the contrary, in the thirteenth and fourteenth centuries, parts of the Islamic world, perhaps most notably Fatimid Spain, provided a much more tolerant cultural and religious environment that would on its face seem to have been more conducive to the development of human rights ideas and practices. The Catholic Counter-Reformation and the intolerance of most ruling Protestant regimes in the sixteenth and seventeenth centuries suggest that early modern Europe was in many ways a particularly *un*supportive cultural milieu for developing human rights ideas. The late sixteenth and early seventeenth centuries, it is important to remember, were an era of violent, often brutal, internecine and international religious warfare. Certainly no widely endorsed reading of Christian scriptures before the mid-seventeenth century supported the idea of a broad set of equal and inalienable individual rights held by all human beings—or even all Christians.

Although Western culture did not cause Westerners to develop ideas and practices of human rights, it did become increasingly supportive of the idea and practice of equal natural rights. At the risk of gross oversimplification, I suggest that capitalist markets and absolutist states lie behind both the rise of human rights ideas and practices and the modernization of Western economies, societies, polities, and cultures.

Ever more powerful (capitalist) markets and (sovereign, bureaucratic) states disrupted, destroyed, or radically transformed "traditional" communities and their systems of mutual support and obligation, with traumatic consequences. Rapidly expanding numbers of (relatively) separate families and individuals faced a growing range of increasingly unbuffered economic and political threats to their interests and quality of life. New kinds of what Henry Shue aptly calls "standard threats" to human dignity provoked a variety of remedial responses.[14] By the late seventeenth century, claims of natural rights began to become a preferred mechanism for securing new visions of human dignity in these new social, economic, and political conditions.

At roughly the same time, the Protestant Reformation disrupted the unity of Christian Europe, often quite violently. By the middle of the seventeenth century, however, states, due to exhaustion at least as much as conviction, began to stop fighting over religion. (The Westphalia settlement of 1648 is conventionally presented as the start of "modern" international relations.) Although full religious equality remained very far off, religious toleration (for selected Christians sects) gradually became the European norm and provided an important foundation for broader ideas of human rights. If individual choice was permitted on the most important of all issues, the salvation of one's immortal soul, why not allow it on issues of lesser magnitude as well?

Add to this the growing possibilities for physical and social mobility and we have the crucible out of which contemporary human rights ideas and practices were formed. Privileged ruling groups faced a growing barrage of demands from an ever widening range of dispossessed groups, first for relief from particular legal and political disabilities, and eventually for full inclusion on the basis of equality. Such demands took many forms, including appeals to scripture, church, morality, tradition, justice, natural law, order, social utility, and national strength. Claims of equal and inalienable natural/human rights, however, became increasingly common.

These processes of threat and response occurred first in modern Europe. Modern markets and states, however, have spread to all corners of the globe, bringing with them roughly the same threats to human dignity. This has created a *functional universality* for human rights. Human rights represent the most effective response yet devised by human ingenuity to a wide range of threats to human dignity that have become nearly universal across the globe.

Although it was no coincidence that the idea and practice of human rights developed first in early modern Europe, this was more an accident or an effect than a cause. Westerners had no special pre-existing cultural proclivity to human rights. Rather, they had the (good or bad) fortune to experience first the indignities of modern markets and states. These new forms of suffering and injustice called forth new remedies. One increasingly popular and effective response was claims of equal and inalienable individual human rights. And nothing better has yet been devised. Socialism and various forms of developmental dictatorship, the leading alternatives of the cold war era, proved themselves in practice to be dismal failures. Human rights remain the only proven effective mechanism for assuring human dignity in societies dominated by markets and states.

The functional universality of human rights depends on human rights providing attractive and effective remedies for some of the most pressing systemic threats to human dignity faced by individuals and groups. In the contemporary world, human rights do precisely that for a growing number of people in all regions. The functional universality of internationally recognized human rights is historically contingent. Today, however, universality rather than relativity most deserves emphasis. We all face the problems of modern markets and states, and we all need equal and inalienable universal human rights to protect us.

5. INTERNATIONAL LEGAL UNIVERSALITY

If this argument is sound, we ought to find substantial and widespread active endorsement of internationally recognized human rights. And indeed, international human rights law provides striking and important evidence of such endorsement.

Virtually all states accept the Universal Declaration of Human Rights as an authoritative statement of international human rights norms. The 1966 International Human Rights Covenants, as of October 2005, had over 150 parties. The treaties on racial discrimination, women's rights, torture, and the rights of the child had, respectively, 170, 180, 140, and 192 parties.[15] These six core international human rights treaties today have on average 164 parties, a truly impressive 85 percent ratification rate. For the purposes of contemporary international relations, "human rights" means, roughly, the rights in the Universal Declaration and the six supporting treaties. I call this *international legal universality.*

International legal universality, like functional universality, is contingent and relative. It depends on the decision of states, international organizations, transnational actors, and various national groups to treat the Universal Declaration and the Covenants as an authoritative statement of internationally recognized human rights. Human rights today are universal in the sense that there is an international legal consensus that all states are bound by, and are legitimate only to the extent that they respect and protect, internationally recognized human rights. Thus we increasingly see not only states but civil society organizations and movements of political opposition waging their struggles for social justice under the banner of human rights.

International legal universality, like functional universality, is ultimately about people, states, and other political actors deciding for themselves that human rights are essential to protecting their visions of a life of dignity. States and other national and international political actors may in the future no longer accept or give as much weight to such principles. Today, however, the overwhelming evidence is that they have chosen, and are continuing to choose, human rights over competing conceptions of national and international political legitimacy.

6. OVERLAPPING CONSENSUS UNIVERSALITY

Is international legal universality replicated at the level of moral and political theory? I argue that it is, in an incomplete but significant form.

John Rawls distinguishes "comprehensive religious, philosophical, or moral doctrines," such as Islam, Kantianism, utilitarianism, Confucianism, and Marxism, from "political conceptions of justice." Political conceptions of justice address only the political structure of society, defined (as far as possible) independent of any particular comprehensive doctrine. Adherents of different comprehensive doctrines thus may be able to reach an "overlapping consensus" on a political conception of justice.[16]

Such a consensus is overlapping, partial rather than complete. It is political rather than moral or religious. Rawls developed the notion to understand how "there can be a stable and just society whose free and equal citizens are deeply divided by conflicting and even incommensurable religious, philosophical, and moral doctrines."[17] The idea, however, has an obvious extension to a culturally and politically diverse international society. I argue that there is an emerging and deepening international overlapping consensus on the Universal Declaration of Human Rights.

Human rights, as I suggested in §2.3, can be readily grounded in a variety of moral theories. For example, they can be seen as encoded in the natural law, called for by divine commandment, political means to further human good or utility, or institutions designed to produce virtuous citizens. The increasing political prominence of human rights over the past few decades has led growing numbers of people among an expanding range of comprehensive doctrines to endorse human rights—but only as a political conception of justice.

It should be emphasized that such an overlapping consensus on human rights operates in the Western world no less than in the broader international community. Catholic natural law theory and **utilitarianism**, for example, agree about little at the level of comprehensive doctrine. Nonetheless, many, probably most, contemporary Catholics and utilitarians endorse human rights as a political conception of justice.

This, however, is a rather recent phenomenon. Jeremy Bentham, often considered the founder of modern utilitarianism, famously described natural rights as "simple nonsense" and imprescriptible natural rights as "nonsense upon stilts."[18] Until the mid-twentieth century, virtually all utilitarians were hostile to natural or human rights. Human rights were also absent from Catholic social teaching. In the past half century, however, prominent Catholic political theorists have enthusiastically embraced human rights,[19] and human rights language has become increasingly central to church social teaching. Utilitarian defenses of human rights today are also common. And in ordinary day-to-day politics, most Catholics and utilitarians not only have no difficulty accepting human rights but often embrace them with considerable enthusiasm.

Much the same is true more generally as well. Virtually all Western religious and philosophical doctrines through most of their history have either rejected or ignored human rights. Today, however, adherents of most Western comprehensive doctrines endorse human rights. There is no logical reason why a similar transformation could not happen elsewhere. In fact, if the medieval Christian world of crusades, serfdom, and hereditary aristocracy could become today's world of liberal and social democratic welfare states, it is hard to imagine a society where a similar transformation is inconceivable.

Consider traditional Hinduism, which not only stressed categorical, qualitative moral differences among descent-based groups (castes) but even denied moral significance to the category of human beings. Gandhi, however, showed that it is possible to reinterpret even such a seemingly inegalitarian comprehensive doctrine in fundamentally egalitarian terms that support human rights. And in practice, India has been, both at home and abroad, one of the leading Third World supporters of internationally recognized human rights.

No particular culture or comprehensive doctrine is by nature either necessarily compatible or necessarily incompatible with human rights. Cultures are immensely malleable, as are the political expressions of comprehensive doctrines. It is an empirical, not a theoretical, question whether (any, some, or most) members of a culture or exponents of a comprehensive doctrine support human rights as a political conception of justice. Today, in all regions of the world, adherents of most comprehensive doctrines, and virtually all deeply egalitarian doctrines, increasingly participate in an emerging and deepening "universal" international overlapping consensus on human rights.

All major civilizations have for long periods treated some significant portion of the human race as "outsiders" not entitled to guarantees that could be taken for granted by "insiders." For most of their histories, all literate civilizations have assigned social roles, rights, and duties primarily on the basis of characteristics such as birth, age, and gender. Most regions of the globe, for example, have practiced and justified slavery or some other form of human bondage.

Today, however, the fundamental moral equality of all human beings is not merely accepted but strongly endorsed by all leading comprehensive doctrines in all regions of the world. This convergence, both within and among civilizations, provides the foundation for a convergence on the rights of the Universal Declaration. In principle, a great variety of social practices other than human rights might provide the basis for realizing foundational egalitarian values. In practice, human rights are rapidly becoming the preferred option. I call this *overlapping consensus universality.*

7. VOLUNTARY OR COERCED CONSENSUS?

Both overlapping consensus and international legal universality rest on the idea of a broad, effectively global consensus. Is this consensus more voluntary or coerced? This question is crucial to determining the depth of the penetration of international human rights norms.

The importance of the example and advocacy of the world's leading power, the United States, and its principal allies should not be underestimated. I suggest, however, that example has been more significant than advocacy. Human rights dominate political discussions not only, or even primarily, because of the support of materially dominant powers but also because they respond to some of the most important social and political aspirations of individuals, families, and groups in most countries of the world. Some governments may feel coerced into endorsing the Universal Declaration. The assent of most societies and individuals, however, is largely voluntary.[20] The international consensus on the Universal Declaration largely reflects its cross-cultural substantive attractions. People, when given a chance, usually (in the contemporary world) choose human rights, irrespective of region, religion, or culture.

Few "ordinary" citizens (in any country) have a particularly sophisticated sense of what a commitment to human rights means. They respond, instead, to the general idea that they and their fellow citizens are entitled to equal treatment and certain basic goods, services, protections, and opportunities. My argument is that the list of rights in the Universal Declaration is likely to be very similar to the list that they would come up with, irrespective of culture, after considerable reflection. More precisely, there is almost nothing on the list in the Universal Declaration that they would not put there, although one could imagine a global constitutional convention coming up with a somewhat larger list. In other words, the Universal Declaration is a pretty good substantive first approximation. I thus conclude that we see something very close to a voluntary overlapping consensus on the Universal Declaration, which is mirrored in the strong international legal consensus.

8. ONTOLOGICAL UNIVERSALITY

Overlapping consensus implies that human rights can, and in the contemporary world do, have multiple, diverse "foundations." A single transhistorical moral foundation for human rights would provide a very different kind of universality. Such *ontological universality*, as I call it, cannot logically be ruled out. However, I argue that it is profoundly implausible and that for a variety of important practical reasons, it should be vigorously rejected.

A single moral code may indeed be objectively correct and valid at all times and in all places. Many theories, both secular and religious, claim such a status. In the West, for example, natural law theories typically present morality as a natural or divinely ordained fact to be discovered by reason. At least three problems with such arguments, however, are practically, although not logically, fatal.

First, no matter how strenuously adherents of a particular philosophy or religion insist that (their) values are objectively valid, they cannot marshal arguments that adherents of other religions or philosophies find persuasive. Those making the argument may simply not yet have developed the analytical or persuasive skills to construct a compelling case. The rest of the world may, for a variety of reasons, be (innocently or perversely) unwilling or unable to accept what are in fact objective truths. Whatever the reason, though, the absence of compelling arguments leaves us politically in much the same position as if there were no objective values at all; that is, we are thrown back on arguments of functional, international legal, and overlapping consensus universality (understood now, perhaps, as imperfect reflections of a deeper ontological universality).

Second, virtually all comprehensive doctrines have for large parts of their history ignored or actively denied human rights. Thus, even if some comprehensive doctrine is indeed objectively correct, it is highly unlikely that human rights in general, and the list in the Universal Declaration in particular, are ontologically universal.

Third, the ontological universality of human rights implies that virtually all moral and religious theories through much of their history have been objectively false. This may indeed be correct. Before we embrace such a radical idea, though, I think we need much stronger arguments than are currently available to support ontological universality.

Overlapping consensus does not make human rights groundless. Quite the contrary, it gives them multiple grounds. This seems to me, in addition to its analytical and philosophical virtues, of great practical utility. Those who want to make ontological claims for their comprehensive doctrines can do so, and thus be faithful to their own views, without the need to convince or compel others to accept this particular, or even any, foundation. Furthermore, treating human rights as a political conception of justice may allow us to handle a wide range of issues of political justice and right while circumventing inconclusive and divisive disputes over moral foundations.

9. UNIVERSAL RIGHTS,
NOT IDENTICAL PRACTICES

Elsewhere I have developed a three-tiered scheme for thinking about universality, however it is conceptualized.[21] I have argued that human rights are relatively universal at the level of the *concept*, the broad formulations characteristic of the Universal Declaration such as the claims in Articles 3 and 22 that everyone has "the right to life, liberty and security of person" and "the right to social security." Particular rights concepts, however, usually have different defensible *conceptions*, introducing a very real element of relativity among universal human rights. Furthermore, any particular conception is likely to have many defensible *implementations*. At this level—for example, the design of electoral districts to realize the claim in Article 21 of the Universal Declaration that "Everyone has the right to take part in the government of his country, directly or through freely chosen representatives"—the range of legitimate variation/relativity is substantial.

Functional and overlapping consensus universality lie primarily at the level of human rights concepts; the arguments that support these kinds of universality usually operate at a high level of abstraction that rarely reaches very far into the level of conceptions, let alone implementations. International legal universality much more regularly requires particular conceptions and occasionally even mandates particular forms of implementation. The resulting, quite substantial, range of legitimate variability means that universal human rights do not require identical human rights practices. In fact, substantial second-order variations, by country, region, or other grouping, are fully compatible with the relative universality of internationally recognized human rights.

Striking legitimate variations exist even within regions. For example, conceptions and implementations of many economic and social rights differ dramatically between the United States and most of the countries of Western Europe. Important variations exist even within Europe. For example, Robert Goodin and his colleagues demonstrate important systematic differences between the welfare state of Germany and that of the Netherlands.[22]

In evaluating arguments supporting particular variations in conception and implementation, three criteria, based on the vision of universality defended above, provide substantial guidance.[23]

1. Important differences in the character of the threats being faced are likely to justify variations, perhaps even at the level of concepts. Although providing perhaps the strongest theoretical justification for even fairly substantial deviations from international human rights norms, in practice such arguments rarely are empirically defensible in the contemporary world. (Indigenous peoples may be the exception that proves the rule.)
2. Variations that appeal to important principles or precepts in underlying comprehensive doctrines involved in the overlapping consensus deserve special consideration.
3. Arguments claiming that a particular conception or implementation is, for cultural or historical reasons, deeply embedded within or of unusually great significance to some significant group in society deserve, on their face, sympathetic consideration.

All three kinds of justifications, however, can be accepted only with the proviso that both the particular variations and the resulting set of human rights are generally consistent with the overarching concepts of the Universal Declaration. Although space prohibits much detail, let me offer two brief examples.

A. Freedom of Religion

Article 18 of the Universal Declaration reads, in its entirety, "Everyone has the right to freedom of thought, conscience and religion; this right includes freedom to change his religion or belief, and freedom, either alone or in community with others and in public or private, to manifest his religion or belief in teaching, practice, worship and observance." Islam, like many other religions and secular philosophies, strongly supports the concept of freedom of religion. Most Islamic countries and communities respect the right of adherents of other religions to practice their beliefs (within the ordinary constraints of public order). Most schools of Islamic law and scholarship, however, deny Muslims the right to change their religion.

Is prohibition of apostasy by Muslims compatible with the universality of Article 18? Reasonable people may disagree, but I am (reluctantly) inclined to answer, "Probably."

We are dealing here with a variation at the level of conceptions—the limits of the range of application of the principle of freedom of religion—in a context where the overarching concept is strongly endorsed. Given that there is a deeply rooted basis in the underlying comprehensive doctrine, supported by a long tradition of practice, we ought, in principle, to approach such arguments with an attitude of tolerance. We should note, however, two important limitations that have general applicability.

First, we should be much more inclined to endorse a relatively isolated deviation from international human rights norms than the identical deviation when it is part of a series of changes that collectively tend to undermine the overall structure of protections and guarantees. The broader human rights context is important not only in itself but for what it suggests about the intentions of those advocating deviations from international norms.

Second, our tolerance ought to decrease as the level of coercion increases. Dissuasion of apostasy almost certainly lies within the legitimate margin of appreciation. It may even be permissible for the state to impose modest disabilities, such as refusing to recognize or register marriages involving apostates. Executing apostates, however, certainly exceeds the bounds of permissible variation. Violently imposing a particular conception of freedom of religion, let alone one that that is explicitly prohibited by international human rights law, inappropriately denies people basic personal autonomy. Although perhaps justified within a particular comprehensive doctrine, it excessively infringes on the international overlapping consensus and thus is not entitled to international toleration.

Nonetheless, a universalistic rejection of the violent suppression of apostasy is not unproblematic. Human rights are not ends in themselves but a means to achieve more deeply rooted values. A comprehensive doctrine that generally supports internationally recognized human rights but is incompatible with some particular element raises thorny issues for adherents of that doctrine and outsiders alike. Adherents face the difficult choice between reforming or abandoning long and deeply held views or rejecting some important part of the international legal consensus on human rights. Outsiders face the problem of determining how far to extend tolerance to fellow participants in the overlapping consensus on human rights. Such a decision is especially difficult when not only international norms but their own comprehensive doctrines reject the practice in question.

When comprehensive doctrines conflict over matters of deep importance to those doctrines, international legal and overlapping consensus universality may lose much of their force. The result may be a conflict that cannot be resolved by reason and persuasion alone. Whatever the outcome, at least one side may find itself profoundly dissatisfied.

B. Hate Speech

Article 4(a) of the racial discrimination convention requires parties not just to prohibit violence and incitement to violence but also to "declare an offence punishable by law all dissemination of ideas based on racial superiority or hatred." This provision has been rejected by the United States, where the view that freedom of speech includes even "hate speech" is deeply embedded in constitutional history and jurisprudence.

This example is somewhat less difficult because it concerns the proper balance between two competing human rights rather than a conflict between human rights and another social value. Whatever we do will require restricting the range of at least one of these rights. In such a case, any particular resolution that plausibly protects the conceptual integrity of both rights must be described as controversial but defensible. And there are many such resolutions. In the United States, incitement to violence is legally prohibited, thus protecting and giving substantial legal backing to the general prohibition against violence that is the central subject of Article 4(a). The deviation from international norms is thus sufficiently limited and narrow that it deserves international toleration, even from those who sincerely believe that prohibiting hate speech is a much better course of action.

Powerful arguments are required to justify deviating from the international legal consensus represented by the treaty. In this case, however, we have an interpretation that is deeply rooted in legal history and constitutional theory, differing only narrowly with respect to one part of a second-order conception, in a context of general support for the overarching concept, as well as most of the rest of the conceptions in the convention. Furthermore, although targets of hate speech may be harmed, they remain protected against violence and are not subject to any state imposition of a particular substantive vision. And part of the underlying justification for the American practice is that prohibiting speech because of its content harms those whose speech is prohibited and in effect involves state support for or active opposition to particular viewpoints that are expressed without the use or threat of violence. Whatever one may think of such an argument, it clearly involves a (not un)reasonable attempt to balance competing harms. Toleration of the American refusal to prohibit hate speech thus seems justified.

10. UNIVERSALISM WITHOUT IMPERIALISM

These brief arguments are hardly conclusive, perhaps not even correct. Nonetheless, I think that they clearly illustrate that the universality of internationally recognized human rights does *not* require, or even encourage, global homogenization or the sacrifice of valued local practices (see also §7.5). Certainly nothing in this chapter implies or justifies cultural imperialism. Quite the contrary, (relatively) universal human rights protect people from imposed conceptions of the good life whether those visions are imposed by local or foreign actors.

The underlying purpose of human rights is to allow human beings, individually and in groups that give meaning and value to their lives, to pursue their own vision of the good life. Such choices deserve our respect as long as they are consistent with comparable rights for others and reflect a plausible vision of human flourishing to which we can imagine a free people freely assenting. Understanding human rights as a political conception of justice supported by an overlapping consensus *requires* us to allow human beings, individually and collectively, considerable space to shape (relatively) universal rights to their particular purposes—within the constraints at the level of the concept established by functional, international legal, and overlapping consensus universality.

The legacy of imperialism does demand that Westerners in particular show special caution and sensitivity when advancing arguments of universalism in the face of clashing cultural values. Westerners must also remember the political, economic, and cultural power that lies behind even their best-intentioned activities. Anything that in any way appears to involve imposing Western values is likely to be met with readily understandable suspicion in many parts of the world—including much of the Western world.

Caution, however, must not be confused with inaction. Even if we are not entitled to impose our values on others, they are our own values. They may demand that we act on them even in the absence of agreement by others, especially when that action does not involve force. If the practices of others are particularly objectionable, even strongly sanctioned traditions may deserve neither our respect nor our toleration. Consider, for example, societies in which it is traditional to kill the firstborn child if it is female or the deeply rooted tradition of anti-Semitism in the West. Their age and deep cultural roots are, I would argue, no defense against the claims of universal human rights.

I do not mean to minimize the dangers of cultural and political arrogance. The proper solution to the "false" universalism of a powerful actor mistaking its own interests for universal values, however, is not relativism but relative universalism.

American foreign policy in particular has (not unreasonably) been accused of often confusing American interests with universal values. Even if there is no longer an American consensus that "What's good for GM is good for America," it does appear to many people in Europe and in the Third World that most Americans today do subscribe to the view that what's good for the United States is good for the world. And the current American administration is more than willing to chide others, at home and abroad, who don't "get it."

Such arrogant and abusive "universalism" has, I am afraid, tempted even well-meaning critics of American foreign policy to advance misguided arguments for the relativity of human rights. Unfortunately, such critics in effect accept the American self-presentation, equating human rights with American foreign policy. Then, in attacking the arrogance of American foreign policy they end up throwing out the baby with the bath water.

Without authoritative international standards, what is there to hold the United States (or any other power) accountable to? If international legal universality has no force (and arguments of ontological universality remain unpersuasive outside a relatively narrow community), it is hard to find a ground for saying that human rights are not whatever the United States says they are. This is especially true in international relations, where normative disputes that cannot be resolved by rational persuasion tend to end up being resolving by political, economic, and cultural power—of which the United States today has more than anyone else.

Consensus is no philosophical guarantee of truth. Nonetheless, insisting that the universality of internationally recognized human rights lies in significant measure in international legal and overlapping consensus provides important protection against the arrogant "universalism" of the powerful. The relative universality of human rights, besides being "correct," can be a significant resource for calling the powerful, including the United States, to account.

One of the great achievements of the international human rights movement has been the creation of international legal universality, which in addition to its intrinsic value has greatly facilitated the deepening of the overlapping consensus on internationally recognized human rights. Even the United States participates—fitfully and incompletely, to be sure—in both of these consensuses. Both of the Bush administrations and the Clinton administration have regularly raised human rights concerns in numerous bilateral relationships. In most instances, the evidence clearly indicates that these concerns are genuine. (The real problem with American foreign policy is not where it does raise human rights concerns but where it doesn't, or where it allows them to be subordinated to other concerns.)

Human rights have become hegemonic in the post–cold war era largely independent of American power. One might even suggest that American power is in some significant measure an effect, not the cause, of the ideological hegemony of human rights. Human rights thus can be turned against the arrogance of American, or any other state, power. And as controversy surrounding the abuses at Abu Ghraib has shown us, the ideological hegemony of human rights may even mobilize internal political forces that lead to changes in policy in the midst of a war.

Universal human rights are hardly a panacea for the world's problems. They do, however, fully deserve the prominence they have received in recent years. The world is a better place than it would have been without the spread of universal human rights ideas and practices. And for the foreseeable future, universal human rights are likely to remain a vital resource in national, international, and transnational struggles for social justice and human dignity.

DISCUSSION QUESTIONS

1. Make a list of all the arguments you can think of that can be made for cultural relativism. Which of these actually involve *cultural* factors and which involve political, economic, or ideological factors? Are arguments of political relativism as persuasive as arguments of cultural relativism? Why? What about economic relativism? Is the distinction among culture, politics, and economics helpful or revealing? Why?
2. Suppose that there are indeed major cultural differences with respect to human rights in the world today. Should we take those into account? Why?

Should we allow them to alter our international human rights policies and practices? If so, are we then acting on the basis of other people's values? If not, what right do we have to act on the basis of our values when dealing with others who do not share them?

3. *Are* human rights ideas truly universal? Are the differences between cultures and countries really primarily concerned with secondary human rights issues? Do recent changes in international relations have anything to tell us about the universality of human rights? Consider, for example, the fall of the communist bloc and democratization in much of the Third World. Then consider Islamic fundamentalism and the rise of nationalist ethnic hostilities.

4. Does the geographical and political relativity of human rights that arises from the system of national implementation fatally undermine the universality of human rights? How can we assert that human rights are in any significant sense universal when they are subject to such radically different national systems of implementation?

5. Why do so many people, in the Western and non-Western worlds alike, insist that their cultures have had human rights ideas and practices at times when they clearly have not? How much of this can be attributed to the notion that the legitimacy of cultures is somehow dependent on their conformity with "modern" Western ideas?

6. What do you think of the argument that human rights ideas and practices are rooted in social structure rather than culture? What does this imply about the nature of culture?

7. How can we untangle the relative contributions of states and markets to the need for and rise of human rights? Would modern states have been possible without the rise of capitalist markets? Does the notion of functional universality have significant implications for the relationship between civil and political rights and economic, social, and cultural rights?

8. Is it really true that *nothing* except human rights has yet been devised that works tolerably well to protect individuals and communities against the standard threats posed by modern markets and states? List some of the leading alternatives and try to figure out why they have failed and what would have been needed to make them work. Does this suggest anything interesting about the nature of potential alternatives to human rights that might develop in the future?

9. What are some of the principal threats to human dignity that are *not* connected with markets and states? How important is their absence from the list of internationally recognized human rights? If they are very significant, how much does this undermine the claim for even the relative universality of human rights?

10. Is consensus morally important? Politically important? If so, why?

11. How much of the apparent appeal of human rights today is due to their inherent advantages? To the collapse of the leading alternatives? To the power and prestige of Western states that support them?

12.   In assessing claims of relativism, how important is coercion? Isn't the "brainwashing" that goes with ordinary socialization just as coercive? Is the idea of voluntary consent just a myth? To the extent that it is, how can any system of values be justified?

13.   Just how malleable is culture? Even if it is immensely malleable across extended periods of time, is it relatively static over a few decades? Isn't that the time frame of politics?

14.   If practices are changing (or even just capable of change), should international human rights policy respect those practices or exert pressure to modify them so that they are more consistent with international human rights standards? What are the strengths and weaknesses of each approach?

15.   Should the United States be held to the same standards as everyone else? If not, how can we justify holding others to our standards?

SUGGESTED READINGS

The literature on cultural relativism is immense. For my own contributions, which are summarized here, see Chapters 4–7 of *Universal Human Rights in Theory and Practice,* 2nd ed. (Ithaca: Cornell University Press, 2003).

In my opinion, the best short overviews of the issue are provided by Ann-Belinda S. Preis, "Human Rights as Cultural Practice: An Anthropological Critique," *Human Rights Quarterly* 18 (May 1996): 286–315; Andrew J. Nathan, "Universalism: A Particularistic Account," in *Negotiating Culture and Human Rights,* ed. Lynda Bell, Andrew J. Nathan, and Ilan Peleg (New York: Columbia University Press, 2001); Abdullahi A. An Na'im, "Towards a Cross-Cultural Approach to Defining International Human Rights Standards," in *Human Rights in Cross-Cultural Perspectives,* ed. Abdullahi A. An Na'im (Philadelphia: University of Pennsylvania Press, 1992); and Onuma Yasuaki, "Toward an Intercivilizational Approach to Human Rights," in *The East Asian Challenge for Human Rights,* ed. Joanne Bauer and Daniel Bell (Cambridge: Cambridge University Press, 1999). See also, Bhikhu Parekh, "Non-Ethnocentric Universalism," in *Human Rights in Global Politics,* ed. Tim Dunne and Nicholas J. Wheeler (Cambridge: Cambridge University Press, 1999).

For examples of a much more radical relativism, see Adamantia Pollis and Peter Schwab, "Human Rights: A Western Construct with Limited Applicability," in *Human Rights: Cultural and Ideological Perspectives,* ed. Adamantia Pollis and Peter Schwab (New York: Praeger, 1979); Adamantia Pollis, "Liberal, Socialist, and Third World Perspectives on Human Rights," in *Toward a Human Rights Framework,* ed. Peter Schwab and Adamantia Pollis (New York: Praeger, 1982); and Alison Dundes Rentlen, "The Unanswered Challenge of Relativism and the Consequences for Human Rights," *Human Rights Quarterly* 7 (November 1985): 514–540. For a sharp response to such views, see Rhoda E. Howard, "Cultural Absolutism and the Nostalgia for Community," *Human Rights Quarterly* 15 (May 1993): 315–338.

The following are, in my view, the best arguments in support of indigenous non-Western conceptions of human rights: Adbul Aziz Said, "Precept and Practice of Human Rights in Islam," *Universal Human Rights [Human Rights Quarterly]* 1, no. 1 (1979): 63–80; Fouad Zakaria, "Human Rights in the Arab World: The Islamic Context," in *Philosophical Foundations of Human Rights* (Paris: UNESCO, 1986); Majid Khadduri, "Human Rights in Islam," *The Annals* 243 (January 1946): 77–81; Dunstan M. Wai, "Human Rights in Sub-Saharan Africa," in *Cultural and Ideological Perspectives,* ed. Peter Schwab and Adamantia Pollis (New York: Praeger, 1979); Kwasi Wiredu, "An Akan Perspective on Human Rights," in *The Philosophy of Human Rights,* ed. Patrick Hayden (St. Paul, Minn.: Paragon House, 2001); Timothy Fernyhough, "Human Rights and Precolonial Africa," in *Human Rights and Governance in Africa,* ed. Ronald Cohen, Goran Hyden, and Winston P. Nagan (Gainesville: University of Florida Press, 1993); Asmarom Legesse, "Human Rights in African Political Culture," in *The Moral Imperatives of Human Rights: A World Survey,* ed. Kenneth W. Thompson (Washington, D.C.: University Press of America, 1980); Yougindra Khushalani, "Human Rights in Asia and Africa," *Human Rights Law Journal* 4, no. 4 (1983): 403–442; Ralph Buultjens, "Human Rights in Indian Political Culture," in *Moral Imperatives of Human Rights: A World Survey,* ed. Kenneth W. Thompson (Washington, D.C.: University Press of America, 1980); James C. Hsiung, "Human Rights in an East Asian Perspective," in *Human Rights in an East Asian Perspective,* ed. James C. Hsiung (New York: Paragon House, 1985); and Lo Chung-Sho, "Human Rights in the Chinese Tradition," in *Human Rights: Comments and Interpretations,* ed. UNESCO (New York: Columbia University Press, 1949).

The two best recent readers, in my view, are Joanne Bauer and Daniel Bell, *The East Asian Challenge for Human Rights* (Cambridge: Cambridge University Press, 1999), and Lynda Bell, Andrew J. Nathan, and Ilan Peleg, *Negotiating Culture and Human Rights* (New York: Columbia University Press, 2001). Both cover a wide range of views except for radical relativism. Jane K. Cowan, Marie-Benedicte Dembour, and Richard A. Wilson, eds., *Culture and Rights: Anthropological Perspectives* (Cambridge: Cambridge University Press, 2001) is useful for its anthropological perspective, which is often sorely missing in other discussions. Mahmood Mamdani, ed., *Beyond Rights Talk and Culture Talk: Comparative Essays on the Politics of Rights and Culture* (New York: St. Martin's Press, 2000) also seeks to break out of the conventional mold for many of these discussions. Older readers still worth consulting, from which individual articles are cited above, include UNESCO, ed., *Human Rights: Comments and Interpretations;* Pollis and Schwab, eds., *Human Rights: Cultural and Ideological Perspectives;* Thompson, ed., *The Moral Imperatives of Human Rights;* An-Na'im, ed., *Human Rights in Cross-Cultural Perspectives.*

Two superb books that treat the complexities of rights and related ideas in Chinese philosophy and political practice are Stephen C. Angle, *Human Rights and Chinese Thought: A Cross-Cultural Inquiry* (Cambridge: Cambridge University Press, 2002), and Marina Svensson, *Debating Human Rights in China* (Lanham, Md.: Rowman and Littlefield, 2003). Both are extremely sympathetic to the similarities and the differences between Chinese and Western ideas and their significant changes over time.

Even for readers with no special interest in China, these books are well worth reading. They offer careful and detailed understandings of complex issues that are far too often handled in glib generalities. Ann Elizabeth Mayer, *Islam and Human Rights: Tradition and Politics,* 4th ed. (Boulder: Westview Press, 2006) does much the same for the Islamic world.

4

◄○►

The Domestic Politics of Human Rights:
The Case of the Southern Cone

Although this book deals primarily with the international politics of human rights, national politics largely determines how human rights are protected or violated in a world of sovereign states. National case studies can both illustrate this important point and provide concreteness to the notion of "human rights violations." This chapter looks in some detail at violations in the Southern Cone of South America. Chapters 5 and 6 include briefer examinations of human rights violations in South Africa and Central America, two cold war focal points for international human rights action. Chapters 7 and 8 consider China and the former Yugoslavia, two prominent post–cold war examples. In these later chapters, the focus is primarily on international responses to national human rights violations. Here, however, my focus is primarily on national violations.

The geographical area known as the Southern Cone of South America includes the countries of Argentina, Chile, Paraguay, and Uruguay, as well as southern Brazil. In this chapter, we look at three of these countries, Argentina, Chile, and Uruguay, which for convenience I refer to as the countries of the Southern Cone. They suffered under a distinctive style of intensely repressive military rule in the 1970s and 1980s and provided an impetus for some important developments in international human rights policies.

1. POLITICS BEFORE THE COUPS

In Chile, military rule had been rare since the mid-nineteenth century. After World War II, a stable three-party democratic system emerged. In 1970, Salvador Allende became the world's first freely elected Marxist president. Allende dramatically intensified the economic and social reforms begun under his Christian Democratic predecessor, Eduardo Frei. Large agricultural estates were expropriated. Key private

59

industries and banks were nationalized, including Chile's (largely U.S.-owned) copper industry. Social services were expanded.

These changes were both lavishly praised and reviled, both within Chile and abroad. The resulting ideological polarization helped to set the stage for a military coup in September 1973. Allende died during the coup, and a repressive military regime was installed that ruled until 1990.

In Uruguay, the military had not intervened in politics since the 1860s. Furthermore, beginning in the first two decades of the twentieth century, under President José Batlle y Ordóñez, Uruguay implemented a series of model social and political reforms that created a widely admired social democratic welfare state that provided education and health care for all. The system, however, began to collapse in the late 1960s.

Political stalemate between its two dominant parties weakened Uruguay's government. The economy faced high inflation and labor unrest. And the Tupamaros were waging a dramatic campaign of guerrilla terrorism. In response, some civil liberties were suspended in 1968, 1970, and 1971 and even more seriously restricted in 1972. In June 1973, President Bordaberry suspended most remaining constitutional rights, closed the National Assembly, and for three years provided a public face for the military government—until he too was forced from office.

Argentina has a more checkered political history. Following independence in 1821–1822, Argentine politics were noted for violent struggles among provincial bosses *(caudillos)* and for leadership in the capital, Buenos Aires. Later in the century, however, a less violent political order emerged. Argentina even experienced a period of democratic rule from 1916 until 1930.

After World War II, populist leader Juan Perón ruled Argentina as an elected president for a decade. In 1955, however, he was overthrown in a military coup. Civilian governments were also prevented from completing their terms in office by coups in 1966 and 1973. The military, however, was not able to impose its preferred candidates when the country returned to civilian rule. Marcelo Cavarozzi aptly characterized this alternation of ineffective civilian and military regimes as the "failure of 'semi-democracy.'"[1]

In the mid-1970s, an already unstable political situation was made much worse by the incompetence and corruption of the civilian government. Meanwhile, the Argentine state and society were under guerrilla attacks by the Montoneros and the Revolutionary Army of the People (ERP). The political right, with the support of the military and security forces, responded with assassinations of leftist students, lawyers, journalists, and trade unionists, in addition to guerrillas. In October 1975, five months before the overthrow of the civilian government, Army Commander in Chief Jorge Rafaél Videla warned that "as many people will die in Argentina as is necessary to restore order."[2] The following year, Videla, who had become president, delivered on his promise of violence, if not order.

2. TORTURE AND DISAPPEARANCES

A distinguishing feature of repression in the Southern Cone was the extensive use of **disappearances**, that is, extrajudicial detentions, usually accompanied by torture, often followed by death.[3] The politics of disappearances were most highly developed in Argentina.

> Task forces of the armed services . . . were detailed to arrest suspected subversives without warrant; to avoid identification of the captors; to take the detainees to clandestine detention camps, generally within military or police facilities; and to disclaim any knowledge of the whereabouts of their prisoners. In those camps, prisoners were interrogated under the most severe forms of torture . . . The camps were deliberately shielded from any judicial or administrative investigation so that the torturers could be free to use any methods, and to deny even the existence of their prisoners, without fear of punishment . . . The overwhelming majority of those who entered the system of "disappearances" were never seen alive again.[4]

After the return of civilian government, the Argentine National Commission on Disappeared Persons (CONADEP, the Sabato Commission) documented 8,960 disappearances, a figure that probably underestimates the total by one-third or more. The commission identified 340 clandestine detention and torture centers, involving about 700 military officers, organized in 5 zones, 35 subzones, and 210 areas. The kidnappers operated with such impunity that three-fifths took place in the home of the victim, with witnesses present during the abduction. The mere passing of an unmarked green four-door Ford Falcon, the car of choice of the arresting squads, was enough to spread terror.

The Navy Mechanics School (ESMA) in Buenos Aires was Argentina's most important clandestine detention center. Torture at ESMA became a routine, bureaucratic activity. A trip to ESMA typically began with "Caroline," a thick broom handle with two long wires running out the end. The victim was stripped and tied to a steel bed frame. "Caroline" was attached to a box on a table that supplied the current. Then the electricity was applied to the victim, who often was periodically doused with water to increase the effects.

> It was unhurried and methodical. If the victim was a woman they went for the breasts, vagina, anus. If a man, they favored genitals, tongue, neck . . . Sometimes victims twitched so uncontrollably that they shattered their own arms and legs. Patrick Rice, an Irish priest who had worked in the slums and was detained for several days, recalls watching his flesh sizzle. What he most remembers is the smell. It was like bacon.[5]

Children were tortured in front of their parents, and parents in front of their children. Some prisoners were kept in rooms no longer or wider than a single bed. And the torture continued for days, weeks, months, even years, until the victim was released or, more often, killed. The sadistic brutality did not always even end with the death of the victim. "One woman was sent the hands of her daughter in a shoe box." The body of another woman "was dumped in her parents' yard, naked but showing no outward signs of torture. Later the director of the funeral home called to inform her parents that the girl's vagina had been sewn up. Inside he had found a rat."[6]

Most bodies, however, were never recovered. At ESMA, which also served as a disposal site for other naval camps, corpses were initially buried under the sports field. When this was filled, the bodies were burned daily, at 5:30 in the afternoon, usually after having been cut up with a chain saw. Finally, those in charge of destroying the evidence of their crimes hit on the idea of aerial disposal at sea. Once they had mastered the currents—at first bodies washed up in Buenos Aires, then in Montevideo— there was no trace to be found. Other units encased their victims in cement and dumped them in the river. The army's preferred method seems to have been to drive the corpses to the cemetery and register them as "NN," Name Unknown.

Repression in Chile was very similar, although the number of deaths was much lower. The Uruguayan style, however, was significantly different. Almost all the disappeared reappeared, usually in prison, after having been severely tortured. Only forty-four Uruguayans who disappeared in Uruguay remained unaccounted for at the end of military rule. The per capita rate of permanent disappearances in Uruguay was only about one-fifth that of Chile and one-twentieth that of Argentina. But about 60,000 people, roughly 2 percent of the population, were detained, giving Uruguay the highest per capita rate of political prisoners and torture victims in all of Latin America. Virtually everyone in the country knew someone who had been detained—an extraordinarily powerful technique of state terror.

Uruguay developed a grotesque division of labor between clandestine detention centers, which specialized in physical abuse, and official prisons, which specialized in psychological abuse. The prison regimen was carefully calculated to dehumanize and break people who had already suffered excruciating physical torture. Prisoners were never referred to by name, always by number or insulting epithet: "cockroach," "rat," "*apesto*" (diseased one). Peepholes and listening devices were common, and broken prisoners were used as informants. Cellmates were often chosen based on psychological profiles in order to cause one another the most annoyance. Even families were incorporated into the routine of torture. For example, children were sometimes permitted to visit their parents once a month, but only if the parent demonstrated no sign of affection.

Prisoners were allowed outside only one hour a day. When they were in their cells, they were often required to stand except during designated sleeping hours. Every aspect of existence was regulated by ominously arbitrary rules. Violations were typically punished by isolation in a windowless cell with a bare electric light bulb that burned twenty-four hours a day. In the most extreme case, nine top Tupamaro leaders, following months of vicious physical torture, were kept in complete solitary confinement for over a decade. One spent an extended period of his confinement at the bottom of a dry well. Mauricio Rosencof reported: "In over eleven and a half years, I didn't see the sun for more than eight hours altogether. I forgot colors—there were no colors."[7]

3. THE NATIONAL SECURITY DOCTRINE

Some of the brutality reflected simple sadism.

> At ESMA the complete licence they [the torturers] had to do what they wanted with their prisoners seems to have acted on them like an addiction. Sometimes they would stay in the torture room for a full 24 hours, never taking time off or resting; or else they would go home, and then return a couple of hours later, as though the atmosphere of cruelty and violence had drawn them back.[8]

Much of the violence, however, was the work of professionals pursuing what they saw as defense of the nation.

National security doctrines, which drew heavily on French and U.S. counterinsurgency doctrines of the 1950s and 1960s, provided an all-encompassing ideological framework for the military regimes of the Southern Cone. The state was viewed as the central institution of society. The military in turn was seen as the central institution of the state, the only organization with the combined insight, commitment, and resources needed to protect the interests and values of the nation.

A. The "Subversive" Threat

The nation and its values were seen as under assault from an international conspiracy that was centered on, but by no means limited to, international communism. For example, a diagram used at Argentina's Air Force Academy depicts a tree of subversion with three roots: Marxism, Zionism, and Freemasonry.[9] Progressive Catholicism appears at the top, and new growths at the bottom include human rights organizations, women's rights, pacifism, nonaggression, disarmament, the Rotary Club, Lions Club, and junior chambers of commerce. The main branches off the trunk are communist parties, the extreme totalitarian right (Nazism and fascism), socialist parties, liberal democracy, revolutionary front parties, Protestants, sectarians and anti-Christians, armed revolutionary organizations, and "indirect aggression." The branches off the limb of "indirect aggression" are particularly striking: drug addiction, alcoholism, prostitution, gambling, political liberalism, economic liberalism, lay education, trade union corruption, "hippieness," pornography, homosexuality, divorce, art, newspapers, television, cinema, theater, magazines, and books.

All-out war was the only "reasonable" response to such a pervasive threat. The process would not always be pretty, especially when applied to the agents of "indirect aggression." But even if many "subversives" were more misdirected or gullible than malicious, they were still guilty and had to be treated as such. As General Iberico Saint Jean, military governor of Buenos Aires, put it in May 1976, "First we will kill all the subversives; then we will kill their collaborators; then . . . their sympathizers; then . . . those who remain indifferent; and finally we will kill the timid."[10]

The metaphor of disease was also common. "Subversives" were an infection, the armed forces the nation's antibodies. An infected member of the body politic had to be isolated (detained) to stop the spread of the disease. If treatment was possible, so much the better—although even a cure might be painful (torture). If the member was beyond repair, though, permanent surgical removal (death) was demanded. What mattered was the long-run health of the body politic.

This paranoid vision helps to explain the wide range of victims. Violence against terrorists was not unexpected; in both Argentina and Uruguay it had been official policy even before the coups. Most of the disappeared, though, had no connection at all to the guerrillas.[11] Yet they too were considered guilty because of their "dangerous" political views.

Uruguay carried this ideology to its totalitarian extreme, creating Certificates of Democratic Background. An "A" rating indicated political reliability. A "B," or suspect, rating subjected one to police scrutiny and harassment. Those rated "C"— sometimes for an "offense" as minor as having been involved in a protest march twenty years earlier—were absolutely banned from public employment, a serious penalty in a country where the state was the largest employer. Many had trouble finding even private-sector jobs because hiring a "C" (or even a "B") citizen often led to harassing government audits and ominous questions about the employer's own loyalty.

The military sought to penetrate and "purify" all aspects of Uruguayan life. Each school received a new, politically reliable director. Every class had a "teacher's aide" to take notes on the behavior of students and teachers. A permit was required to hold a birthday party. Elections for captains of amateur soccer teams were supervised by the military, which could veto the results. A public performance of Ravel's *Piano Concerto for the Left Hand* was banned because of its sinister title.

B. Economic Reform and Economic and Social Rights

National purification also had a major economic dimension. In Chile, the Pinochet government tried to reverse not only Allende's reforms but also those of the 1960s. In 1975 the junta applied "Shock Treatment" *(Plan Shock)*. Government spending declined by more than one-fourth, and public investment was cut in half. Uruguay and Argentina pursued similar plans somewhat less vigorously. The aim was to privatize the economy and weaken or destroy organized labor, which was seen as a focal point for subversion. In Argentina, as many as half of the disappeared were labor activists.

This forced march toward "free" markets produced a rapid decline in living standards. For example, real wages in Chile were one-third lower in 1976 than in 1970. Infant mortality increased dramatically. But after the initial shock, there was limited economic recovery, especially in Chile. Although most of the benefits of growth were concentrated in the hands of a small elite, employment and wages increased while inflation declined. Economic success helped to calm at least some of the discontent with military rule. In fact, all three military governments relied on economic growth to deflect attention from, or compensate for, political repression.

The beneficiaries of the national security state were somewhat less clear than the victims. Some members of the upper and middle classes profited from the privatization of the economy and the lifting of government controls. Industrialists seem to have strongly supported military control over labor. But neither local industrialists nor multinational corporations seem to have had much influence on economic policies. Furthermore, many local industrialists were left extremely vulnerable to foreign competition. And although the military amply rewarded itself—for example, between 1968 and 1973, Uruguayan spending on education declined from 24.3 percent to 16.6 percent of the budget, while military spending rose from 13.9 percent to 26.2 percent—economic advantage seems to have been a secondary concern.[12] In their economic policies as much as in their political strategies, ideology was central to the policies of the military regimes of the Southern Cone.

4. HUMAN RIGHTS NGOS

If the Southern Cone provides a particularly striking example of human rights violations, it also provides one of the most moving examples of resistance. On April 30, 1977, fourteen middle-aged women, frustrated in their search for their disappeared children, met publicly in the Plaza de Mayo (the main square of Buenos Aires) in front of the Casa Rosada (the president's residence and the seat of government). The weekly Thursday afternoon vigil of the Mothers of the Plaza de Mayo—white scarves on their heads, silently walking around the square—became a symbol of both the cruelty of the military regime and the refusal of at least some ordinary people to bow to repression. Although subject to harassment and even attack—nine people associated with the mothers, including two French nuns, permanently disappeared on December 10, 1977, after evening mass—the mothers persevered and grew in numbers and in strength. By 1980, they had almost 5,000 members and were able to set up a small office.

The following summer, similar groups from several Latin American countries joined to form the Federation of Families of Disappeared Persons and Political Prisoners (FEDEFAM). Its first president was Lidia Galletti, one of the leaders of the mothers. Patrick Rice, the Irish priest mentioned earlier who survived his trip to ESMA, became its volunteer secretary, operating out of a small office with a borrowed typewriter in Caracas, Venezuela. FEDEFAM became an important source of information and a focus for concerted international action by relatives' groups throughout Central and South America.

The Grandmothers of the Plaza de Mayo were organized in October 1977 to deal with one of the most bizarre aspects of Argentina's "Dirty War," the traffic in children. Young children and infants were occasionally picked up with their parents. Others were born while their mothers were in captivity. The total numbered around eight hundred. They were usually given or sold to childless military couples. One torturer estimated that about sixty babies passed through ESMA and that all but two—whose heads were smashed against the wall in efforts to get their mothers to talk—were sold.[13] Even today, the grandmothers continue to try to trace and recover these victims.

Several other human rights NGOs operated in Argentina. For example, the Center for Legal and Social Studies (CELS) was established in summer 1979 to investigate individual cases involving the security forces. Within a year of its founding, CELS had become affiliated with both the Geneva-based International Commission of Jurists and the New York–based International League for Human Rights. The Argentine Human Rights Commission (CADHU) was formed in 1975 to protest right-wing death-squad killings. It was forced into exile in 1976 but opened branches in Geneva, Mexico, Rome, and Washington to spread information about the nature of the repression in Argentina. Adolfo Pérez Esquivel, a leader of the Service for Peace and Justice (SERPAJ), received the Nobel Peace Prize in 1980, three years after having been imprisoned and tortured by the military regime. Important work was also done by the Permanent Assembly for Human Rights (APDH) and the Families of Those Detained and Disappeared for Political Reasons.

The Argentine Catholic Church, however, despite the disappearance or assassination of two bishops and twenty priests, nuns, and seminarians, was never a vocal critic of the military. Although SERPAJ was a religious organization and the Ecumenical Movement for Human Rights was active, the church as an institution was not part of the opposition. In fact, some military chaplains actively participated in the system of torture.

In Chile, by contrast, the church was at the center of the human rights movement. The Committee of Cooperation for Peace (COPACHI) was formed in October 1973, the month after the coup, under the joint leadership of the bishops of Chile's Catholic and Lutheran churches. A month later, a legal-aid organization was established in space provided by the Catholic Church. By August 1974, COPACHI had more than one hundred employees in the capital of Santiago alone.

When Pinochet ordered COPACHI dissolved in November 1975, the Catholic Church responded by organizing the Vicaría de la Solidaridad (Vicariate of Solidarity).[14] The Vicaría provided aid and support for relatives of the disappeared and legal assistance to victims of state terror. Its Health Department organized soup kitchens and child-nutrition programs, especially in poorer urban areas that had been severely affected by Pinochet's economic reforms. Peasant organizations and unions, which had been special targets of repression, also received special support. And as military rule dragged on, the Vicaría began an extensive program of documentation and analysis. Although some lay human rights groups were also active, particularly the Chilean Human Rights Commission, in Chile, as in much of the rest of Latin America, the Catholic Church could do things that were impossible for lay organizations and even other churches.

In addition to aiding victims and their families, human rights NGOs were an important source of information. In fact, the lists of disappeared people prepared by CELS and APDH provided much of the factual basis for initial UN and OAS action. Given the efforts of the juntas to hide the scope of their violence, this may have been a significant achievement.

Human rights NGOs also allowed Argentineans and Chileans a limited opportunity to struggle against, rather than simply acquiesce in, military rule and the Dirty War. (In Uruguay the system of repression was so totalitarian that no effective local human rights NGOs were able to function until the final two or three years of military rule.) Taken together, NGO activities probably played a significant role in the failure of the military governments to "normalize" their rule.

5. THE COLLAPSE OF MILITARY RULE

The Argentine military, ironically, finally fell from power after it lost a conventional war with Britain over control of the obscure Falkland Islands. Argentina had long protested British occupation and control of the Malvinas, as they are known in Latin America. In April 1982, the junta decided to reclaim them by force, a ploy to deflect public attention from the collapse of the economy during the global recession of the early 1980s.

When Britain decisively repulsed the invasion, though, the military's humiliation was complete. Having attacked its own people, brought the economy to the brink of ruin, and then embarrassed itself and the country before the entire world, the Argentine military had little choice but to permit a return to civilian government. On October 30, 1983, Raúl Alfonsín won the national presidential election. He took office on December 10, the thirty-fifth anniversary of the adoption of the Universal Declaration of Human Rights.

In Chile, the economy also collapsed in the early 1980s. In 1982, per capita gross domestic product declined by one-sixth. By March 1983, one-third of the labor force was unemployed. The minimum wage lost between one-fifth and one-half of its purchasing power. Close to half of Chile's children were malnourished, an appalling situation in a country that had previously been relatively prosperous. A wave of bankruptcies brought hard times even to the middle and upper classes.

As the junta approached its tenth anniversary in power, opposition increased in all sectors of society. Working-class residential neighborhoods began to organize. The old political parties (especially the centrist Christian Democrats, which had never been forced entirely underground) began to act, cautiously, in public. Strikes by truck drivers and copper miners in June 1983 were labor's first major challenge since the coup, followed by a successful general strike in July. Between May and November, several Days of National Protest culminated in a demonstration by close to one million people in Santiago.

The military, however, also found new resolve. As opposition grew, so did repression. Several deaths and over 1,000 arrests accompanied the July general strike. Mass arrests increased dramatically, as did banishments, exiles, torture, and political deaths. By late 1984, the government was forced to reimpose a state of siege, and repression became more brutal. For example, two young Chileans were set on fire by the police during a protest demonstration, killing one and savagely maiming the other. Although the government claimed that the youths had accidentally set themselves aflame with a Molotov cocktail, a third victim was torched a week later, as if to remind opponents that it had been no accident.

Popular resistance, however, could not be crushed this time. In October 1988, the military tried a plebiscite to legitimate its rule. The majority of Chileans, however, rejected a new eight-year term for Pinochet. On December 14, 1989, an opposition alliance of seventeen parties, led by Patricio Aylwin, won the first free elections in Chile in nearly two decades.

The Uruguayan military was also hit hard by the economic crisis of the early 1980s. By 1984, real wages were less than one-half their 1968 levels, and more than 10 percent of the population had left the country, including one-seventh of the country's university graduates and close to one-fifth of the economically active population of the capital city of Montevideo.[15] But the military, after some initial indecision, was unwilling to adopt the Chilean strategy of increased repression in the face of growing opposition. Elections were held in 1984, and a freely elected civilian government returned to power in 1985, even without a Falklands-like blunder.

6. *NUNCA MÁS*: SETTLING ACCOUNTS WITH TORTURERS AND THE PAST

Elections, or at least the transfer of power from one elected civilian government to another (as occurred in both Argentina and Uruguay in 1989, and in Chile in 1993), are sometimes seen as the solution for human rights problems. But a nation that has suffered gross and systematic violations of human rights remains no less scarred than individual victims, their families, friends, and acquaintances. Furthermore, successor regimes face the problem of dealing with those responsible for human rights violations under the old order.

When the torture stops, it may not be clear how to deal with those responsible—especially when they retain political influence and control the weaponry that supported their dictatorial rule. Defining the terms of retributive justice is part of a process of national reconciliation necessary to keep the wounds inflicted under military rule from festering. The experience of the countries of the Southern Cone, however, provides some sobering lessons. Similar problems have been faced in the post–cold war world in Central and Eastern Europe, as well as in South Africa, Cambodia, and a number of other countries.

Two weeks before the election that brought a return to civilian rule, the Argentine junta issued a Law of National Reconciliation that created a blanket amnesty for all offenses connected with the "war against subversion." In his first week as president, however, Raúl Alfonsín delivered on his campaign promise to prosecute all nine members of the three military juntas that had run Argentina from 1976 to 1982.

No less significant was Alfonsín's decision to create the CONADEP, which would conduct an official investigation of the Dirty War. CONADEP's September 1984 report contained over 50,000 pages of documentation and provided an extensive, official, public accounting of the Dirty War. The summary, published under the title

Nunca Más (Never Again)—a phrase that first attained wide political currency in the aftermath of the Holocaust—became an instant best-seller.

Where so much of the violence was clandestine, to know the nature of the crime was the essential first step to overcoming its legacies. *Nunca Más,* at minimum, finally recognized and publicly memorialized the victims, whose very existence had for so long been officially denied. Truth, however, is only a first step. Punishment or pardon usually follows, and preventing future abuses must be a high priority.

Argentina made several changes in domestic law and ratified several international human rights treaties. The military command structure was reorganized. Military spending declined from 4.3 percent of gross domestic product in 1983 to 2.3 percent in 1987. In April 1988, a new Law of Defense defined the role of the armed forces as protecting against external aggression, effectively renouncing the national security doctrine.

Punishment was pursued through the courts. A defense of obedience to orders, however, effectively pardoned ordinary soldiers and lower-ranking officers. In a gesture to the dignity of the military, the Supreme Council of the Armed Forces was given initial jurisdiction to deal with its own through the system of military justice. But when the supreme council could find nothing illegal in any actions of the military government, the civilian Federal Court of Appeals took over the cases.

Sentences were handed down on December 9, 1985, the day before the second anniversary of the return of civilian government. Five leaders of the juntas received prison sentences, including life sentences for General Videla, the leader of the first junta, and Admiral Massera, the commander most intimately associated with the Dirty War. In addition, the court left open the possibility of further trials against more than 650 additional members of the armed forces.

Under extreme pressure from the military and its supporters, Alfonsín in December 1986 pushed through the *Ley de Punto Final*—literally, the Law of Full Stop (period), or the "final deadline." No new prosecutions could be filed after sixty days. The hope was that the legendary slowness of the Argentine judicial bureaucracy would leave most officers untouched. *Punto Final,* however, actually spurred monumental efforts by human rights groups and the courts. Judges even canceled their summer vacations to meet the deadline. Four hundred new indictments were registered against over one hundred officers.

On April 15, 1987, rebellious soldiers occupied several garrisons throughout the country and forced Alfonsín to push through a Law of Due Obedience, which limited prosecutions to chiefs of military areas. Even this, though, was not enough for the hard-liners. In January and December 1988 and in December 1990, new (but much less effective) revolts broke out, suggesting a precarious balance of power between hard-liners and moderates in the military and between the armed forces and the government.

Argentina's second civilian government, under President Carlos Menem, pardoned thirty-nine senior military officials in October 1989, effectively halting ongoing investigations of high leaders such as General Galtieri, the leader of the last junta. Hundreds involved in the military uprisings were also pardoned. Another eight senior officers, including General Videla, were pardoned at the end of December 1990. Although neither side was satisfied—Julio Strassera, who had prosecuted Videla, resigned from his position as Argentina's representative to the UN Commission on Human Rights, while General Videla publicly indicated that even this gesture was not enough, asking instead for a full vindication of the military—Argentine politics has since increasingly left the past behind.

Uruguay's new civilian government, when it took power in 1985, faced the even more difficult task of dealing with a military that had not been humiliated on the battlefield. It is thus not surprising that President Sanguinetti chose to accept the military's self-amnesty. In December 1986, Uruguay adopted the Law of Limitations, which protected the military against prosecution for crimes committed while it ruled the country.

The reaction against *impunidad* (impunity) for the military—there had not been a single prosecution, or even an official investigation—was dramatic.[16] In February 1987, a campaign was launched to hold a national referendum. By Christmas Eve, petitions had been signed by 634,702 people, out of a total population of about 3 million. This was equivalent to obtaining nearly 50 million signatures in the United States.

In the April 16, 1989, plebiscite, however, a majority chose to let the amnesty stand. Despite heavy rain, voter turnout was over 80 percent. Fifty-three percent voted "yellow," to let the amnesty stand. Forty-one percent voted "green," to overturn it. The example of military resistance in Argentina seems to have been the deciding factor—especially after public statements by highly placed members of the Uruguayan military suggested that they would not allow the amnesty to be overturned.

Although not an entirely free choice, Uruguayans had the opportunity to choose whether to try to punish the military. Many victimized nations have not had even that much. For example, in Guatemala the military declared an amnesty just before leaving office in 1986. And to remind everyone where real power still resided, five dozen mutilated bodies appeared in various places in the country in the first three weeks of "civilian" rule. There was no plebiscite, nor even an investigation of the tens of thousands of disappearances and arbitrary executions.

Chile, following the lead of Uruguay and the lesson of Argentina, chose to forgo prosecutions, which the military made clear it would not permit. In April 1990, however, President Aylwin created the Commission for Truth and Reconciliation (CVR, the Rettig Commission). Its March 1991 report documents close to 1,000 disappearances that resulted in death. (The commission's mandate did not include other violations, including tens of thousands of cases of torture.)

The outcome of such efforts, in the Southern Cone as in other countries grappling with legacies of political repression and brutality, will be determined by a complex interplay among the political will and skill of the government, its popular support, and the tolerance or intransigence of the military. These efforts do suggest, however, that even where punishment is impossible, the guilty may be denied complete impunity.

"Men are unable to forgive what they cannot punish."[17] These words of Hannah Arendt, which have often been cited by those in the Southern Cone struggling against impunity, capture the central problem with military-imposed amnesties. Pardon is an act of charity or compassion. Punishment is an act of justice (and a deterrent to injustice). New civilian regimes are often unable to punish because the guilty retain considerable political power. The pardons thus received by torturers and murderers may have legal effect, but morally they are profoundly defective. This corruption of both punishment and pardon by power also makes preventing future abuses more difficult.

The task of prevention, however, is likely to be greatly aided by the truth, which can sometimes be a partial substitute for punishment or pardon. A public declaration of the crimes of the guilty may help to put the past behind and focus a country's energy and attention on preventing future abuses. At the very least, a nation unable to acknowledge its past publicly is less likely to be able to prevent new human rights violations.

The official name of Chile's Rettig Commission was thus particularly well chosen: Commission for Truth and Reconciliation. Especially where suffering has been denied, truth may permit mourning and provide a public solace that may help to make reconciliation possible. There may even be a punishment of sorts in being forced to face a public demonstration of one's crimes. South Africa's truth commission, under the leadership of Nobel Laureate Bishop Desmond Tutu, has been particularly forceful and effective in its efforts to uncover, and thus help to overcome, the horrors of the past.

Truth alone is never enough. Sometimes, though, it may make inroads against power. In any case, the task of human rights advocacy is to speak truth to power, in the name of past and present victims and in the hope of preventing future victims.

> *accuracy is essential*
> *we must not be wrong*
> *even by a single one*
> *we are despite everything*
> *the guardians of our brothers*
> *ignorance about those who have disappeared*
> *undermines the reality of the world.*[18]

Nunca Más. Never again. Never *this* horror again. Ultimately, this is the meaning of the struggle against systematic violations of human rights.

7. POSTSCRIPT: MAINTAINING CIVILIAN RULE

Perhaps the most remarkable aspect of the return of civilian rule in the Southern Cone has been its persistence. Although the military remains an important institution, especially in Uruguay, soldiers have remained in their barracks. Even in times of severe economic and political crisis, they have not threatened to retake power.

Argentina provides perhaps the most striking example. The financial crisis that began in July 1997 in East Asia spread in 1998 to Russia, then Brazil, and at the end of the year, Argentina. After a series of failed internal measures in 1999, Argentina was forced to negotiate a $7.2 billion agreement with the International Monetary Fund (IMF) in March 2000, followed by a massive $40 billion package of assistance in December. The country nonetheless plunged into deep depression, forcing Argentina into default on its international loans.

Real GDP declined every year from 1999 through 2002, with a staggering 10.9 percent decline in 2002 alone. In 2002, the inflation rate was over 40 percent, and well over 100 percent when measured in world prices (reflecting the collapse of the Argentinian peso, which lost three-quarters of its value during the year). Unemployment was approaching 20 percent, and well over half of the population was in poverty (as compared to less than 40 percent before the crisis). Perhaps most ominously, in light of the history of the 1970s, in December 2001 Buenos Aires and other major cities experienced significant episodes of looting and rioting. Nonetheless, the military did not intervene, despite a series of questionable decisions by the civilian governments in their attempts to deal with the crisis.

The deepening of the consensus on civilian rule can also be seen in the fate of General Pinochet in Chile. Although Pinochet stepped down as head of state in 1990, he continued to head the military until 1998, when he was named senator for life—a position that granted him parliamentary immunity. However, in October 1998 a Spanish special judge issued an international arrest warrant, which was served on Pinochet while he was visiting London. After a period of detention, the British government decided that he was not fit to be extradited and allowed him to return to Chile in March 2000.

On returning to Chile, Pinochet was stripped of his parliamentary immunity and arrested. In July 2002, however, the case against him was dismissed by the Chilean Supreme Court, on the (highly debatable) technical grounds of mental incapacity. But his legal troubles continued. In May 2004, the Chilean Supreme Court reversed itself and found him mentally competent, and in August 2004, the Supreme Court confirmed the stripping of his immunity for many of his crimes connected with Operation Condor during the Dirty War. In June 2005, he also was stripped of immunity in a huge tax evasion case. In September 2005, he lost his immunity for another Dirty War campaign, Operation Colombo, in which 114 leftist activists disappeared. In November 2005, bail was denied on the tax fraud charges, forcing him back into house arrest, where he spent his ninetieth birthday. The next day, Pinochet was charged in a case involving six disappearances during Operation Colombo. In December, he lost his immunity from prosecution in another case involving 29 additional disappearances.

Whether Pinochet will ever stand trial, let alone be convicted, is far from clear. Earlier efforts to prosecute him on human rights violations have been overturned on a variety of technical legal grounds. Nonetheless, on a very personal level, General Pinochet has been denied impunity.

Throughout all of these wranglings, the Chilean military has remained in the background. Although still a significant political force, they seem to have accepted the idea that their influence is to be exercised only from their barracks. Even more encouraging, in January 2005, the Chilean army formally accepted institutional responsibility for past abuses.

It would be foolish to proclaim civilian rule absolutely safe in light of the dramatic changes that have occurred over the past thirty-five years. Nonetheless, democratic rule and respect for human rights seem to be deeply entrenched. The people of Argentina, Chile, and Uruguay deserve most of the credit for this achievement. Nonetheless, international action, especially the global and regional spread of human rights values, does seem to be a significant part of the story, both in supporting local human rights advocates and in delegitimating their opponents, in the 1980s as well as the post–cold war era.

DISCUSSION QUESTIONS

1. When we talk about human rights violations, numbers of victims can take on a strangely abstract character. To make the suffering behind the numbers more concrete, try this simple exercise. Count all the people you know personally. For most people, the number will be several hundred. This is far fewer than the number disappeared in Argentina or Chile. It is about the number of people killed in a single day in June 1989 in Tiananmen Square in China. Now add all the people you know of (actors, writers, celebrities, people in the news). The total will probably be a few thousand. In Argentina, more people disappeared than you can even name. In the early 1980s in Guatemala and El Salvador, this many people were being killed every few months.

2. Are there situations in which torture or disappearances could be justified? (Don't answer too quickly, whatever your initial inclination.)

3. How can people become torturers? Even if they are not applying the electric shocks to the victims, how can people work in institutions that regularly practice torture or arbitrary execution? Consider the following possibilities:

   Sadism: They enjoy it.

   Commitment: They believe it is necessary to achieve a higher good.

   Self-interest: They see an opportunity to get ahead.

   Coercion: They are forced to participate.

   Cowardice: They find themselves in a system they are afraid to resist.

   Denial: They try to convince themselves that things are other than they appear.

   Inertia: They go with a flow that they don't try to resist.

   Does it make a difference why people engage in torture and commit murder? Does it make a *moral* difference? At what point in your thinking about "justification" does the issue of motive become relevant?

4. Chile and Uruguay had long and relatively well-established democratic traditions. Nonetheless, they endured more than a decade of extraordinarily repressive military rule. How can this be explained? Although you may lack the factual information to make a truly informed judgment, speculating on possible reasons can be useful, particularly if we want to use these cases to think about prospects for democracy elsewhere.

5. Is it easier to build or to destroy a democracy? Once it is destroyed, how (and how easily) can it be fixed? Does the way it was destroyed—and the length of time it took—have a significant impact on the prospects for recovery or repair? Does the particular way that democracy was (re-)instituted have an impact on its future prospects?

6. It obviously makes sense to distinguish between large and small numbers of human rights violations. But does it make sense to distinguish between different types of violations? If so, which ones are especially heinous? Why?

7. Is there a qualitative difference between a regime that tortures people but feeds everyone well and one that allows people to suffer from malnutrition but tortures no one? Or between a regime that allows free political participation but requires everyone to work sixty-hour weeks and one that provides thirty-five-hour workweeks but no political participation? There are differences, certainly, and they are likely to be of considerable political importance. But are the differences of any *moral* significance?

8. Are the only important (moral) distinctions between human rights violations ultimately quantitative? This would seem to be the implication of the claim that all human rights are interdependent and indivisible. But is the moral difference really just the number of people and the number of rights violated?

9. However you have answered the preceding set of questions, you can construct a list of human rights violations and then rank them from more to less severe. Having done that, what foreign policy implications can you draw? Suppose we concentrate on the worst cases. The reasons to do so are fairly obvious, but are there drawbacks? Suppose someone were to suggest that we focus on *less* severe violators because the chances for improving practices there are greater. Or consider the claim that we should focus on the trend in a given country. If we accept this, should an improving or a worsening trend receive greater weight? What other relevant considerations can you think of? States clearly cannot concentrate on all human rights violators equally, but how should they prioritize cases?

10. How should new governments deal with former torturers and dictators and the members of the repressive apparatus of the old regime? Suppose that there are no political constraints imposed by the continuing power of these forces. Who should be punished—and who shouldn't—for what, and how severely? How should vengeance, justice, mercy, and reconciliation be balanced? Now suppose that the old forces of repression do still hold considerable power. How far should the demands of justice be pressed? At what point does bowing to power corrupt or undermine the new political order? Is there a practical alternative to accepting the lesser of two evils? Are practical alternatives the only ones that should be adopted?

11. Although economic, social, and cultural rights received some attention in this chapter, the central focus was on violations of civil and political rights. This reflects the focus of international discussions of human rights viola-

tions in the Southern Cone. Is that focus the best one? Was the distinctive character of human rights violations in the Southern Cone significantly connected with economic, social, and cultural rights? Even if the distinctive nature of the repression concerned civil and political rights, should there have been greater international attention to economic and social rights?

SUGGESTED READINGS

Readers interested in more information on human rights violations in the Southern Cone should begin with Ian Guest, *Behind the Disappearances: Argentina's Dirty War Against Human Rights and the United Nations* (Philadelphia: University of Pennsylvania Press, 1990). Guest, a journalist who covered the United Nations Commission on Human Rights for a number of years, begins with an account of the repression following the coup in Argentina. His telling of the story is particularly powerful because of the effective use of personal accounts of some of the victims. Guest then moves on to the halting efforts of the United Nations to deal with disappearances in Argentina (and elsewhere), followed by an extended discussion of U.S. policy during both the Carter and the Reagan years. Somewhat narrower, but even more moving for being a first-person account by a journalist victim of the Dirty War, is Jacobo Timerman, *Prisoner Without a Name, Cell Without a Number* (New York: Knopf, 1981). Eric Stener Carlson, ed., *I Remember Julia: Voices of the Disappeared* (Philadelphia: Temple University Press, 1996) is also powerful and evocative.

John Simpson and Jana Bennett, *The Disappeared: Voices from a Secret War* (London: Robson Books, 1985) is another useful example of political journalism, providing detailed information on the internal politics of the Dirty War. A much more idiosyncratic, but penetrating, analysis by a cynical external observer can be found in V. S. Naipaul, *The Return of Eva Perón* (New York: Vintage Books, 1981). For a more general discussion of disappearances as a technique of human rights violations, see Amnesty International USA, *Disappearances: A Workbook* (New York, 1981). Jeffrey A. Sluka, ed., *Death Squad: The Anthropology of State Terror* (Philadelphia: University of Pennsylvania Press, 2000) offers interesting comparative case studies.

The horror of the Dirty War is difficult to capture even in good journalism (let alone in dry academic prose). Literary representations can thus be particularly useful. Among fictional accounts, I particularly like Lawrence Thornton, *Imagining Argentina* (New York: Doubleday, 1987), a novel in the "magic realist" tradition of García Márquez. Among poets, one might begin with Marjorie Agosín, *Zones of Pain/Las Zonas del Dolor* (Fredonia, N.Y.: White Pine Press, 1988), and *An Absence of Shadows* (Fredonia, N.Y.: White Pine Press, 1998), two bilingual collections of poems on the human consequences of military rule in Chile and Argentina.

For an excellent academic account of the human rights movement in Argentina, see Alison Brysk, *The Politics of Human Rights in Argentina* (Stanford: Stanford University Press, 1994). On Chile, Pamela Lowden, *Moral Opposition to Authoritarian Rule in Chile, 1973–1990* (Houndmills, U.K.: Macmillan Press, 1996) is strong on domestic opposition. Darren G. Hawkins, *International Human Rights and Authoritarian Rule in Chile* (Lincoln: University of Nebraska Press, 2002) thoroughly reviews the record of international human rights diplomacy.

Another journalistic account, Lawrence Weschler, *A Miracle, A Universe: Settling Accounts with Torturers* (New York: Pantheon Books, 1990), is perhaps the best place to begin further reading and reflection on the difficult process of overcoming the legacy of repression. The second half of the book, which began as two articles in the *New Yorker,* is a brilliant and moving discussion of the system of repression in Uruguay and the politics of the amnesty referendum. The first half, which deals with Brazil and thus is, strictly speaking, outside the scope of this chapter, is also valuable.

Among the now immense academic literature on reconciliation and transitional justice, the following volumes are useful for their breadth of coverage and extensive comparative case studies: Neil J. Kritz, ed., *Transitional Justice: How Emerging Democracies Reckon with Former Regimes,* 3 vol. (Washington, D.C.: United States Institute of Peace Press, 1995); A. James McAdams, ed., *Transitional Justice and the Rule of Law in New Democracies* (Notre Dame: University of Notre Dame Press, 1997); Carol A. L. Praeger and Trudy Govier, eds., *Dilemmas of Reconciliation: Cases and Concepts* (Waterloo, Canada: Wilfred Laurier University Press, 2003); and Chandra Lekha Sriram, *Confronting Past Human Rights Violations: Justice vs. Peace in Times of Transition* (London: Frank Cass, 2004) all cover both general issues and comparative case studies. Ruti G. Teitel, *Transitional Justice* (Oxford: Oxford University Press, 2000) is a good topical overview from a more legal perspective. Other useful volumes include Mark R. Amstutz, *The Healing of Nations: The Promise and Limits of Political Forgiveness* (Lanham, Md.: Rowman and Littlefield, 2005), and Mark Philip Bradley and Patrice Petro, eds., *Truth Claims: Representation and Human Rights* (New Brunswick, N.J.: Rutgers University Press, 2002). Mark Ensalaco, *Chile Under Pinochet: Recovering the Truth* (Philadelphia: University of Pennsylvania Press, 2000) is excellent on Chile.

On broader issues of human rights in transitional societies, see Shale Horowitz and Albrecht Schnabel, eds., *Human Rights and Societies in Transition: Causes, Consequences, Responses* (Tokyo: United Nations University Press, 2004), Elizabeth Jelin and Eric Hershberg, eds., *Constructing Democracy: Human Rights, Citizenship, and Society in Latin America* (Boulder: Westview Press, 1996), Luis Roninger and Mario Sznajder, *The Legacy of Human Rights Violations in the Southern Cone: Argentina, Chile, and Uruguay* (Oxford: Oxford University Press, 1999), and Rachel May and Andrew Milton, eds., *(Un)civil Societies: Human Rights and Democratic Transitions in Eastern Europe and Latin American* (Lanham, Md.: Lexington Books, 2005). The Web site of the International Center for Transitional Justice, http://www.ictj.org/, is useful for recent information on transitional justice issues around the world. The Truth Commission Digital Collection, http://www.usip.org/library/truth.html, provides basic information. For useful links, see the Truth Commissions page on the site of the Transitional Justice Forum, http://tj-forum.org/files/Truth-comms-from-JE.html#reps.

On General Pinochet and his fate at the hands of the legal system, Peter Kornbluth, ed., *The Pinochet File: A Declassified Dossier on Atrocity and Accountability* (New York: New Press, 2003) provides an extensive review of the evidence. See also Roger Burbach, *The Pinochet Affair: State Terrorism and Global Justice* (London: Zed Books, 2003), and Ariel Dorfman, *Exorcising Terror: The Incredible Unending Trial of General Augusto Pinochet* (New York: Seven Stories Press, 2002).

5

◄○►

The Multilateral
Politics of Human Rights

The preceding chapters have set the stage for a detailed examination of international human rights practices. The remaining chapters fall into two parts. Chapters 5 and 6 focus on the cold war era, when most multilateral human rights institutions were established and human rights became an important issue in foreign policy. In these chapters, we also consider general issues of multilateral and bilateral human rights diplomacy. Chapters 7 through 10 explore the changing human rights environment of the post–cold war world by examining one case (international responses to the Tiananmen massacre) and three broad issues (humanitarian intervention, globalization, and terrorism) in some depth.

At several points I use the concept international regime. An **international regime** is a set of principles, norms, rules, and decision-making procedures accepted by states (and other international actors) as binding within an issue area.[1] International human rights principles and norms were discussed in Chapters 1 and 2. In this chapter we consider the leading international and regional regimes and their decision-making and implementation procedures. Human rights in bilateral foreign policy is addressed in Chapter 6.

Decision-making procedures in international regimes can be roughly grouped into promotional, implementation, and enforcement activities. International promotion involves the exchange of information and efforts to encourage or assist national implementation of international norms. International implementation includes international monitoring of practices and procedures involving the regular use of an international forum to coordinate policies that remain under national control. International enforcement involves binding international decision making (and perhaps also very strong forms of international monitoring and policy coordination).

Regimes can be classified by the "highest" procedure available, with each type further divided into relatively strong or weak. We must also add the class of declaratory regimes, which involve international norms but no international decision making

79

(except in the creation of norms). Table 5.2 below provides a summary overview of the evolution of the major international human rights regimes from the founding of the United Nations in 1945 through 2005.

1. THE UNITED NATIONS COMMISSION ON HUMAN RIGHTS

The United Nations is the world's leading multilateral political forum. It is not, however, a world government. It is an intergovernmental organization, a "club" whose members are sovereign states. Few UN decisions create binding international legal obligations. Even fewer can be effectively enforced. Nonetheless, when the United Nations acts on the basis of consensus, as it often does in the field of human rights, it may be said to speak for the international **society of states**.

The General Assembly (GA) is the center of the UN system. It sets guidelines for the organization, both through formal resolutions and through cues provided by its discussions and political dynamics. Each member has one vote in the General Assembly, which must give final UN approval to all human rights treaties. On occasion, the GA has even made important drafting decisions. For example, the final compromises on the 1984 Convention Against Torture were worked out there. The GA was also a major actor in international campaigns against racism and colonialism.

The United Nations, however, is a political body composed of sovereign states that use the organization to further their own national interests. Because the General Assembly is the preeminent political institution of the UN, the temptation to politicize human rights issues is especially strong there. For example, during the 1970s, public human rights criticism in the GA was restricted almost exclusively to the pariah regimes of South Africa, Israel, and Chile. Although these countries richly merited international condemnation, comparable violations elsewhere were ignored, for political reasons.

Until recently, the UN Commission on Human Rights, a permanent subsidiary body of the Economic and Social Council (ECOSOC), showed somewhat less political bias, often functioning in the 1940s, 1980s, and 1990s as a *relatively* nonpartisan forum. And in the area of standard setting, the Commission has always been relatively nonpartisan, operating on the basis of consensus. Therefore, the Commission has historically been the single most important institution of the global human rights regime.

The Commission initially devoted its principal efforts to working on the Universal Declaration of Human Rights and the International Human Rights Covenants. For twenty years, however, it undertook no monitoring or enforcement activities. ECOSOC Resolution 75 in 1947 denied the Commission even the right to see complaints that were sent to the UN. Underlying this practice was a very strong conception of **sovereignty**, that is, a narrow reading of the range of international human rights activities permitted by the principle of **nonintervention**. It also reflected the ambiguous position of intergovernmental human rights bodies.

The sovereign states that are the members of the UN are both the principal subjects of international human rights obligations and the principal violators of those rights. They are thus unlikely to grant the organization strong enforcement powers. Furthermore, the members of the Commission on Human Rights are state representatives, not independent experts. The Commission's decision not to act on human rights complaints was thus legally justifiable and politically understandable—although no less disappointing to victims and human rights advocates.

In 1967, ECOSOC Resolution 1235 finally authorized the Commission to discuss human rights violations in particular countries. Although hardly forceful action, the UN at least began to break its complicitous silence on particular human rights violations. In 1970, ECOSOC Resolution 1503 authorized the Commission to investigate "communications" (complaints) that suggested "a consistent pattern of gross and reliably attested violations of human rights and fundamental freedoms." This is commonly referred to as the **1503 procedure**. In 2000, procedures for handling communications were reorganized. If the Working Group on Communications determines that there appears to be a consistent pattern of gross violations, it may refer a country's practices to the Working Group on Situations, which may in turn refer the case to the full commission.

Stringent criteria of admissibility, however, limit the cases that can be considered.[2] Only situations of gross and systematic violations are covered; particular abuses and individual cases cannot be examined. The procedure is confidential until a final report is made to ECOSOC. Although confidentiality may encourage cooperation by states, it can dramatically slow an already cumbersome process. For example, genocide against Paraguayan Indians remained under scrutiny for nine years without any action. A decision on Uruguay, after seven years of scrutiny, came only after the guilty government had been removed from office. Things improved a bit after the end of the cold war, but the 1503 procedure could not be called efficient or timely. Nonetheless, more than eighty countries have been subject to scrutiny under Resolution 1503.[3]

Few states fear the direct political power of the UN. Its findings, though, do have a certain authority. Domestic human rights NGOs and opposition parties may draw support from UN decisions and reports, which are also used by international NGOs and foreign governments. Confidentiality thus represents a major concession by the UN. Whether it is compensated by an increased willingness of states to cooperate with the Commission in order to avoid adverse publicity is hard to assess.

The most important limitation, however, is that in the end "enforcement" means making publicly available the evidence that has been acquired, along with the Commission's views on it. Furthermore, only a handful of cases have reached this stage. The 1503 procedure is thus a promotional device involving only sporadic and limited semi-independent monitoring.

Nonetheless, given the sensitivity of human rights questions, even this may have practical value, especially where a government cares about its international reputation. We should not ignore the value of publicizing violations and trying to shame states into better compliance with international human rights norms. Even vicious governments may care about their international reputation, and publicity often does help some of the more prominent victims of repression. The limitations of the procedure, however, deserve at least as much emphasis as its achievements.

Much the same is true of the Commission's other activities. For example, the twenty-six-member Sub-Commission on the Promotion and Protection of Human Rights (known until 1999 as the Sub-Commission on the Prevention of Discrimination and Protection of Minorities) has undertaken a number of useful studies. Together with the Commission, it has helped to focus international public opinion on conditions in several countries (for example, South Africa and Chile) and on selected violations and issues such as disappearances, torture, religious liberty, human rights defenders, migrant workers, and indigenous peoples.

Particularly important in this regard are the Commission's "global" or "thematic" procedures involving working groups and special rapporteurs on a wide range of topics including disappearances, torture, and summary or arbitrary executions. For example, in 1980 the Commission created a Working Group on Disappearances to assist families and friends in determining the whereabouts of disappeared persons (see Chapter 4). After examining communications offering details of a disappearance, the Working Group transmits the case to the government in question. If necessary, reminders are sent, at least once a year. Over 19,000 cases were handled in the group's first decade of work. In roughly one case in ten, government responses established the whereabouts or fate of the individual. Special urgent-action procedures for disappearances within the three months preceding the communication—when most victims suffer torture or execution, but also when they are most likely to reappear—have resolved about one case in five. There is good reason to believe that a significant number of those identified by this procedure owe their lives to it.

Ironically, the first urgent inquiry concerned Mohamed al-Jabiri, Iraq's representative to the Commission. He had been active in establishing the Working Group and was slated to be its first chair. But al-Jabiri apparently ran afoul of Iraqi dictator Saddam Hussein, was recalled to Baghdad, and disappeared. Theo van Boven, director of the Division of Human Rights, began diplomatic inquiries and threatened to publicize the case. About a week later, van Boven received a handwritten note from al-Jabiri saying that he had decided to retire.

It is uncertain what al-Jabiri's fate would have been without immediate UN intervention. His case does suggest, though, that aggressive international procedures can help at least a few victims. Furthermore, the Working Group's annual inquiries about unresolved cases, even when they are ignored, are a reminder that someone is watching and still cares.

The Commission on Human Rights has also made increasing use of country rapporteurs, who have examined situations even in moderately high-profile countries such as Guatemala, Iran, and Burma. Like their thematic counterparts, the country rapporteurs are individual experts who report to the Commission, rather than the voice of the Commission as a whole. They thus operate with fewer diplomatic and political constraints. In addition, their narrow mandate allows them to maintain sustained, focused attention and in some cases even develop a constructive exchange of views with a government.

The limitations of all of these procedures, however, are tragically illustrated by the case of Rwanda. Sufficient information was coming into the Commission to lead to

Rwanda being discussed confidentially under the 1503 procedure in 1992 and 1993. In addition, the report of the Special Rapporteur on Extrajudicial Executions was discussed in the spring of 1994, just before the outbreak of the genocide. In it, he confirmed reports of official involvement in the massacre of civilians and explicitly suggested that genocidal acts were already occurring. Nonetheless, it was not until May 25—seven weeks after the genocide began—that the Commission even appointed a country rapporteur.

The Commission on Human Rights, however, was never intended to have implementation or enforcement powers, let alone the capacity to stop human rights violations before they occurred. It does, though, engage in useful promotional activities, particularly as a source of authoritative information and publicity. Unlike most other international human rights institutions, it may (in principle) examine any human rights practices in any country of the world. Furthermore—and most importantly—its role in developing international human rights norms has been, and remains, vital and irreplaceable. Most of the now substantial body of international human rights law was largely developed through extended negotiations in the Commission.

Through the 1990s, the United Nations Commission on Human Rights was in many ways the heart of the global human rights regime. Sadly, though, over the past several years it has become increasingly politicized. The current membership includes particularly egregious human rights violators, such as Sudan and Zimbabwe, as well as Cuba, Paraguay, Saudi Arabia, and Pakistan, which have some of the worst human rights records in their regions. As a result, Human Rights Watch has described it as "an 'abusers club' of governments hostile to human rights."[4] Not surprisingly, the Commission has increasingly failed to address situations of serious human rights violations.

Given this embarrassing situation, many serious and sympathetic observers have become disillusioned with the Commission. (The election of Libya as chair in 2003 seems to have crystallized a growing sense of frustration.) The Secretary-General even recommended that it be replaced by a new Human Rights Council—ostensibly to increase the prominence accorded to human rights within the United Nations system, but in large measure because the crude politicization of the Commission in recent years has made it as much a liability as an asset in the global struggle for human rights. By a nearly unanimous vote in March 2006, the UNGA decided to create a new Human Rights Council.

2. THE HIGH COMMISSIONER FOR HUMAN RIGHTS

The Commission's complaints procedure, thematic initiatives, and country discussions and rapporteurs reflect an information-advocacy model of human rights implementation. They seek to acquire and disseminate authoritative information on violations, along with whatever political pressure or prestige the Commission can muster, to encourage governments to improve their practices. Their basic logic relies on the desire of states to be respected by their peers and on the damage to state reputations that can be caused by well-publicized systematic human rights violations.

The position of United Nations High Commissioner for Human Rights, created after the 1993 Vienna World Conference, personifies this information-advocacy approach. The High Commissioner has the global reach of the Commission, without its cumbersome procedures and politicization. Like the special rapporteurs, the High Commissioner may deal directly with governments to seek improved respect for internationally recognized human rights—but with the added advantage of an explicit mandate to deal with all governments on all issues.

The first High Commissioner, José Ayala Lasso (1994–1997), a former foreign minister and UN ambassador of Ecuador, was actively involved in the negotiations that led to creating the office. A UN insider, he adopted a very low profile, focusing on getting the office up and running and embedded within the UN bureaucracy, with a reputation for impartiality. This laid the foundation for the blossoming of the office under its second incumbent, Mary Robinson (1997–2002), the former president of Ireland. A tireless advocate with good political skills and a diplomatic but assertive public style, she transformed the office into a central actor in the global human rights regime. The current High Commissioner, Louise Arbour, took office in 2004. A Canadian jurist, previously chief prosecutor at the International Criminal Tribunal for the former Yugoslavia and a justice on the Supreme Court of Canada, she has continued in the Robinson mold.

Today, the High Commissioner is widely accepted as an authoritative, impartial authority on human rights. Furthermore, her office has become a respected source of information, particularly legal information, especially through its admirable Web site (http://www.unhchr.ch). The Office of the High Commissioner has also greatly improved its technical assistance services, although these remain woefully underfunded. Due to the growing politicization of the Commission, the UN's human rights machinery has shifted its focus to the High Commissioner, although the Commission remains the key actor in the development of new international norms and legal instruments.

3. TREATY-REPORTING SYSTEMS

An important cluster of global human rights institutions derive their authority from multilateral human rights treaties. (See Table 5.1.) The principal activity of the committees created by these treaties is to review reports on compliance submitted by the parties.

A. The Human Rights Committee and the Committee on Economic, Social, and Cultural Rights

The Human Rights Committee (HRC) is a group of eighteen independent experts elected by the parties to the International Covenant on Civil and Political Rights. Although it does not address issues of economic, social, and cultural rights—which are monitored by the separate, weaker Committee on Economic, Social, and Cultural Rights—its broad scope makes it closer to the general country-oriented procedures of the Commission on Human Rights than its thematic procedures. The work of the HRC, however, focuses not on investigations but on the review of periodic reports submitted by states.

Reports are discussed in a public session, often lasting a full day, in which state representatives are questioned. Committee members often pose penetrating and critical questions. Sometimes the responses are serious and thoughtful. In such cases, the result is a genuine exchange of views that provides a real element of international monitoring.

The representative of the reporting state, however, need not answer any question, let alone answer to the satisfaction of the questioner. Many reports contain little more than extracts from laws and the constitution or obviously false or evasive claims of compliance. And whatever the quality of the report, once it has been reviewed, the monitoring process typically ends until the next report is due, in five years. The committee cannot even assure timely submission of reports.

Despite these weaknesses, the HRC can draw public attention to a country's record. This may occasionally embarrass a state into altering its practices. The need to report to an impartial international body may be a minor check on contemplated violations. The reports of some countries may even provide ideas and models for others, as may the committee's comments. And the national work of preparing a report can help to highlight areas where change is needed or possible. (The strengths and weaknesses of reporting systems are discussed in §5.3.C.)

The HRC may also consider complaints from individuals in the 105 states that, as of October 2005, are parties to the Covenant's (first) Optional Protocol.[5] Through May 2004, 1,279 communications had been registered concerning 77 countries. Of the cases concluded, a bit more than half were either discontinued or found to be inadmissible (in almost all cases, apparently reasonably). Where the committee stated its views, though, it found a violation in more than three-quarters of the cases.[6] The procedure seems to be relatively open and independent, providing genuine if limited international monitoring, which in at least a few cases has altered state practice. For example, Canada has changed legislation concerning the rights of Indians living off their tribal lands, Mauritius changed legislation on women's rights, and the Netherlands has altered discriminatory social security legislation. The committee's relatively aggressive use of these powers is clear in its innovative decision to treat a state's failure to respond as an admission of culpability. (The strengths and weaknesses of individual petition mechanisms are discussed in §5.7.)

The Committee on Economic, Social, and Cultural Rights (CESCR) provides a parallel process for economic, social, and cultural rights. Reports under the International Covenant on Economic, Social, and Cultural Rights were originally reviewed by an ECOSOC Working Group. In 1985, however, the CESCR was created. Its review of reports is very similar to the HRC. There is, however, no complaint procedure for economic, social, and cultural rights.

One further activity of some significance carried out by both committees is the formulation of "general comments." General comments represent the committee's understanding of the nature of particular treaty obligations. The HRC has issued general comments on eighteen substantive articles, as well as comments on the nature of the general obligations imposed by the Covenant.

General comments represent an effort to develop a kind of jurisprudence for authoritatively interpreting international human rights obligations, in the absence of judicial or quasi-judicial mechanisms.[7] It is too soon to predict the impact, which will be incremental and in particular areas, of this creative and promising avenue for elaborating and deepening international human rights norms. General comments, however, have been used by a variety of national and transnational advocates, and even by some states and international organizations. In this regard, the CESCR general comments on water, food, health care, and housing seem to be emerging as particularly important.

B. Racial Discrimination, Women's Rights, Torture, and Children

Regimes on racial discrimination, women's rights, torture, and the rights of the child have developed around similar treaty-based reporting schemes.[8] Basic data on the relevant committees are shown in Table 5.1. These treaties give greater range, precision, and force to the general formulations of the Universal Declaration and the Covenants, as well as added international prominence to the particular rights addressed. The mandated periodic review of reports provides additional international scrutiny of state practices in these areas.

Single-issue treaties and committees are typically situated at the core of a more extensive international regime. For example, the work of the Committee on the Elimination of Discrimination Against Women (CEDAW) is supplemented by the UN Commission on the Status of Women, a permanent functional commission of ECOSOC. In the case of racial discrimination, the 1960 UNESCO Convention Against Discrimination in Education and ILO Convention No. 111 Concerning Discrimination in Respect of Employment and Occupation provide supporting norms and monitoring procedures.

The torture regime includes an unusually varied array of supporting principles and institutions. The 1955 Geneva Standard Minimum Rules for the Treatment of Prisoners and the 1988 Body of Principles for the Protection of All Persons Under Any Form of Detention or Imprisonment provide supporting norms, as do regional torture conventions in Europe and the Americas. As noted earlier, the UN Commission on Human Rights has a special rapporteur on torture. The Commission's Working Group on Arbitrary Detention addresses a problem often closely associated with torture. The UN Voluntary Fund for Torture Victims provides financial assistance for victims, support groups, and research on strategies to help torture victims and their families.

In addition, there has been unusually close and fruitful cooperation among states, NGOs, and intergovernmental organizations on the issue of torture. For example, both the convention and the special rapporteur owe much to the intensive lobbying and public information activities of Amnesty International over more than a decade.

In a very different vein, Copenhagen is the home of an international Rehabilitation and Research Center for Torture Victims, a location that reflects the leading role of Denmark in international action against torture. Similar centers operate in Canada, Norway, and other countries.

In all the treaty-based committees, members, who are independent experts, prepare for the review of reports individually, as they see fit. This often allows NGOs to have significant, if indirect, input by providing information not included in a report. At the public session, members are free to raise any question they deem appropriate. In many instances, the result is careful scrutiny of certain areas of state practice.

The major difference between the committees, other than the personalities of the members, concerns their treatment of individual communications. The Committee on the Rights of the Child (CRC) has no powers to receive or review individual complaints. The Committee for the Elimination of Racial Discrimination (CERD) is technically authorized to consider individual communications, but the procedure is largely moribund. The Committee on the Elimination of Discrimination Against Women (CEDAW) received such powers under the Optional Protocol, which came into force at the end of 2000 and currently applies to seventy-two parties. To date, however, CEDAW has issued only three decisions under the procedure. The Committee Against Torture (CAT) is the only body (besides the HRC) that has an active and significant individual complaint procedure. It has been authorized by fifty-six states to receive individual communications and has reached decisions in more than one hundred cases from sixteen states.

C. Assessing Treaty-Reporting Systems

The weakness of treaty-reporting schemes as an "enforcement" mechanism is widely acknowledged. However, these systems do provide incentives for states to improve their human rights practices. Preparing a report provides a concrete periodic reminder to officials of their international legal obligations. And the review process, whatever its defects, assures that at least one international body periodically monitors the actions of those responsible for implementing internationally recognized human rights.

We should be careful, however, not to think of reporting in overly adversarial terms. Reporting procedures cannot force recalcitrant states to alter their practices. Preparing a report, though, does require a national review of law and practice. If thorough and conscientious, it can uncover areas where improvement may be needed or possible. Such review may be particularly valuable in newly democratic or liberalizing countries and is likely to have some use in all democratic countries. Reporting as an implementation technique thus functions primarily through the good intentions of states and their desires for a good international reputation. Recalcitrant states can violate human rights with something approaching impunity.

Supervisory bodies therefore must struggle to make the most of the opportunities for influence available during the review of reports. In some cases, instead of attempting to chastise or embarrass a state, it may be more productive to try to establish a constructive dialogue. "Weaker" and less adversarial techniques may sometimes have a greater effect.

TABLE 5.1   Major Treaty-Based Supervisory Committees

	HRC	CESCR	CERD	CEDAW	CAT	CRC
Treaty in force	3/23/1976	3/1/1976*	1/4/1969	9/3/1981	6/26/1987	9/2/1990
Parties (10/2005)	154	151	170	180	140	192
Committee members	18	18	18	23	10	10
Sessions per year	3	2	2	2	2	3
Length of session (in weeks)	3	3	3	3	3	3
Reporting cycle (in years)	5	5	4	4	4	5

HRC = Human Rights Committee (International Covenant on Civil and Political Rights).

CESCR= Committee on Economic, Social, and Cultural Rights (International Covenant on Economic, Social, and Cultural Rights)

CERD = Convention/Committee on the Elimination of All Forms of Racial Discrimination.

CEDAW = Convention/Committee on the Elimination of All Forms of Discrimination Against Women.

CAT = Convention Against Torture and Other Cruel, Inhuman, or Degrading Treatment or Punishment; Committee Against Torture.

CRC = Convention/Committee on the Rights of the Child.

For additional information on all these bodies, see http://www.ohchr.org/english/bodies

*The CESCR was not established until 1985, the Covenant having made no provision for a supervisory committee.

The constraints imposed by sovereignty also suggest special consideration for initiatives directed not at the worst cases but toward states with less bad, or even relatively good, records. Such states, by their behavior, have given concrete evidence of (relatively) good intentions. They are thus likely to be more open to persuasion and more concerned about their international reputation.

The result is a paradox: Reporting is likely to have an impact where it is not critically needed, that is, where human rights records are relatively good. Nevertheless, any victim who is helped is a victory for international action, wherever that person resides.

One might even argue that the greatest virtue of treaty-reporting systems is their ability to address violations that are not sufficiently severe to merit scrutiny by the Commission on Human Rights, a special rapporteur, or the High Commissioner. Particularly for countries and violations that do not have a high international profile, reporting may actually provide greater scrutiny. Small-scale incremental progress, which is a realistic possibility in the case of any state that takes its reporting obligation seriously, is not to be sneered at—especially when we consider the typically modest impact of higher-profile investigatory or complaint procedures. And even if stronger mechanisms are available, the periodic self-study that reporting requires is a valuable contribution.

The proliferation of international human rights reporting systems, however, has created difficulties for even well-intentioned states. Late reports are a serious and pervasive problem. At the end of 2005, the six principal treaties had an average of 212 outstanding overdue reports, that is, half again as many outstanding late reports as parties.[9] The pervasive problem of late reports reflects not merely indifference but the administrative burden of reporting, especially in small or poor states. Without the skills or resources required for a conscientious review, reporting is an empty formality, even if the government is well intentioned. The impact of reporting systems thus could be significantly improved by linking them to a system of technical and financial support. Although many states would not avail themselves of such help, some would. (Countries that have recently undergone a change of government would be particularly promising candidates.) But the now chronic financial problems of the organization makes major budgetary additions difficult (although perhaps not impossible, especially if the discussions on reform that began in 2004 and 2005 bear fruit).

Another way to ease the reporting burden would be to standardize reporting systems. After more than a decade of discussion, some progress may be achieved soon. Draft guidelines for standardizing and consolidating reporting procedures are being seriously discussed, and the issue was raised directly by the Secretary-General in his call for reform of the overall system.

4. ADDITIONAL SINGLE-ISSUE REGIMES

In addition to the treaty-based regimes considered in the preceding section, more diffuse single-issue regimes on workers' rights, apartheid, genocide, and minority rights have been important in the development of multilateral human rights procedures.

A. Workers' Rights

The first international human rights regime was the workers' rights regime developed in the International Labor Organization (ILO). Major ILO conventions (treaties) have dealt with freedom of association, the right to organize and bargain collectively, forced labor, migrant workers, and indigenous peoples, as well as a variety of issues of working conditions and workplace safety. Even nonbinding ILO recommendations provide an important international reference point for national standards.

ILO monitoring procedures, which date back to 1926, have been the model for other international human rights reporting systems. The Committee of Experts meets annually to review periodic reports submitted by states on their implementation of ratified conventions. If apparent problems are uncovered, the committee may issue a "direct request" for information or for changes in policy. Over the past two decades, more than a thousand such requests have brought changes in national policies. If the problem remains unresolved, the committee may make "observations," that is, authoritative determinations of violations of the convention in question.

The Conference Committee, which is made up of ILO delegates rather than independent experts, provides an additional level of scrutiny with greater political backing. Each year, it selects cases from the report of the Committee of Experts for further review. Government representatives are called upon to provide additional information and explanation. Special complaint procedures also exist for violations of the right to freedom of association and for discrimination in employment.

No less important than these inquisitorial or adversarial procedures is the institution of "direct contacts," a program of consultations and advice, often initiated by a government concerned about improving its performance with respect to a particular convention. The ILO is a leader in cooperative resolution of problems before they reach international monitoring bodies.

Part of the ILO's success can be attributed to its unique "tripartite" structure. Nearly all other intergovernmental organizations are made up solely of state representatives. NGOs often participate in deliberations but have no decision-making powers. In the ILO, however, workers' and employers' representatives from each member state are voting members of the organization, making it much more difficult for states to hide behind the curtain of sovereignty. The trans-ideological appeal of workers' rights has also been important to the ILO's success. In addition, the Committee of Experts, the ILO's central monitoring body, deals principally with technical issues such as hours of work, minimum working age, workplace safety, and identity documents for seamen. In monitoring such technical conventions, the committee develops and confirms expectations of neutrality that can help to moderate controversy when more contentious "political" issues do arise.

The ILO is, however, an international organization and is thus not entirely immune from political pressures and biases. For example, ILO criticisms of Israel for labor practices that went uncriticized in many other countries led the United States to withdraw temporarily in the late 1970s. Nonetheless, the ILO has been unusually active, effective, and impartial in its human rights work and a model for other international monitors.

B. Apartheid

The most extensive and vigorous of all international human rights regimes was also its narrowest, the regime against apartheid. For nearly half a century, South Africa was synonymous with **apartheid**, a distinctive style of unusually wide-ranging systematic racial domination. Officially abolished in 1992, apartheid was a major international human rights issue for thirty years and provides a good illustration of the strengths and weaknesses of multilateral mechanisms.

A System of Racial Domination.   Racial discrimination in South Africa goes back to the initial Dutch colonization in 1652. Indigenous hunters (San, or "Bushmen") were largely killed off or pushed out, and local herding peoples (Khoikhoi, "Hottentots") were forced off their lands. Slaves began to be imported in 1658. Blacks, discriminated against in voting from the very beginning, lost the formal right to vote in 1936. They were legally excluded from many jobs after 1911.

With the electoral victory of the conservative Nationalist Party in 1948, race became the basis for regulating all aspects of life in South Africa. The Nationalist government created a totalitarian bureaucracy to enforce racism throughout South African society.

The official rationale was racial and cultural preservation—separation and separate development. In practice, though, apartheid meant white privilege and domination.

The Population Registration Act of 1950, the cornerstone of apartheid, required racial registration of each person at birth. The Group Areas Act of 1950 (amended in 1957) consolidated and extended earlier laws designating land by race. The 1954 Natives Resettlement Act provided for forced removals of blacks from white-designated land.

These racial designations, however, did not necessarily have any connection to previously existing facts. For example, in 1956 and 1957, Sophiatown, a black free-hold section of Johannesburg, was rezoned white and the residents forcibly removed. In 1966, District Six of Capetown was declared white, although the population was 90 percent Coloured. Over 3.5 million blacks were removed from "white" areas, and more than a million were forced to relocate within designated black areas, often great distances away from their actual home.

Controls on the movement of nonwhites resulted in a series of pass laws and regulations that made it illegal for most blacks to be in urban areas for more than seventy-two hours without special permission. The result was the creation of black "townships," with inferior housing, education, and social services, on the outskirts of (white) cities, often two hours away from where residents worked. Because of the absurdities of the system of restrictions on movement, the ordinary nonwhite was subject to the constant threat of prosecution. More than one-fifth of the nonwhite population could expect to be prosecuted for pass-law violations within a ten-year period, a staggering level of legal intrusion on the basis of just one set of rules. And because prosecutions often led to expulsion from the area and the loss of a person's only source of income, the pass laws were an extraordinarily powerful instrument of social control.

According to the 1980 official census, 48 percent of all blacks were living in white areas. And it was a good thing, for the land defined as black "Homelands" was largely barren and completely unable to support the population.[10] Getting everyone where they "belonged" would have produced mass starvation for blacks and the collapse of white standards of living and the white economy, which were built around cheap (black) labor.

Interracial marriage and sexual relations between whites and nonwhites were prohibited. The 1953 Reservation of Separate Amenities Act removed the formal legal requirement that racially segregated facilities be equal. The Native Laws Amendment Act of 1957 prohibited holding classes, church services, or any meeting by blacks in designated white areas. The euphemistically named Extension of University Education Act of 1959 effectively removed nonwhites from most existing universities and established new, and decidedly inferior, ethnic universities.

Increasingly repressive internal-security laws were passed to prevent political opposition. By 1967, few legal safeguards remained for those suspected of political offenses. At least one hundred people died while being detained by the police or security forces, usually after having been tortured. The best-known victim was black-consciousness activist Steve Biko.

Many who were not formally detained were brought in by the authorities for questioning, often as a not-so-subtle warning. Any organization could be banned (that is, outlawed), and the printing or dissemination of any publication prohibited. South Africa also "banned" individuals, restricting their movements, limiting whom they might see (sometimes to their immediate family), and prohibiting them from speaking publicly or being quoted in the media. Most nonparliamentary opposition was thus forced underground.

This does not mean that there was no resistance. The African National Congress (ANC), the leading political group in contemporary South Africa, was founded in 1912. The 1952–1953 pass-law demonstrations marked the beginning of organized resistance to apartheid. But resistance took new forms after the police fired on a group of peaceful demonstrators on March 21, 1960, killing sixty-nine people and wounding about two hundred others in what quickly came to be known as the Sharpeville Massacre.

When the ANC and several other groups were banned, a number of leading activists of the 1950s, including Nelson Mandela, concluded that peaceful protest alone could not be successful and launched a (not very effective) sabotage campaign. When Mandela and several other leaders were convicted in 1964 and sentenced to life imprisonment, the ANC was forced into exile. The government weathered mass protests and riots in 1976 and 1977 through a combination of force, new restrictions, and minor concessions.

Peaceful opposition also continued, despite government efforts to make it illegal. South African churches became particularly important, since almost all overtly political opposition organizations were banned. The award of the Nobel Peace Prize in 1984 to Bishop Desmond Tutu symbolized this struggle. Black trade-union activity also increased and became politically important in the mid-1980s.

New and unusually violent uprisings in the townships broke out in fall 1984 and lasted for nearly two years. Torture and abuse of those detained increased dramatically. Official violence against those not detained also increased. Symbolic of all this was the widely seen footage of armed security force personnel popping up from their hiding place inside a passing vehicle and opening fire on unarmed children. Even more ominous was the dramatic increase in violence by police-sponsored vigilante groups.

Direct repression was accompanied by no less severe social and economic exploitation and degradation. For example, the average white under apartheid had an income more than twelve times that of the average black. A black child was eight to ten times more likely to die before the age of one than a white child. Other standard statistical measures revealed a similar picture.

The International Campaign Against Apartheid.   Although the United Nations addressed racial discrimination in South Africa as early as 1946, it became a priority only after the 1960 Sharpeville Massacre. In the subsequent thirty years, a flood of resolutions sought to mobilize international support for the national and international struggle against apartheid.

In 1962, the UN General Assembly called on states to break diplomatic relations and boycott all trade with South Africa. The decisions of the General Assembly, however, are only recommendations, and until the 1980s they were largely ignored by most powerful states. The Security Council, which does have the authority to impose mandatory sanctions, established only a voluntary arms embargo in December 1963.

A mandatory arms embargo finally was approved in November 1977, after the murder of Steve Biko and the ensuing riots and repression in Soweto (Johannesburg's largest black township). Both nationally and internationally, the death of the charismatic Biko was a crucial turning point in South African history. Although a comprehensive, mandatory trade embargo was never established, several states did reduce or end diplomatic, cultural, and commercial relations with South Africa (see §6.4).

The UN developed a complex web of procedures and forums to pressure South Africa. The Special Committee on Apartheid, created in 1962, promoted a broad international campaign against apartheid. National support committees were formed, and opinion leaders in several countries were targeted. In 1975, a Trust Fund for Publicity Against Apartheid was established. The United Nations Educational and Training Program for Southern Africa, established in 1964, made more than 20,000 grants to South Africans studying abroad. The United Nations Trust Fund for South Africa, established in 1965, provided more than $30 million in legal, educational, and humanitarian assistance to the victims of apartheid, including refugees. The 1973 International Convention on the Suppression and Punishment of the Crime of Apartheid came into force in 1976 and had eighty-eight parties by the end of 1990, when apartheid was on its last legs.

Reiteration of anti-apartheid norms and associated condemnations of South Africa became a regular feature of most international organizations. For example, the ILO paid considerable attention to questions of workers' rights in South Africa. Other specialized agencies, such as the World Health Organization, also closely scrutinized South African policies in their areas of competence. Others instead excluded South Africa, beginning with the International Telecommunications Union in 1965. The South African government in 1970 was even prevented from taking its seat in the United Nations General Assembly.

The norm of isolation was applied with particular force in sports, culminating in the 1985 International Convention Against Apartheid in Sports. South Africa was unable to participate in the Olympics from 1964 until 1992. The Special Committee on Apartheid also kept and publicized a list of sporting contacts with South Africa, in an attempt to pressure national sporting federations to join the boycott. Less systematic efforts were made to monitor, deter, and give adverse publicity to entertainment and cultural contacts.

The principal positive influence of the apartheid regime was probably the support, encouragement, and justification it provided for individuals and national and international NGOs trying to alter the foreign policies of individual states. We will see some evidence of this in the discussion of U.S. policy toward South Africa in §6.4. International pressure undoubtedly played a role in the process of reform that led the Botha government to agree to the abolition of apartheid. But the fact that fundamental change in South Africa came only after thirty years of unusually strong and sustained international action underscores the limits of international human rights action in the face of truly recalcitrant violators.

C. Genocide

The 1948 Convention on the Prevention and Punishment of the Crime of Genocide was a central part of the first wave of post–World War II international human rights action. It was the most direct international response to the Holocaust, which played a decisive role in moving human rights onto international agendas. In the ensuing decades, however, the genocide regime remained purely declaratory and had little or no practical effect.

The genocide convention envisions enforcement solely through national and international courts; it establishes no supervisory machinery. The UN Commission on Human Rights, which might have had the authority to explore issues of genocide, has been notably silent on this important class of violations. In fact, genocide, until recently, has been treated largely outside the framework of international human rights law and institutions.

One of the major changes in the post–cold war politics of international human rights has been the development of a practice of multilateral armed intervention against genocide, which is examined in Chapter 8. At the same time, and through closely related political processes, a system of individual criminal responsibility has been established through ad hoc tribunals for Rwanda and the former Yugoslavia and with the creation of the International Criminal Court sitting permanently in The Hague.

The result has been a unique kind of regime, with real powers of international judicial punishment and the capacity to intervene with military force. There are no international parallels (except the European Court of Human Rights, which operates only regionally). Yet the regime still lacks any supervisory mechanism or a clear institutional focus. And international efforts remain largely focused on punishing violators rather than the promotional and preventive activities characteristic of most other international human rights regimes.

D. Minorities and Indigenous Peoples

The final issue I want to consider here is minority rights.[11] Although racial discrimination has been a central international human rights concern at least since the 1960s—the racial discrimination convention was adopted before even the International Human Rights Covenants—discrimination against nonracial minorities was largely ignored until well into the 1980s. In 1992, however, the UN General Assembly adopted the Declaration on the Rights of Persons belonging to National, or Ethnic, Religious and Linguistic Minorities, and the topic has gained attention since then.

The most interesting work, however, is being done within Europe, where the issue of minority rights first received significant multilateral attention (during the interwar period), and where the aftermath of the breakups of Yugoslavia and the Soviet Union have given the issue immense topical significance. Both the Council of Europe and the Organization for Security and Co-operation in Europe have active and innovative promotional programs that involve working with both states and civil society at local, national, and regional levels. The Council of Europe's Framework Convention for the Protection of National Minorities creates an elaborate system of formal regional reporting and monitoring.

A "minorities" issue of special interest is the rights of indigenous peoples, groups that have a unique character and special vulnerabilities. The most important international legal instrument is ILO Convention 169 of 1989. A comprehensive draft declaration on indigenous rights, however, is moving extremely slowly through the Commission on Human Rights, still stuck in a drafting working group after nearly a decade of work. This reflects both the sensitivity of the issues raised and the fact that the working group has allowed unusual access to representatives of NGOs and indigenous peoples, seriously complicating the negotiating process.

5. REGIONAL HUMAN RIGHTS REGIMES

Single-issue regimes supplement the global human rights regime with norms and procedures covering a relatively narrow set of rights. In contrast, regional human rights regimes address a wide range of rights in smaller and more homogeneous groups of states.

A. Europe

A strong regional regime exists among the forty-six members of the Council of Europe. Personal, legal, civil, and political rights are guaranteed by the (European) Convention for the Protection of Human Rights and Fundamental Freedoms (1950) and its protocols. Economic and social rights are laid down in the European Social Charter (1961, revised 1996). The lists of rights in these documents are very similar to those of the Universal Declaration and the Covenants. However, the decision-making procedures of the European regime are of special interest, especially the authoritative decision-making powers of the European Court of Human Rights.[12]

Decisions of the European regional regime have had a considerable impact on law and practice in a number of states. For example, detention practices have been altered in Belgium, Germany, Greece, and Italy. The treatment of aliens has been changed in the Netherlands and Switzerland. Laws concerning freedom of the press were amended in Britain. Wiretapping regulations have been changed in Switzerland. Legal aid practices have been revised in Italy and Denmark. Procedures to speed trials have been implemented in Italy, the Netherlands, and Sweden. Privacy laws were revamped in Italy.

The impact of the European Court is especially strong and important because of its adoption of the principle of "evolutive interpretation." The Court interprets the European Convention not according to the conditions and understandings that existed in 1950 when it was drafted but in light of the current regional practices. This has contributed to national changes, especially in states that lag behind European norms. Examples include corporal punishment in schools in the United Kingdom and discrimination against unmarried mothers and children born outside of marriage in Belgium. More recently, gender issues have been an important area for such evolving interpretations. Europe has also led in the progressive development of the rights of sexual and gender minorities.

A Council of Europe Commissioner for Human Rights was created in 1999. This is an entirely independent institution that aims to promote education and awareness of human rights issues, improve the enjoyment of recognized rights, and identify possible shortcomings in national law and practice. Other than the requirement that she not deal with individual complaints, the Commissioner may look into any aspect of human rights in Europe, deal directly with governments, and issue opinions, reports, and recommendations. Moreover, member states have a positive obligation to facilitate the independent and effective functioning of the Commissioner.

The system for dealing with economic, social, and cultural rights has also been significantly strengthened in the past decade. The substance of the European Social Charter was substantially expanded by protocols in 1988, 1991, and 1995. In 1996 these changes, and some others, were consolidated into a Revised Charter of Social Rights, which entered into force in 1999. The net result was not only to expand the rights covered but to strengthen the supervisory system and to open it more fully to NGOs and "social partners" such as workers' organizations. Rather than judicial settlement, supervision is conducted through a system of reporting and collective complaints to an Independent Committee of Experts, which reports to the Council of Ministers for further action. Such review is much more extensive than that typical of nearly all other international and regional regimes.

The European Parliament, a largely advisory body selected by direct popular election, has shown interest in international human rights issues. For example, it adopts an annual international human rights resolution based largely on the extensive reports of its human rights rapporteur.

There is also a human rights dimension to the activities of the European Union (EU). Economic integration in recent years has been accompanied by efforts to harmonize social policy. This has often had a positive impact on economic and social rights because policies tend to be standardized not according to the lowest common denominator but on the basis of average performers. The EU has also pursued human rights concerns in external relations, including a formal requirement for human rights conditionality in all aid allocations. Diplomatic initiatives on behalf of human rights and individual victims have become a regular practice.

A cynic might argue that the breadth and strength of the European human rights regime simply illustrate the paradox of international action on behalf of human rights: Strong procedures exist where they are least needed. Because they require the permission of the states, they are likely only where states have a high interest and good records.

"Least needed," however, does not mean "unneeded." Even committed governments with good records can fall short of their best intentions. For example, Germany, Italy, and the United Kingdom have been criticized in Amnesty International reports on torture. The enforcement procedures of the European regime are available to victims when slips occur. They also provide subtle but constant pressure on states to meet the highest standards of behavior.

No less important than these adversarial remedial procedures has been the impact of the regime on national political reforms. New constitutions in Greece, Portugal, and Spain after they escaped military rule were written with the European Convention in mind. The previously communist states of Central and Eastern Europe have also reformulated their legal systems with European norms in mind. And in most countries the convention has significantly influenced legislation in many areas.

B. The Americas

The inter-American human rights regime's procedures revolve around a commission and a court. The Inter-American Court of Human Rights, which sits in San Jose, Costa Rica, may take binding enforcement action with respect to the eighteen parties (not including the United States) that have recognized its jurisdiction. The Court has issued more than 130 judgments and has become notably more active in recent years. Historically, however, the real heart of the regime is the seven-member Inter-American Commission of Human Rights (IACHR).

Established in 1959 as a part of the Organization of American States, the authority of the Inter-American Commission does not rest on a separate human rights treaty (although there is a 1969 American Convention on Human Rights). As with the UN Commission on Human Rights, all states that are members of the organization may in principle come under its scrutiny. And the IACHR has aggressively exploited its charge to promote and develop awareness of human rights, make recommendations, prepare studies and reports, handle individual complaints, and conduct on-site investigations throughout the Western Hemisphere.

Individual communications, however, have not been the heart of the work of the Inter-American Commission. Although it receives several hundred communications a year and is authorized to make findings on the merits of individual cases, the decisions of the IACHR have rarely been implemented. This reflects the very different human rights environments in the Americas and Europe.

Because of the generally excellent human rights records of its members, communications in the European regime typically deal with narrow or isolated violations that are not fundamentally threatening to the government. Even when there are serious systematic violations, as during military rule in Greece, the government involved is seen as aberrant. If the behavior persists, the country is treated as a pariah.

Most countries in the Americas, by contrast, have suffered repressive military rule within the past generation. During the entire cold war era, at any given time several OAS member states, and often a majority, were ruled by dictatorial governments. With so many cases of such high sensitivity and with governments so deeply disinclined to change, it is no surprise that the findings of the Commission in individual cases have typically been ignored.

Faced with systematic violations, the Inter-American Commission's greatest impact has come through studies and reports on human rights situations in more than twenty countries. IACHR reports, which have typically used individual communications and on-site visits to document a pattern of violations, have often been an important part of international efforts to publicize violations.

The strengths and weaknesses of this process are illustrated by the Inter-American Commission's response to military rule in Chile (see Chapter 4). Within a week of the coup on September 11, 1973, the Commission cabled Chile expressing its concern and asking for information. In October, its executive secretary, Luis Reque, visited Chile. His report advised a formal on-site visit by the Inter-American Commission, which took place July 22 through August 2, 1974.

During its visit, the Inter-American Commission interviewed government authorities, received 575 new communications, and took statements from witnesses to support previously submitted communications. Commission members also observed military tribunals, studied trial records of military and civil courts, and gathered information on the junta's legislation. Their visits to detention centers led to some minor changes and helped to identify facilities where torture was being practiced.

The Commission's report concluded that the government of Chile was guilty of a wide range of human rights abuses, including systematic violations of the rights to life, liberty, personal security, due process, and civil liberties. In October 1974, this was hardly news. Nonetheless, the report was thorough and tough. It also provided authoritative confirmation of the charges that had been made against the Chilean junta. This made it much more difficult for sympathetic foreign governments to dismiss the complaints of exiles and human rights activists as partisan or unsubstantiated. For example, the IACHR report was a standard source of information in U.S. congressional hearings.

Over the next two years, the Commission focused on individual communications. In 1975 it considered more than 600 cases of torture and 160 disappearances. The government, however, was uncooperative. As noted earlier, individual communications are not well suited to handling systematic, gross violations.

The Commission's second report on Chile, in 1976, applied new pressure on the Pinochet regime. Although noting a decline in some violations, it documented continuing systematic abuses and concluded that government actions and policies continued to be an impediment to the restoration of respect for human rights in Chile. This helped to undercut arguments made by and on behalf of Chile that the situation was returning to normal.

The political organs of the OAS, however, refused to follow the Commission's lead. The first report on Chile provoked an innocuous resolution that did little more than ask for additional information. The OAS was so little moved that in 1975 the members overwhelmingly accepted Chile's offer to host the next session of the OAS General Assembly. Following the IACHR's second report, Chile was asked "to continue adopting and implementing the necessary procedures and measures for effectively preserving and ensuring full respect for human rights in Chile." By implying more progress than had in fact occurred, this resolution was in some ways worse than nothing. And after the third report, in March 1977, the OAS General Assembly did not even extend the formal courtesy of asking for a further study.

This icy reception underscores the limits of even aggressive and independent monitors in an organization with little concern for human rights. Nonetheless, the IACHR persisted. Its annual reports for 1977, 1978, and 1979–1980 included sections on Chile. The reports for 1980–1981 through 1982–1983, in a concession to the generally hostile organizational environment, contained no references to particular countries. But the 1983–1984 report returned to a tougher stand, with a chapter on violations in several states (including Chile).

In May 1984, in response to the worsening situation in Chile, the Commission began work on a new country report, issued in 1985. A resolution criticizing Chile by name failed by a single vote in the OAS General Assembly in December 1985. And the IACHR continued to pressure the Pinochet government until it was finally removed from office.

What can we conclude from all this? A cynic can point to "the bottom line," namely, the persistence of military rule in Chile. If a state is willing to accept the costs to its reputation, which rarely exceed strained relations and reduced foreign aid, it can flout international human rights regimes.

But to expect recalcitrant states to be forced to mend their ways is wildly unrealistic. The Inter-American Commission, like most other multilateral human rights agencies, works primarily with the power of publicity. It can promote the regional implementation of human rights norms. It can monitor and publicize violations and try to persuade states to improve their practices. But it cannot, and is not intended to be able to, force a state to do anything. Sovereignty remains the overriding norm in the inter-American human rights regime—as in all other international human rights regimes except that of Europe.

Nonetheless, in summarizing the Commission's work on Chile, Cecilia Medina, who herself was forced into exile by the military government, has argued that

> in a situation of gross, systematic violations, the constant attention of the international community is of the highest importance; it serves as a support and encouragement for those suffering and opposing repression within the country, and at the same time prompts, and serves as a basis for, further international action by other governmental and nongovernmental international organizations.[13]

This is particularly true when a state is subject to scrutiny in multiple intergovernmental organizations and by several national and international NGOs.[14]

Perhaps the strongest evidence for the importance of international publicity is the diplomatic effort states exert to avoid it. In the late 1970s and early 1980s, both Argentina and Chile devoted much of their diplomacy—in the United Nations, the OAS, and the United States—to avoiding public criticism.[15] If rights-abusive regimes take international condemnation seriously enough to struggle to avoid it, the work of international human rights agencies is unlikely to be entirely pointless.

We must also remember that "the bottom line" includes individuals who are helped. States often respond to international pressure by releasing or improving the treatment of prominent victims. These small victories for international action are victories nonetheless—and of immense significance to individual victims.

In rare cases, there may even be a systematic impact. For example, the 1978 IACHR report on Nicaragua increased the pressure on the dictatorial Somoza government. Furthermore, the OAS call for Somoza to resign in June 1979 shook his political confidence and seems to have hastened his departure.[16]

Reports, though, are only reports. Decisions on individual cases are only nonbinding resolutions. Real change requires additional action by states. This is an inherent shortcoming of almost all international human rights regimes.

Nonetheless, the Inter-American Commission has aggressively exploited its powers, to at least some effect. Its activities have improved the treatment of many thousands of victims of human rights violations. If we compare it not to Europe but to the UN Commission or the single-issue regimes discussed earlier, the cold war–era record of the inter-American regimes stands in a relatively good light.

Elected (although not necessarily fully democratic) governments have been in office in all the mainland countries of the Western Hemisphere since 1991. The OAS General Assembly, which in the early 1980s refused to discuss human rights abuses, has become willing to act on behalf of human rights, most notably in removing the military from power in Haiti. Nonetheless, the inter-American regime does not appear to be moving toward anything like the strength of the European regime. Although states have adopted much less adversarial attitudes toward the Commission, and the Court has become notably more active, the American states have not shown any special enthusiasm for strengthening regional human rights institutions.

C. Africa, Asia, and the Middle East

A third regional human rights regime exists within the Organization of African Unity (OAU) under the 1981 African Charter on Human and Peoples' Rights—or Banjul Charter, as it is often called, after the site of its adoption (Banjul, The Gambia).

The Banjul Charter gives unusual emphasis to collective or peoples' rights. The International Human Rights Covenants recognize the right of peoples to self-determination. The apartheid convention also refers to the rights of peoples to self-determination and equality. The Banjul Charter adds rights to development and to peace. The significance of such rights, however, is a matter of controversy.

One standard dictionary definition of a people is "the persons belonging to a place or forming a group, the subjects or citizens of a state." This is the usual sense in regional and international organizations, with the emphasis on citizens of an already established state. "People" most definitely does not mean "the persons composing a community or tribe or race or nation," another standard definition. For example, Nigerians are a people entitled to self-determination, peace, and development. Nigeria, however, contains such ethnic communities as the Yoruba, Ogoni, and Ibo, who are most definitely not considered subjects of the "peoples' rights" of the African Charter. The Ibo were forcefully reincorporated into Nigeria, with the full support of the OAU, when they attempted to secede (as Biafra) in 1967.

The rights of peoples and states direct our attention to the external threats to human rights posed by foreign governments, international markets, and multinational corporations. These are important and perhaps underemphasized in international human rights discussions. Nonetheless, the great majority of human rights abuses, in Africa as elsewhere, are committed by states against their own nationals.

Peoples' rights also focus attention on the collective dimension of human rights and the connection between the collective goods of peace and development and more traditional individual human rights (which are also recognized in the African Charter). But neither peace nor development, in the ordinary senses of those terms, will guarantee the enjoyment of internationally recognized human rights. For example, the citizens of the Soviet Union enjoyed peace but not human rights for four decades. In numerous countries, a small elite has obtained most of the benefits of national economic development.

The African Charter also places unusual (and problematic) emphasis on individual duties. A system of rights can operate effectively only if individuals attend to their reciprocal duties. Although commonplace, this is well worth repeating. Yet one may ask whether the real human rights problem in Africa (or elsewhere) is that people have too few duties to the state and society. I would suggest instead that far too many states are all too aware of the duties of individuals but insufficiently attentive to their own duties and the rights of their citizens.

The African Charter is also marred by extensive "clawback" clauses. For example, Article 6 recognizes "the right to liberty and to the security of the person" but then goes on to state that "no one may be deprived of his freedom except for reasons and conditions previously laid down by law." Because there are no restrictions on such reasons and conditions—the European convention, by contrast, explicitly restricts permissible grounds—this allows the state free rein, so long as it bothers to pass laws that suspend or abolish these (and many other) rights. Freedom of assembly may be restricted for reasons of national security or "the safety, health, ethics and rights and freedoms of others." Thus, any assembly that may offend anyone else (the ethics of others) may be banned. In good circumstances, this may not be a problem. But human rights are supposed to protect individuals above all in bad times.

Finally, the Banjul Charter's implementation provisions are unusually weak. In addition to reviewing reports, the eleven-member African Commission on Human and Peoples' Rights may consider communications. But only situations, not individual cases, may be discussed. And an in-depth study of a situation requires permission from the OAU's Assembly of Heads of State and Government. This is by far the most politicized of all multilateral procedures. Furthermore, neither state reports nor the Commission's review of them has been promising.

Nonetheless, the African Commission does seem to approach its task with seriousness and energy. It has not merely permitted but has encouraged NGO participation. Given the relatively weak civil societies typical in Africa and the lack of a tradition of independent human rights NGOs, this may prove to be a significant contribution.

Whatever the ultimate fate of this African regional human rights regime, it is already much further advanced than those in the Arab world or in Asia and the Pacific. The Permanent Arab Commission on Human Rights established by the Arab League in 1968 has been notably inactive, except for occasional efforts to publicize human rights violations in Israeli-occupied territory. There are not even authoritative regional norms.

Taken together, Asia and the Pacific compose a large and diverse area that is not a region in any social or political sense. Thus, the lack of a regional human rights regime is not surprising. But the relatively low level of Asian ratifications of the International Human Rights Covenants (the lowest percentage of any geographical region) suggests that more than size and diversity stand in the way of even subregional human rights regimes in Asia.

Even without intergovernmental organizations, there may still be important transnational action on behalf of human rights. For example, more than one thousand NGOs are listed in Human Rights Internet's *Human Rights Directory: Asia and the Pacific*. Most of these groups operate only domestically. Nonetheless, they and their transnational colleagues play an important role, especially in countries with a relatively good human rights records. Even in extremely repressive countries, international human rights NGOs, such as the U.S.-based Human Rights Watch Asia, work hard to assure that human rights violations are not ignored by the international community.

In the Middle East as well, NGO initiatives have tried to compensate for the absence of a functioning regional regime. For example, the Arab Organization for Human Rights (AOHR), founded in 1983, issues annual reports on human rights conditions in the countries of the Arab world. In 1989—through a joint initiative of the Arab Lawyers Union, AOHR, and the Tunisian League for Human Rights, with the support of the UN Center for Human Rights—an Arab Institute for Human Rights was established in Tunis to provide information on human rights conditions and training for both government and nongovernmental personnel. There have also been efforts by Muslim individuals and NGOs to formulate Islamic human rights norms.

The general hostility of governments increases the importance of the activities of national and transnational human rights NGOs. They can help to keep the idea alive and at least on the fringes of political debate. NGOs are also likely to be important in probing the limits of political tolerance and attempting to take advantage of what limited political space exists for action on behalf of internationally recognized human rights.

D. The Helsinki Process

A hybrid, quasi-regional human rights regime exists within the Organization for Security and Co-operation in Europe (OSCE, previously Conference on Security and Co-operation in Europe [CSCE]), an organization made up of European countries (with the breakup of the Soviet Union and Yugoslavia, there are now fifty-four), plus the United States and Canada. The system is often referred to as the Helsinki process, in honor of its central normative document, the Helsinki Final Act of 1975.

The CSCE was convened in 1973 to promote more stable and cooperative East-West relations. The principal Soviet objective was recognition of the territorial and ideological division of Europe. The Soviets also wanted to improve their access to Western technology and trade. During negotiations, however, they reluctantly agreed to include limited human rights provisions, under the novel notion of domestic security for citizens.

The resulting document is a marvel of diplomatic compromise. Three very different "baskets"—dealing with political and military issues (particularly the inviolability of frontiers and the principle of nonintervention), economic relations, and humanitarian relations—are held together in a delicate political balance. Our concern here is solely with Principle VII ("Respect for human rights and fundamental freedoms, including the freedom of thought, conscience, religion or belief") and the human rights provisions of "Basket III" ("Co-operation in Humanitarian and Other Fields").

Basket III deals solely with human contacts (especially family contacts and reunification), the free flow of information, and cultural and educational cooperation. Principle VII, however, includes an agreement to "promote and encourage the effective exercise of civil, political, economic, social, cultural and other rights and freedoms." Much of the history of the Helsinki process can be seen as a struggle over the relative priorities of these provisions. The Soviet bloc states attempted to stick to the narrow focus of Basket III (and even that only reluctantly). Western states, along with human rights NGOs in both the East and the West, stressed the broad language of Principle VII.

Follow-up meetings in Belgrade (1977–1978), Madrid (1980–1983), and Vienna (1986–1989) provided the principal diplomatic arena for this struggle. The Belgrade and Madrid meetings deadlocked and produced little beyond harsh words. But the Vienna meeting, which ended just months before the final crumbling of the Iron Curtain, was more productive. Its concluding document included extensive new language on freedom of religion and the treatment of detainees and established new CSCE procedures for state-to-state consultations over alleged human rights violations. In addition, a separate Conference on the Human Dimension of the CSCE was established. And in Moscow in 1992, new investigatory procedures were adopted. In hindsight, the Helsinki process can be seen as a chronicle of the gradual demise of the cold war and Soviet-style communism in the face of increasing national and international demands to implement internationally recognized human rights.

The Helsinki process also provided important legitimation for dissident groups in the Soviet bloc. The Final Act recognized the "right of the individual to know and act upon his rights and duties," in addition to the Basket III provisions on the free flow of information.

In May 1976, eleven prominent reformers, taking the Helsinki Final Act at its word, formed the Public Group to Assist the Implementation of the Helsinki Accords in the USSR. The purpose of the Moscow Helsinki Group, as it soon came to be known, was "to inform the governments that signed the Final Act in Helsinki, as well as the publics of those countries, of cases of direct violations of the humanitarian articles of the Final Act in the Soviet Union."[17] In six years of work, it prepared more than 150 reports on a great variety of human rights topics and issued numerous statements, letters, and appeals.

Local Helsinki-monitoring groups were also formed in Armenia, Georgia, Lithuania, and the Ukraine. All were harassed, and most were legally punished, often under the charge of anti-Soviet agitation and propaganda. This was a serious offense in Soviet law, and one could be found guilty even if all the facts that one was accused of disseminating were true—as was the case with the Moscow group's reports. From the very outset, members were intimidated into leaving the group or accepting an exit visa from the Soviet Union. By 1980, the group's principal activity had become monitoring the cases of their colleagues. By August 1981, only three members remained at liberty in the country. In September 1982, the Moscow Helsinki Group was forced to disband.

In Czechoslovakia, the coming of the Belgrade follow-up meeting helped to spur Charter 77, a manifesto signed in January 1977 by 242 people, including Václav Havel (who in 1990 became the first elected president of newly democratic Czechoslovakia). During the succeeding decade, Charter 77 became a powerful local human rights group with more than 1,300 public adherents.

As in the Soviet Union, official harassment began immediately. In fact, a car containing Havel and two others was stopped by the security forces while they were on their way to deliver the signed document to the government and the media. Members were physically attacked, fired from jobs, blacklisted, and in some cases arrested. Telephones were cut off, apartments taken away, driving licenses and passports revoked, and individuals detained without charge to prevent them from engaging in group activities. Some were convicted of political crimes. Children and other family members of activists were harassed and discriminated against in employment, residence, and schooling.

Nonetheless, the immense international publicity accorded the activities of the Moscow Helsinki Group both embarrassed Soviet authorities and helped to mobilize private and public political pressure. Formal Helsinki meetings provided a well-publicized forum for airing human rights grievances. And in Czechoslovakia, Charter 77 provided much of the leadership for the Velvet Revolution of 1989.

The revolutions of 1989 in Eastern Europe certainly cannot be attributed to either the formal Helsinki proceedings or the activities of national and international Helsinki monitors. Nonetheless, the combined pressures from above and below helped to open political space for some of the forces that ultimately overthrew communist rule. As the Charter of Paris for a New Europe, adopted at the Paris Summit of Heads of State or Government of the CSCE in November 1990, put it: "The courage of men and women, the strength of the will of the peoples and the power of the ideas of the Helsinki Final Act have opened a new era of democracy, peace and unity in Europe."

Perhaps the greatest testimony to the value of the process is the fact that the new governments of Central and Eastern Europe seem committed to using it to help to consolidate and extend their achievements. The now renamed Organization for Security and Co-operation in Europe undertakes a considerable variety of promotional and monitoring activities in the areas of human rights, democratization, minorities rights, and conflict resolution.[18]

6. THE EVOLUTION OF
INTERNATIONAL HUMAN RIGHTS REGIMES

Table 5.2 summarizes the character of the regimes considered above, considered at fifteen-year intervals, using the categories of declaratory, promotion, implementation, and enforcement regimes laid out at the beginning of this chapter. This section examines the pattern of growth in these regimes. The following, and final, section provides a more evaluative assessment of the character of these regimes.

The most striking pattern is the near complete absence of international human rights regimes in 1945, in contrast to the presence of several in all the later periods. We can also note the gradual strengthening of most international human rights regimes over the past thirty years. Even today, though, promotional regimes remain the rule.

Once states accept norms stronger than nonbinding guidelines, declaratory regimes readily evolve into promotional regimes. It is difficult to argue against promoting the further spread and implementation of norms that one has accepted. However, the move to implementation or enforcement involves a major qualitative jump that most states resist, often with considerable vigor, and usually with success.

National commitment is the single most important contributor to a strong regime; it is the source of the often mentioned "political will" that underlies most strong regimes. If a state has a good human rights record, then not only will a strong regime appear relatively unthreatening, but the additional support it provides for national efforts is likely to be welcomed. The European regime's unprecedented strength provides the most striking example of the power of national commitment.

Cultural community, however, is no less important. In the absence of sociocultural and ideological consensus, strong procedures are likely to appear too subject to partisan use or abuse to be accepted even by states with good records and strong national commitments. For example, opponents of stronger procedures in the global human rights regime and in single-issue regimes include major countries from the First, Second, and Third Worlds with national human rights records that range from good to poor. The very scope of all but the regional regimes undercuts the relative homogeneity that seems almost necessary for movement beyond a promotional regime.

Finally, we must stress the importance of dominant power and ideological hegemony, which should be kept analytically distinct. The effective exercise of even preponderant material power usually requires an ideological justification sufficiently powerful to win at least acquiescence from nonhegemonic powers. The seemingly inescapable ideological appeal of human rights over the past half century, even during the ideological rivalry of the cold war, thus has been an important element in the rise of international human rights regimes. We might even argue that the ideological hegemony of human rights was more important than dominant material power.

A hegemonic idea such as human rights may actually draw power to itself; power may coalesce around, rather than create, hegemonic ideas, such as human rights and the regimes that emerge from them. Hegemonic ideas thus can be expected to draw acquiescence to relatively weak regimes. But to move beyond promotional activities—

TABLE 5.2 International Human Rights Regimes, 1945–2005

	1945	1960	1975	1990	2005
GLOBAL REGIME					
Norms	None	Declatory	Promotional	Strong Promotional	Strong Promotional
Procedures	None	Guidelines	Standards with exemptions	Global norms with exemptions	Authoritative global norms
	None	Weak promotion	Promotion	Strong promotion/ monitoring	Strong promotion/ monitoring
REGIONAL HUMAN RIGHTS REGIMES					
European Regime					
Norms	None	Promotional/Implementation	Implementation/Enforcement	Enforcement	Strong Enforcement
Procedures	None	Guidelines/regional norms	Regional norms	Authoritative regional norms	Authoritative regional norms
	None	Promotion/monitoring	Regional decisions with exemptions	Regional decisions	Binding regional decisions
Inter-American Regime					
Norms	None	Declaratory	Promotional	Strong Promotional	Strong Promotional
Procedures	None	Guidelines	Standards with exemptions	Regional norms	Authoritative regional norms
	None	None	Promotion/monitoring	Monitoring/very limited regional decisions	Monitoring/very limited regional decisions
African Regime					
Norms	None	None	None	Declaratory	Declaratory
Procedures	None	None	None	Guidelines	Weak standards with exemptions
	None	None	None	Weak promotion	Weak promotion
Asia	None	None	None	None	None
Middle East	None	None	None	None	None
SINGLE-ISSUE REGIMES					
Worker's Rights					
Norms	Promotional	Strong Promotional	Strong Promotional	Strong Promotional	Strong Promotional
Procedures	Limited guidelines	Standards with exemptions	Strong standards with exemptions	Strong standards with exemptions	Strong standards with exemptions
	Promotion/monitoring	Promotion/monitoring	Promotion/monitoring	Promotion/monitoring	Promotion/monitoring
Racial Discrimination					
Norms	None	None	Promotional	Strong Promotional	Strong Promotional
Procedures	None	None	Standards with exemptions	Strong standards with exemptions	Strong standards with exemptions
	None	None	Promotion/weak monitoring	Promotion/weak monitoring	Promotion/weak monitoring
Women's Rights					
Norms	None	None/Very Weak Declaratory	Declaratory	Strong Promotional	Strong Promotional
Procedures	None	None/Limited guidelines	Guidelines	Standards with exemptions	Standards with exemptions
	None	None	Weak promotion	Promotion/weak monitoring	Promotion/weak monitoring
Torture					
Norms	None	None	Declaratory	Strong Promotional	Strong Promotional
Procedures	None	None	Guidelines	Strong standards with exemptions	Authoritative global norms
	None	None	None	Promotion/monitoring	Promotion/monitoring
Genocide					
Norms	None	Very Weak Declaratory	Very Weak Declaratory	Very Weak Declaratory	Declaratory/Ad hoc Enforcement
Procedures	None	Guidelines	Guidelines	Guidelines	Authoritative global norms
	None	None	None	None	Ad hoc Enforcement
Children					
Norms	None	None	None	Declaratory/Promotional	Promotional
Procedure	None	None	None	Guidelines	Standards with exemptions
	None	None	None	None	Promotion/weak monitoring

which requires significant sacrifices—something more, typically external material power or internal substantive commitment, is needed. Hegemony thus also points toward the pattern of limited growth, with strong barriers at the threshold between promotional and implementation regimes.

7. ASSESSING MULTILATERAL HUMAN RIGHTS MECHANISMS

How do we assess the welter of multilateral institutions we have examined in this rather lengthy chapter? I will focus on differences in regimes that arise from the source of their authority (based on a treaty or rooted in a wider international organization), their range or focus, and the character of their powers. Each type of mechanism has its own strengths and weaknesses.

Human rights institutions based in international and regional organizations can draw on the prestige and influence of the broader organization. This is one of the greatest resources of the High Commissioner for Human Rights and the UN Commission on Human Rights. Organization-based institutions may also benefit from internal political linkages. The other objectives states are pursuing within the organization may constrain them from resisting the organization's human rights initiatives.

In addition, the decisions of international organizations represent the collective activities of states, with their associated power resources. This may allow mobilizing a different kind of influence than that available to committees of independent experts. For example, the impact of IACHR activities on Chile and Argentina was increased by the support of the regional hegemon, the United States, especially during the Carter presidency.

Politicization, however, is the price often paid for the political power of multilateral organizations. For example, in the UN during the cold war, countries were singled out for scrutiny largely on the basis of their (lack of) international political support. Even though serious violations were addressed, the procedures were corrupted by the taint of political partisanship. The position of the IACHR in the 1970s and 1980s also illustrates the problems that can arise if the broader organization is substantially less interested in human rights.

Committees of independent experts have been relatively nonpartisan. Even during the cold war, the Human Rights Committee, for example, was far less politicized than even the UN Commission, let alone the General Assembly. Given the heavy reliance on publicity and persuasion, a reputation for integrity and fairness can be a powerful tool.

Combining these two lines of argument suggests that an international human rights institution can maximize its impact if it is backed by a broader organization while avoiding the taint of politicization. This assessment is confirmed by the record of the UN and Inter-American Commissions and the European Court. The Inter-American Commission was far more aggressive, and effective, than the highly politicized OAS General Assembly. The UN Commission, especially in the 1980s and early 1990s, was able to draw on the combination of a reputation for relative impartiality and the prestige of the broader organization. This enabled, for example, improved access for special rapporteurs in unusually closed countries such as Iran and Burma. Likewise, the widespread voluntary compliance with the decisions of the European regime rests on a combination of the Council of Europe's prestige and influence and the unparalleled reputation for neutrality of its human rights machinery. This line of argument also helps to explain the emergence of the High Commissioner as a major international actor.

I noted earlier that single-issue and country-specific initiatives have largely complementary strengths and weaknesses. Because thematic or single-issue mechanisms avoid singling out individual countries, even when they do address particular state practices, the inquiry is likely to be less threatening. Thematic and single-issue initiatives also may appear less threatening because they do not address the full range of human rights issues.

Although initiatives on single issues may appear timid and almost beside the point in countries guilty of gross violations, significant incremental improvements in particular areas may result from single-issue mechanisms even where systematic violations persist. Whether the initiatives are countrywide or issue specific, the concrete achievements usually are, at best, incremental improvements in limited areas, such as the release of prominent political prisoners or the modification of particular laws, decrees, or administrative practices.

In examining particular implementation mechanisms, we again see a picture of complementary strengths and weaknesses. The principal tools available within these various regimes are (1) state reports, characteristic of the treaty-based regimes; (2) information-advocacy procedures, such as those undertaken by the IACHR or the UN Commission's thematic and country rapporteurs; and (3) individual communications (complaints), as in the European regime and the activities of the HRC under the Optional Protocol. The strengths and weaknesses of reporting systems were considered in §5.3.C. Here I focus on investigations and communications.

The individual petition system in Europe often appears to be the ideal mechanism. From an individual victim's point of view, the near-universal compliance with the decisions of the European Court are undoubtedly preferable to the uncertainties of reporting and investigatory-diplomatic methods. The Inter-American system, however, suggests that it is not so much the formal availability of individual petitions that is crucial but the commitment of states not simply to abide by the resulting quasi-judicial proceedings but to do the tough domestic legal and political work of implementing regional decisions. Regional or global petition systems thus are best seen as modest supplementary elements in an effective system of enforcing human rights. This is particularly true where, as with the HRC and the Inter-American Court, the procedure is optional, presenting a striking example of the typical trade-off between the scope and the strength of international procedures. Even the European regime is an example of the strongest procedures applying only to a relatively small group of states with relatively good human rights records.

The other obvious drawback of individual complaint mechanisms is the small number of cases they can address. The European and Inter-American courts and the HRC together have taken decisions on only about 4,000 complaints.

Nonetheless, the focus on individual cases gives these procedures a valuable specificity and concreteness. Because violations are personalized and detailed evidence of individual violations is provided, it is more difficult for states to deny responsibility.

Individual petitions, like the other kinds of procedures, occupy a special niche. They are particularly desirable where violations are either narrow or sporadic. But widespread adherence to individual complaint mechanisms is more an effect than a cause of high levels of implementation of internationally recognized human rights.

Investigation and reporting mechanisms will continue to be needed for a very long time. I am even tempted to argue that they are the heart of multilateral human rights activity. In a world still organized around sovereign states, the international contribution to implementing human rights rests on persuasive diplomacy, which itself rests considerably on the power of shame that lies at the heart of investigatory and reporting mechanisms.

If this is true, the key to change in state practices probably lies not in any one type of forum or activity but in the mobilization of multiple, complementary channels of influence. This would seem to be the lesson of the international campaign against apartheid and against military rule in the Southern Cone, the two principal examples considered in this chapter.

DISCUSSION QUESTIONS

1. You have read in this chapter about a large number of multilateral human rights regimes. What kind of overall evaluation would you draw? Clearly there is a reasonably large amount of international activity. What sort of impact has it had? Is that impact worth all the effort?

2. There is a diverse array of multilateral human rights bodies and procedures: global and regional, comprehensive and single issue, individual and situation oriented, political and legal. What are the strengths and weaknesses of each type? Is there, in your view, one type that is preferable to the others? What is the relationship between the best type and the other possible types in this area?

3. How would you assess international reporting schemes? Be sure to consider not only what they have (and have not) accomplished, but also what the costs have been and what the alternatives are.

4. Make an inventory of alternative multilateral approaches that either have not yet been tried or in your view have not been adequately exploited. Then consider why they haven't been used and whether these impediments are likely to persist.

5. I have suggested that international human rights procedures are likely to have their greatest impact where the human rights abuses are less egregious. What does this suggest about the most effective forms of international action? Are you comfortable with the idea of writing off the worst cases (which some may conclude is the central policy implication of this argument)? Is there a practical alternative?

6. Multilateral human rights institutions concentrate heavily on civil and political rights. What are the reasons for this? Is this a defensible allocation of resources and attention? What would have to change to bring about a more comprehensive system of international human rights monitoring?

7. Even when we consider only civil and political rights, we find that monitoring focuses on a relatively small number of rights, especially egregious violations of personal liberty and bodily integrity and cases of discrimination. There has been very little attention to the *political* aspects of civil and political rights. How can this be explained? How should it be evaluated? What are the alternatives, both theoretical and practical?

8. Return now to the issue of national implementation of international human rights norms. Do we have the right mix of national and international mechanisms of implementation and enforcement? How does your answer to this question change when you shift between moral and political perspectives? Is national implementation anything more than an unfortunate compromise with the realities of a world of sovereign states?

SUGGESTED READINGS

The bulk of the literature on international human rights regimes is written by international lawyers. As a result, much of it is far more technical and legalistic than the average reader of this book would desire. Nonetheless, no one who has read this chapter should feel intimidated. Almost everything listed below is accessible to a conscientious undergraduate student. Where the analysis veers off into highly technical legal issues, it usually can be easily skipped over. One must be prepared, however, for often rather dry and detailed discussions.

Philip Alston, ed., *The United Nations and Human Rights: A Critical Appraisal* (Oxford: Clarendon Press, 1995) provides an excellent comprehensive assessment of the UN role. Although some chapters are beginning to show their age, this is an excellent starting point for further reading on the global human rights regime. Other useful volumes that offer a wide-ranging assessment of the global regime include Anne F. Bayefsky, ed., *The UN Human Rights Treaty System in the 21st Century* (The Hague: Kluwer Law International, 2000), Hurst Hannum, ed., *Guide to International Human Rights Practice*, 4th ed. (Ardsley, N.Y.: Transnational Publishers, 2004), Janusz Symonides, ed., *Human Rights: International Protection, Monitoring, Enforcement* (Aldershot and New York: Ashgate/UNESCO, 2003), and Manfred Nowak, *Introduction to the International Human Rights Regime* (Leiden, the Netherlands: Martinus Nijhoff, 2003). Bertrand G. Ramcharan, *Human Rights and Human Security* (The Hague: Martinus Nijhoff, 2002) provides a fairly comprehensive review from a human security perspective. Henry J. Steiner and Philip Alston, *International Human Rights in Context: Law, Politics, Morals,* 2nd ed. (Oxford: Oxford University Press, 2000) is an immense volume that is more wide ranging but covers international and regional regimes well.

The standard work on treaty monitoring is Philip Alston and James Crawford, eds., *The Future of UN Human Rights Treaty Monitoring* (Cambridge: Cambridge University Press, 2000). It covers the full range of venues and issues. Michael O'Flaherty, *Human Rights and the UN: Practice Before the Treaty Bodies,* 2nd ed. (The Hague: Martinus Nijhoff, 2002) is also wide ranging. Much briefer and more accessible is a pamphlet prepared by the Office of the High Commissioner for Human Rights, "The United Nations Human Rights Treaty System," http://www.ohchr.org/english/about/publications/docs/fs30.pdf. Many of the chapters in the Bayefsky volume cited in the preceding paragraph are also directly relevant. For up-to-date information of ratification of the major human rights treaties, see http://www.ohchr.org/english/countries/ratification/index.htm. Christof Heyns and Frans Viljoen, *The Impact of United Nations Human Rights Treaties on the Domestic Level* (The Hague: Kluwer International, 2002) provides considerable illustrative material on the domestic impact of international human rights treaties.

There are three comprehensive studies of the Human Rights Committee: Ineke Boerefijn, *The Reporting Procedure Under the Covenant on Civil and Political Rights: Practice and Procedures of the Human Rights Committee* (Antwerp: Intersentia, 1999); Dominic McGoldrick, *The Human Rights Committee: Its Role in the Development of the International Covenant on Civil and Political Rights,* rev. ed. (Oxford: Clarendon Press, 1996); and Kirsten A. Young, *The Law and Process of the U.N. Human Rights Committee* (Ardsley, N.Y.: Transnational Publishers, 2002). None is easy reading, but each covers close to the full range of evidence with care and insight. The chapter by David Kretzner, "The Human Rights Committee," in *The UN Human Rights Treaty System in the 21st Century,* ed. Anne F. Bayefsky (The Hague: Kluwer Law International, 2000) is a useful brief overview. See also the UN pamphlet "Civil and Political Rights: The Human Rights Committee," http://www.ohchr.org/english/about/publications/docs/fs15rev.1_en.pdf.

On the Committee on Economic, Social, and Cultural Rights, perhaps the best discussion is in Matthew Craven's book *The International Covenant on Economic, Social, and Cultural Rights: A Perspective on Its Development* (Oxford: Clarendon Press, 1995). For good short introductions, see "The Committee on Economical, Social, and Cultural Rights," by Scott Leckie in *The Future of UN Human Rights Treaty Monitoring,* ed. Philip Alston and James Crawford (Cambridge: Cambridge University Press, 2000) and the UN pamphlet "Fact Sheet No. 16: The Committee on Economic, Social and Cultural Rights," http://www.ohchr.org/english/about/publications/docs/fs16.htm. On the issue of individual communications, see Philip Alston, "No Right to Complain About Being Poor: The Need for an Optional Protocol to the Economic Rights Covenant," in *The Future of Human Rights in a Changing World: Fifty Years Since the Four Freedoms Address. Essays in Honour of Torkel Opsahl,* ed. A. Eide and J. Helgesen (Oslo: Norwegian University Press, 1991).

Howard Tolley's book *The U.N. Commission on Human Rights* (Boulder: Westview Press, 1987) remains the best source on that body, despite its age. Several pamphlets by the Office of the High Commissioner provide useful introductions to particular dimensions of the activity of the Commissioner. For an overview of country and thematic procedures, see http://www.ohchr.org/english/bodies/chr/special/index.htm. Also useful are "Seventeen Frequently Asked Questions about United Nations Special Rapporteurs," http://www.ohchr.org/english/about/publications/docs/factsheet27.pdf; "Fact Sheet No. 26, The Working Group on Arbitrary Detention," http://www.ohchr.org/english/about/publications/docs/fs26.htm; "Fact Sheet No. 6 (Rev.2), Enforced or Involuntary Disappearances," http://www.ohchr.org/english/about/publications/docs/fs6.htm; and "Fact Sheet No. 11 (Rev.1), Extrajudicial, Summary or Arbitrary Executions," http://www.ohchr.org/english/about/publications/docs/fs11.htm. See also the relevant chapters in the general volumes cited in the second paragraph of suggested readings above.

On women's rights, Marjorie Agosín, ed., *Women, Gender, and Human Rights: A Global Perspective* (New Brunswick, N.J.: Rutgers University Press, 2001) is a good general reader with a multidisciplinary perspective. Rebecca J. Cook, ed., *Human Rights of Women: National and International Perspectives* (Philadelphia: University of Pennsylvania Press, 1994) is older but still well worth examining. Also useful is Patricia Grimshaw, Katie Holmes, and Marilyn Lake, eds., *Women's Rights and Human Rights: International Historical Perspectives* (Basingstoke, U.K.: Palgrave, 2001). For a more legal perspective, see Kelly D. Askin and Dorean N. Koenig, eds., *Women and International Human Rights Law* (Ardsley, N.Y.: Transnational, 1999). On the national use of international human rights law, see Andrew Byrnes, Jane Connors, and Lum Bik, eds., *Advancing the Human Rights of Women: Using International Human Rights Standards in Domestic Litigation* (London: Commonwealth Secretariat, 1997). "Fact Sheet No. 22, Discrimination Against Women: The Convention and the Committee," http://www.ohchr.org/english/about/publications/docs/fs22.htm, is a good brief introduction. See also the chapters in the Alston and Bayefsky volumes cited above.

The principal scholarly monograph on the Committee Against Torture is Chris Ingelse, *The UN Committee Against Torture: An Assessment* (The Hague: Kluwer, 2001). "Fact Sheet No. 17, The Committee against Torture," http://www.ohchr.org/english/about/publications/docs/fs17.htm, provides a good brief overview. Nigel S. Rodley, *The Treatment of Prisoners Under International Law*, 2nd ed. (Oxford: Clarendon Press, 1999) is authoritative on the broader legal framework. On the torture procedures within the European regional regime, there are two comprehensive books by Malcolm Evans and Rod Morgan: *Preventing Torture: A Study of the European Convention for the Prevention of Torture and Inhuman or Degrading Treatment or Punishment* (New York: Oxford University Press, 1998), and *Protecting Prisoners: The Standards of the European Committee for the Prevention of Torture in Context* (New York: Oxford University Press, 1999).

On the broader issue of torture, Amnesty International, *Torture Worldwide: An Affront to Human Dignity* (New York: Amnesty International, 2000), and Duncan Forrest (for Amnesty International), ed., *A Glimpse of Hell: Reports on Torture Worldwide* (New York: New York University Press, 1996) provide good, accessible introductions. Sanford Levinson, ed., *Torture: A Collection* (Oxford: Oxford University Press, 2004) is also excellent. For current information, see Amnesty International's torture homepage, http://www.amnestyusa.org/stoptorture/index.do.

Lawrence J. LeBlanc, *The Convention on the Rights of the Child: United Nations Lawmaking on Human Rights* (Lincoln: University of Nebraska Press, 1995) offers a thorough survey with a less technical legal focus than Geraldine Van Beuren, *International Law on the Rights of the Child* (The Hague: Kluwer Law International, 1998), Sharon Detrick, *A Commentary on the United Nations Convention on the Rights of the Child* (The Hague: Martinus Nijhoff, 1999), or Deirdre Fottrell, ed., *Revisiting Children's Rights: 10 Years of the UN Convention on the Rights of the Child* (The Hague: Kluwer Law International, 2000). Gerison Lansdown, "Reporting Process Under the Convention on the Rights of the Child," in *The Future of UN Human Rights Treaty Monitoring*, ed. Philip Alston and James Crawford (Cambridge: Cambridge University Press, 2000) is a good brief introduction.

The UN pamphlet "Fact Sheet No. 18 (Rev. 1), Minority Rights," http://www.ohchr.org/english/about/publications/docs/fs18.htm, offers a good brief overview of the issue of minority rights. Kristin Henrard, *Devising an Adequate System of Minority Protection: Individual Human Rights, Minority Rights and the Right to Self-Determination* (The Hague: Martinus Nijhoff, 2000) provides a comprehensive legal survey. Jennifer Jackson Preece, *National Minorities and the European Nation-State System* (Oxford: Oxford University Press, 1998) covers European practice in the twentieth century from a political rather than legal perspective. Her new book *Minority Rights Between Diversity and Community* (Cambridge: Polity Press, 2005) is an excellent general survey of minority rights as an issue in international politics.

On the International Labor Organization, see Hector Bartolomei de la Cruz, Geraldo von Potobsky, and Lee Swepston, *The International Labor Organization: The International Standards System and Basic Human Rights* (Boulder: Westview Press, 1996). Ernst B. Haas, *Human Rights and International Action: The Case of Freedom of Association* (Stanford: Stanford University Press, 1970) is a classic that despite its age is still worth examining.

Two standard comprehensive legal reviews of the European regional regime are Robert Blackburn and Jörg Polakiewicz, *Fundamental Rights in Europe: The European Convention on Human Rights and Its Member States, 1950–2000* (Oxford and New York: Oxford University Press, 2001), and P. van Dijk and G. J. H. van Hoof, *Theory and Practice of the European Convention on Human Rights*, 3rd ed. (The Hague: Kluwer Law International, 1998). On the impact of regional human rights law, see Robert Blackburn, ed., *The Impact of the European Convention on Human Rights in the Legal and Political Systems of Member States* (London: Mansell, 1996). Michael O'Boyle, "Reflections on the Effectiveness of the European System for Protection Human Rights," in *The UN Human Rights Treaty System in the 21st Century*, ed. Anne F. Bayefsky (The Hague: Kluwer Law International, 2000) is a good short introduction. The Web site of the Council of Europe (http://www.coe.int/T/E/Human_rights/) is an excellent and comprehensive source of information. On the human rights dimensions of the European Union, see Philip Alston, ed., *The EU and Human Rights* (Oxford: Oxford University Press, 1999).

On the Inter-American regime, David J. Harris and Stephen Livingstone, eds., *The Inter-American Human Rights System* (New York: Oxford University Press, 1998) provides a thorough overview. Also useful are J. Scott Davidson, *The Inter-American*

Human Rights System (Aldershot, U.K.: Dartmouth, 1997), and Thomas Buergenthal and Dinah Shelton, *Protecting Human Rights in the Americas: Cases and Materials*, 4th ed. (Kehl, Germany: Engel, 1995). Claudio Grossman, "The Inter-American System of Human Rights and the New Hemispheric Reality," in *Innovation and Inspiration: Fifty Years of the Universal Declaration of Human Rights*, ed. P. R. Baehr, C. Flinterman, and M. Senders (Amsterdam: Royal Academy of Arts and Sciences, 1999) is a useful chapter-length introduction. Cecilia Medina Quiroga, *The Battle of Human Rights: Gross, Systematic Violations and the Inter-American Regime* (Dordrecht, the Netherlands: Martinus Nijhoff, 1988) is excellent on the cold war era.

Daniel C. Thomas, *The Helsinki Effect: International Norms, Human Rights, and the Demise of Communism* (Princeton: Princeton University Press, 2001) provides an excellent, readable account of the impact of the Helsinki process, from a political rather than a legal perspective. Walter A. Kemp, ed., *Quiet Diplomacy in Action: The OSCE High Commissioner on National Minorities* (The Hague: Kluwer Law International, 2001) focuses on an area where the OSCE has been especially creative and effective. For additional information, see the official Web site, www.osce.org.

One final type of actor, not directly addressed in this chapter, also deserves mention, namely, international commissions. An excellent recent book surveys many of the most prominent examples of the past thirty years, frequently touching on human rights issues: Ramesh Thakur, Andrew F. Cooper, and John English, eds., *International Commissions and the Power of Ideas* (Tokyo: United Nations University Press, 2005). For readings on human rights NGOs, see the last paragraphs of the suggested readings for Chapter 6.

6

Human Rights and Foreign Policy

The preceding chapter dealt with the multilateral politics of international human rights. This chapter considers national foreign policy, the bilateral politics of international human rights. It is divided into four principal parts. The first four sections are devoted to the United States, with special emphasis on the 1970s and 1980s, when human rights matured as an issue in international politics. In addition to the cases of South Africa and the Southern Cone, introduced in the two preceding chapters, we look at American policy toward Central America. The next two sections offer a much briefer comparative analysis of the international human rights policies of some other Western countries. Three additional sections deal with general issues of human rights and foreign policy. The final two sections expand out from the narrow topic of bilateral foreign policy, briefly addressing the role of NGOs and the overall system of international accountability represented by the multilateral and bilateral mechanisms considered in this and the preceding chapter.

1. ANTICOMMUNISM AND AMERICAN EXCEPTIONALISM

Chapter 1 provided a brief overview of major events in postwar international human rights. For the United States, we can distinguish six phases.

- 1945–1948: initial enthusiasm, culminating in the adoption of the Universal Declaration of Human Rights
- 1949–1973: human rights concerns subordinated to anticommunism and cold war rivalry with the Soviet Union
- 1974–1980: emergence of human rights as a prominent element in the public diplomacy of the United States, first in the Congress and then during the Carter presidency
- 1981–1988: the (ultimately unsuccessful) Reagan attempt to subordinate human rights to the (new) cold war

- 1989–2001: post–cold war spread and deepening of human rights concerns
- 2001–present: partial subordination of human rights to antiterrorism.

This chapter concentrates on the first four periods, which were dominated by anticommunism.

Even during the "liberal" Democratic presidencies of Truman, Kennedy, Johnson, and Carter, fear of communism was an overriding concern. The Korean War began under Truman. U.S. advisers and then troops were committed to Vietnam under Kennedy and Johnson. Carter's Central American policy was strongly shaped by the desire to avoid "another Cuba." Individual presidents certainly disagreed on strategy and tactics. Anticommunism, however, had the highest foreign policy priority in every administration from Truman through Reagan. As a result, the United States usually supported avowedly anticommunist governments. Whether this was good foreign policy or bad, its human rights consequences were disastrous.

Totalitarian, Soviet-style communism, which today persists only in isolated enclaves such as China, North Korea, and Cuba, systematically violates most internationally recognized civil and political rights. But the fact that anticommunist regimes were often guilty of serious, and sometimes no less severe, violations did not stop the United States from regularly equating anticommunism with the pursuit of "freedom" and human rights. In country after country—Bolivia, Chile, Guatemala, Haiti, Iran, Liberia, Pakistan, Paraguay, Somalia, South Africa, Sudan, South Vietnam, South Korea, and Zaire, to name just a few—the United States supported repressive military dictatorships and narrow civilian oligarchies (along with U.S. economic and geopolitical interests) in the name of democracy and human rights.

This confusion of anticommunism with human rights has been strengthened by what students of domestic politics in the United States call **American exceptionalism**, the belief that the United States is different from (and generally superior to) most other countries, in large part because of its domestic commitment to individual rights. The isolationist variant of American exceptionalism, expressed with particular clarity in George Washington's Farewell Address, has seen the country as a beacon of hope for an oppressed world—but only an example, not an active participant in the struggle for freedom overseas. No less powerful, however, has been interventionist exceptionalism, which stresses an active American mission to spread its values through direct foreign policy action and even military force.

This interventionist strand has often led to identifying the international interests of the United States with democracy and human rights. During the cold war, the logic typically ran roughly this way: Communism is opposed to human rights; the United States favors human rights; therefore, American action against communism is action on behalf of human rights.

Even where it has not led to intervention, American exceptionalism has often been associated with a narrow and self-serving definition of human rights. Americans typically act as if human rights problems exist only in places that must be reached by crossing large bodies of salt water. Other countries have human rights problems. The

United States is said to suffer from, for example, police brutality or a health care crisis, which are spoken of as if they were qualitatively different from torture or denial of the right to health care. Although strictly speaking beyond the scope of this book, which is about international human rights, this pervasive reluctance of Americans to look at themselves through the lens of internationally recognized human rights cannot be ignored.[1]

The interaction of exceptionalism and anticommunism has contributed to an American tendency to denigrate economic and social rights. Only civil and political rights (plus certain elements of the right to property) are constitutionally guaranteed in the United States. Because most Americans think first of constitutional rights when they hear the term human rights, there has been a strong tendency to view economic and social rights as much less important (see §2.4). For example, homelessness or lack of access to medical care is rarely presented as a human rights problem. The fact that communist regimes emphasized economic and social rights created a sort of guilt by association.

During the cold war, U.S. foreign policy reacted suspiciously to action on behalf of economic and social rights (other than the right to private property), especially when it involved redistributing wealth. By labeling economic and social reformers "communists" and "subversives," right-wing rulers could generally retain U.S. support for systematic repression to protect their own wealth, power, and privilege, often under an American banner of "democracy."

Beyond the devastating human rights consequences, such policies frequently prevented the achievement of professed U.S. goals. For example, repressive military dictatorships often eliminated not only the far left but also the political moderates that the United States claimed to support. There is more than a touch of irony in the fact that in all of Central America in the 1980s, only in "Marxist" Nicaragua (and disarmed Costa Rica) did a democratic opposition acquire power through peaceful electoral means.

The incoherence of American policy is especially clear in U.S. attitudes toward elections. Although Americans in general have a deep, even exaggerated, faith in elections, U.S. foreign policy during the cold war has consistently ignored restrictions on political participation, corruption, intimidation of voters, or outright fraud by "friendly" regimes. The United States regularly, and rightly, criticized one-party elections in communist countries. But the mere existence of elections in anticommunist countries was usually accepted as evidence of the ruling regime's democratic character. And when the United States disapproved of governments brought to power through free and fair elections, it was not above using force to remove them. Sponsorship of the 1954 military coup in Guatemala, subversion in Chile in the early 1970s, and continued support for the Nicaraguan contras after the 1984 election are striking examples.

Such inconsistencies were rationalized by anticommunist ideology. Elections that brought (alleged) communists to power were bad and had to be overturned. When force or fraud brought anticommunists to power, that was an acceptable price to pay to keep communists out of power and on the run. And the United States, the leader of the "Free World," was the self-appointed judge of "democratic" credentials.

2. CENTRAL AMERICA AND
U.S. HUMAN RIGHTS POLICY

Central America is the geographical area that lies between North America (Canada, the United States, and Mexico) and South America. It became a major international human rights concern in the 1980s largely because of U.S. support for the conservative government of El Salvador and parallel U.S. efforts to overthrow the leftist government of Nicaragua.

A. Human Rights in El Salvador and Nicaragua

El Salvador.   Salvadoran independence from Spain in the 1820s was in many ways less significant than the economic reforms in the second half of the nineteenth century that transferred one-third of the country's land to a small coffee oligarchy. For the following half century, protests by dispossessed peasants were ruthlessly suppressed, culminating in the systematic killing of at least 10,000 people and as many as 30,000 in the *matanza* (massacre) of 1932.

After World War II, the Salvadoran economy grew, but the benefits of growth were distributed extremely unequally. In the mid-1970s, more than two-thirds of the children under five suffered from malnutrition. Three-fourths of rural families (which made up about two-thirds of the total population) were landless. Less than 40 percent had access to piped water. Half lacked the income necessary for a minimum healthy diet. Urban poverty was only somewhat less extreme.[2] Not only was distributing the benefits of growth to the mass of the population largely ignored, but the ruling oligarchy regularly used force against those seeking a more egalitarian society.

Elections were held regularly, but the official military-backed party used patronage, threats, and when necessary, blatant fraud to assure victory for its candidates. As disillusionment grew, "popular organizations" emerged that engaged in direct nonviolent action—sit-ins, strikes, demonstrations, civil disobedience. A few opponents also turned to armed insurrection, but in the mid-1970s they were of negligible political significance.

The security forces and their paramilitary supporters responded to peaceful protest and guerrilla activity alike with violence. The government of General Carlos Humberto Romero, installed after the fraudulent elections of 1977, imposed total press censorship, outlawed not only strikes but also public meetings of all sorts, and suspended judicial due process. Death squads, which worked closely with both the party and the Salvadoran national security agency, became a regular part of the Romero regime's repressive apparatus.

In an attempt to head off civil war, reformist junior officers staged a coup in October 1979. In January 1980, however, all the civilian members of the cabinet resigned because of the government's inability to control the security forces. For example, military sharpshooters opened fire from the top of the National Palace on a peaceful demonstration commemorating the *matanza* of 1932, killing between twenty and fifty people. A second junta collapsed in March, again because the military refused to allow civilian political control. This was vividly illustrated by the assassination on

March 24, 1980, of Archbishop Oscar Arnulfo Romero. As opposition continued to grow, the government declared a state of siege.

Although the intensification of repression led all other civilian political parties to refuse to participate, the conservative wing of the Christian Democrats, led by Jose Napoleon Duarte, joined the third junta. Political deaths jumped from under 2,000 in 1979 to 12,000 in 1980. In November 1980, six leaders of the Democratic Revolutionary Front (FDR), a party made up principally of Social Democrats and the left wing of the (centrist) Christian Democrats, were dragged from a meeting and brutally murdered. After this, most of the remaining leaders of the nonviolent opposition went underground or into exile. Duarte, however, remained in the fourth junta, which instituted a reign of terror. Americas Watch estimated that out of a total population of less than 5 million, there were more than 30,000 government-sponsored murders in 1980–1983 alone (roughly equivalent to killing 1.25 million Americans).

Duarte's election as president in 1984 (largely as a result of U.S. pressure) helped to reduce the level of violence. The human rights situation, however, remained dismal. The government estimated that death squads were killing "only" about thirty people a month in 1985, but most independent observers put the number substantially higher. Torture continued. The number of political prisoners even increased, apparently because of the decline in political murders.

El Salvador thus settled into a sad routine of reduced, but still widespread and systematic, human rights abuses. At the end of the decade, most civil and political rights were still being regularly violated. The country's poor economic situation remained, at best, unchanged (and that only because of massive U.S. aid). The guerrillas, whose strength grew along with the repression in the early and mid-1980s, continued to operate, but with no real success. Peaceful political opposition, and economic organization by workers and peasants, remained dangerous.

The electoral transfer of power between civilian governments in March 1989 was a notable event in Salvadoran political history. But under Alfredo Cristiani's right-wing National Republican Alliance (ARENA) government, political space in El Salvador actually contracted in 1989. At least seventy human rights activists were arrested, labor activists came under increased attack, the offices of COMADRES (Committee of Mothers of Political Prisoners, Disappeared, and Assassinated in El Salvador) were bombed, and six Jesuit priests and two lay women were murdered by the military.

A UN-mediated end to the civil war was agreed to at the end of 1991, and UN monitors arrived in 1992. This stopped the fighting and initiated efforts at structural political reform (especially greater civilian control over the armed forces). Although serious human rights issues remain, they now involve little direct state violence against the people. But throughout the 1980s, when it was a principal subject of U.S. human rights policy, El Salvador was either a brutal military dictatorship or a somewhat less brutal military-civilian oligarchy.

Nicaragua.   Nicaragua's early political history was not much different from that of El Salvador. In 1936, however, Anastasio Somoza Garcia seized power and initiated what would be more than forty years of authoritarian family rule. When Somoza was assassinated in 1956, power passed first to his son Luis Somoza Debayle and then to his younger son, Anastasio Somoza Debayle, who ruled until overthrown in 1979.

The Somozas retained the forms of democracy, but elections were rigged, and civil and political rights were regularly violated. (Large-scale systematic killings, though, were not part of their repertoire.) Economic and social rights were also systematically infringed, both through the predatory accumulation of immense personal wealth by the Somozas and their cronies and through disregard of social services. For example, in the early 1970s, the Nicaraguan government spent three times as much on defense as on health care, whereas its neighbors typically spent about equal amounts on each.

Massive corruption in the cleanup and recovery effort following the 1972 earthquake in the capital city of Managua, which left perhaps ten thousand dead and hundreds of thousands homeless, exacerbated and highlighted the endemic problems of inequality. Two years later, Somoza was reelected in a contest that even by Nicaraguan standards was farcical. In January 1978, the pace of disaffection accelerated after the assassination of Pedro Joaquín Chamorro, the leader of the moderate opposition. Even the business community turned against Somoza, under whom it had profited, organizing a general strike to protest Chamorro's death. Eighteen months later, Somoza was forced into exile.

Somoza was swept from power by a mass popular revolt incorporating many different social and political groups. Its military forces were led by the Sandinista National Liberation Front (FSLN), established in 1961 as a radical breakaway from the Soviet-oriented Nicaraguan Socialist Party. During his final two years in power, Somoza was opposed even by Nicaragua's traditional and conservative Catholic Church and by the United States, the Somozas' traditional patron.

The revolution, although widely supported, had immense human and economic costs. About one-fifth of Nicaragua's population of roughly 2.5 million became refugees. Casualties included 40,000–50,000 people killed, 150,000 wounded, and perhaps 40,000 orphaned. The war also disrupted agricultural production and most other sectors of the economy. The nation's gross domestic product fell by one-fourth in 1979 and by another one-fifth in 1980. Direct economic losses from the revolution were about $2 billion, or roughly Nicaragua's entire annual gross domestic product.

Human rights conditions generally improved in revolutionary Nicaragua. The Sandinista government increased spending on social programs, especially health care, and redirected spending for education toward mass literacy. Personal and legal rights were fairly widely respected. Internationally recognized civil liberties were extensively implemented for the first time in Nicaraguan history. Mass political participation was actively fostered, and the 1984 election was generally considered by outside observers to have been relatively open and fairly run.

The government itself admitted serious human rights violations during the forced relocation of Indian populations on the Atlantic Coast. Restrictions on freedom of the press, freedom of association, and due process were imposed. Sandinista mass popular organizations and the government-controlled media received preferential treatment. Nonetheless, political opponents operated under fewer constraints, and with far less fear of retaliation, than Somoza's opponents had. Human rights NGOs such as Americas Watch consistently judged the human rights situation to be significantly better than in neighboring El Salvador and Guatemala.

This record, although acceptable only in relative terms, was noteworthy because the Sandinista government was under intense attack from U.S.-financed "contras" (a shortened form of the Spanish for counterrevolutionaries). The contras originated in the Nicaraguan Democratic Forces, a group of former Somoza national guardsmen led by Colonel Enrique Bermudez. In 1981, the U.S. Central Intelligence Agency (CIA) began financial and logistical support, which by 1983 involved $100 million provided to a force that had grown to more than 10,000 guerrillas.

Contra strategy emphasized terrorism, including attacks on farms, schools, and health clinics, indiscriminate attacks on civilian economic targets, kidnappings, and assassinations. Nonetheless, the rights to life and security of the person were surprisingly consistently respected by the Nicaraguan government. In sharp contrast, U.S.-supported governments in neighboring Guatemala and El Salvador typically justified state terrorism by the need to combat guerrilla violence.

With the winding down of the contra war in 1988 and 1989, respect for civil and political rights again improved. Peaceful political opposition was generally tolerated during the 1989–1990 election campaign. And in national elections in February 1990, the Sandinistas were voted out of power. This was particularly noteworthy because it involved not merely a change in government, as in neighboring El Salvador and Guatemala, but a change in social and political philosophy.

The new government of President Violeta Chamorro tried to set aside ideological and political disputes in the name of national reunification. Her government achieved a solid record on civil and political rights and restored the economy to a relatively solid foundation, following the devastation of the revolution and the contra war. But economic and social rights, especially for the poor, generally stagnated or suffered. The October 1996 presidential election saw the second defeat of Sandinista leader Daniel Ortega, this time by Arnoldo Alemán. In the municipal elections of 2000, the FSLN did well in many urban areas, including winning in Managua. But in 2001, Ortega lost again, in the country's fourth free and fair election since 1990.

B. U.S. Policy in Central America

In the early twentieth century, U.S. policy in Central America was directed toward establishing military, economic, and political hegemony. Central America was strategically significant for its proximity to the United States, the Panama Canal, and Caribbean sea-lanes. U.S. pressure and intervention were also regularly used to further the interests of U.S. banks and corporations. By the 1920s, Central America had become a special U.S. sphere of influence, "our backyard," as it was still often put in the 1980s.

Since World War II, however, the role of economic concerns in U.S. policy has declined dramatically. Although the 1954 U.S.-backed overthrow of the freely elected government of Jacobo Arbenz Guzmán in Guatemala reflected the interests of the United Fruit Company, which had special influence in both the State Department and the CIA, anticommunism was probably a stronger motivating force. By the

1980s, when Central America reemerged as a central issue in U.S. foreign policy, economic interests were largely irrelevant. For example, U.S. exports to Nicaragua averaged just under $200 million per year from 1976 to 1978, and total U.S. direct foreign investment was a meager $60 million.

Human rights concerns, however, did not replace economic interests. "Human rights is a residual category in United States policy toward Latin America; it (along with economic development) is what policy emphasizes when there is no security problem on the horizon."[3] During the cold war, U.S. policy was instead driven by the fear that domestic instability might increase support for local communists and their Soviet (and Cuban) backers. U.S. policy in Central America thus oscillated between neglect during periods of domestic calm and intervention at times of domestic instability. In both modes, though, U.S. policy usually supported the military and traditional civilian elites, to the detriment of the rights of most Central Americans.

Consider Nicaragua. In 1912, U.S. troops prevented a liberal political revolution and then remained until 1933, except for eighteen months between 1925 and 1927. Furthermore, the United States was the leading force behind the creation of the National Guard, the principal base of Somoza power. Economic interests and strategic concerns over a potential second canal through Nicaragua explain the initial U.S. involvement. But after World War II, the Somozas' support of U.S. cold war policies became their major asset. The (probably apocryphal) assessment of the senior Somoza attributed to Franklin D. Roosevelt aptly summarized the relationship: "He's a son of a bitch, but he's *our* son of a bitch." Even when the United States was not actively backing the Somozas, its toleration of their dictatorial rule was widely seen as tacit support.

U.S. policy in Guatemala and El Salvador was similar. Following the overthrow of Arbenz in 1954, the United States supported a series of vicious Guatemalan military governments. In El Salvador, although dictatorship was established with little American involvement, the United States supported a series of military-dominated governments.

The postwar U.S. record on economic and social rights in Central America was more mixed. The Alliance for Progress, a major foreign aid initiative for Latin America launched in 1961, brought substantial increases in U.S. aid to Central America. This seems to have contributed to rapid economic growth in the 1960s and early 1970s. U.S. aid also helped to improve life expectancy and literacy. The benefits of growth, however, were distributed so unequally that the gap between rich and poor widened in the 1960s and 1970s. And in El Salvador, Guatemala, and Nicaragua alike, U.S.-backed governments regularly used their power against political parties, trade unions, peasant organizations, and most other groups that tried to foster more rapid reforms or structural changes in society or the economy.

There were signs of U.S. uneasiness. For example, after martial law was imposed in Nicaragua in 1974, the Ford administration moved to distance itself from Somoza (although not so far as to support any alternative). Nonetheless, the logic of anticommunism dominated U.S. policy in Central America in the first three decades after World War II.

The Carter administration entered office in 1977 intent on giving human rights at least equal place in its policy. In Central America, the administration took both concrete and symbolic action. Early in 1977, Guatemala's military government announced that it would not accept U.S. aid if it was contingent on public U.S. reporting of Guatemalan human rights practices. Neither Congress nor Carter, however, was willing to leave it at that. Military assistance credits to Guatemala were banned in 1978, and the U.S. refused to support multilateral loans to Guatemala in 1979 and 1980. The United States also carried out an active program of public diplomacy, including a well-publicized visit by Assistant Secretary of State William Bowdler. In summer 1977, the administration announced that continued military aid to Nicaragua would be contingent on human rights improvements.

Although notable, such changes were also limited. For example, although new military aid to Guatemala was cut off, already committed ("pipeline") aid was continued. And Carter never seriously pressed for major structural reforms. For example, when Somoza lifted censorship regulations and the state of siege, the United States largely dropped the issue of human rights.

When Nicaragua did emerge as a major concern of U.S. foreign policy, in fall 1978, internal turmoil rather than human rights was the major American concern. Carter's goal was to remove Somoza without yielding power to the Sandinistas, who were seen as too closely tied to Cuba and the Soviet Union. The desire to avoid "another Cuba" dominated policy.

The United States tried to strengthen the political center, but it was suffering under political and financial retaliation by Somoza, and the assassination of Pedro Joaquín Chamorro had deprived it of its most respected and effective leader. After four frustrating months of U.S. mediation, Somoza simply refused to leave. Carter responded with wide-ranging sanctions. Military and economic aid was terminated, the Peace Corps was withdrawn, and the size of the U.S. embassy in Managua was reduced by more than one-half. But when these sanctions failed to convince Somoza to step down, there was little that could be done short of the use of force—which Carter refused to consider, for reasons of principle and policy alike.

In June 1979, when the Sandinistas (FSLN) launched their "final offensive," the United States again tried to promote a centrist "third force." The pace of events, however, combined with the moderate opposition's lack of organization and foresight, proved fatal. When Somoza left in July, power passed to a provisional coalition government dominated by its most astute and best-organized faction, the FSLN.

The Carter administration attempted to set aside its suspicions. Food and medical supplies were sent almost immediately. When Carter left office in January 1981, eighteen months after Somoza's fall, the United States had provided $118 million in aid to Nicaragua. This was more than the United States gave to any other Central American country in the same period and was the largest amount provided to Nicaragua by any Western government. In addition, the United States supported $262 million in World Bank and Inter-American Development Bank loans.

In El Salvador, because of human rights concerns, the United States backed the October 1979 coup led by reformist military officers. But when most of the civilians in the junta resigned in January 1980 to protest the government's inability to control the military or halt human rights violations, the Carter administration remained supportive (although it still did not restore military aid). Even after Colonel Majano, the leader of the reformist faction in the military, was forced out of the junta in December 1980, the United States continued to characterize the Salvadoran government as reformist, despite massive and mounting violations of civil and political rights and lack of progress on land reform and economic and social rights.

It is also important to note that even Carter's limited efforts on behalf of human rights met with substantial domestic opposition. For example, in June 1979 more than one hundred members of Congress signed a full-page ad in support of Somoza that ran in the *New York Times* under the headline "Congress Asks: Please, Mr. President, Not Another Cuba!" The Carter administration itself also included skeptics among its high officials, most prominently National Security Adviser Zbigniew Brzezinski. As these elements increasingly came to dominate policymaking, the Carter administration began moving the United States toward what would become Reagan's new approach.

Reagan's approach to Central America was rooted in radical anticommunism. Although Soviet power prevented efforts to "roll back" communism in Central and Eastern Europe, the Third World did present opportunities. Central America (along with Afghanistan) became a test case for Reagan's new global political strategy. By summer 1981, the CIA was working with the contra military opposition in Nicaragua. On March 14, 1982, the war began when two bridges were destroyed by former members of the National Guard who had been trained by the CIA.

The "Kirkpatrick Doctrine" provided a rationale for this new approach. In an influential article that helped to earn her the position of U.S. ambassador to the UN, Jeane Kirkpatrick argued that Carter had failed to understand that the most serious threats to human rights were posed not by authoritarian dictatorships but by totalitarian communists. Furthermore, because many authoritarian dictatorships were U.S. allies, Carter's policy hurt U.S. friends while giving insufficient attention to communism, the most serious threat to human rights.[4] As one conservative group summed up the Carter approach, "Faced with the choice of an occasionally deplorable ally and a consistently deplorable enemy, since 1977 the United States has aided its adversary and alienated its ally."[5] For the Reagan administration, global strategic rivalry with the Soviet Union *was* a struggle for human rights, regardless of the actual human rights practices of the governments in question.

Many in Congress, however, had a more complex vision of Central America, and they were supported by a wide range of liberal interest groups. The Reagan administration thus faced constant, but only sporadically successful, resistance to its requests for aid to the contras. Although aid was suspended by Congress in July 1983, "humanitarian" assistance resumed in June 1985, and military aid was approved the following summer. Not until February 1988, during Reagan's last year of office, was military aid again stopped.

The Reagan administration blocked multilateral loans to Nicaragua, cut the import of Nicaraguan sugar by 90 percent in 1983, and imposed a complete trade embargo in May 1985. The United States orchestrated a massive assault on Nicaragua, using the full range of resources short of the direct use of U.S. troops—but including illegally mining Nicaraguan harbors in 1984. Funds were even illegally diverted to the contras, and those responsible lied under oath to Congress.

This campaign of military and economic aggression had devastating consequences. As many as 40,000 people were killed, and at least a quarter million displaced. Food production declined by at least one-fourth. Advances in health care and social services were reversed by terrorist attacks on clinics, schools, and social service offices. By 1988, the Nicaraguan economy had been destroyed, with hyperinflation raging at 31,000 percent per year.

The intense U.S. opposition to the government of Nicaragua contrasted sharply with the strong U.S. support for the government of El Salvador. The human rights situation in El Salvador in the late 1970s and early 1980s was far worse than in Nicaragua under either Somoza or the Sandinistas. Salvadoran security forces regularly used indiscriminate violence against civilians. Clandestine paramilitary death squads, with links to the security forces and right-wing political parties, operated with impunity, kidnapping and killing politicians, labor leaders, peasant activists, intellectuals, church activists, and other civilians believed to sympathize with the guerrillas.[6] And in addition to the tens of thousands of Salvadorans killed, Americans were also victims. In December 1980, four American churchwomen were abducted, raped, and murdered. In March 1981, two officials of the American Institute for Free Labor Development were assassinated in the San Salvador Sheraton Hotel. Yet massive aid continued—about $500 million a year in 1984 and 1985 (compared to less than $100 million in 1979 and 1980 combined), totaling almost $4 billion for the decade.

To release American aid, Congress required the president to certify that the government of El Salvador was respecting internationally recognized human rights and had gained control over the armed forces. The first such certification came in January 1982, after a year in which the Salvadoran government and its paramilitary allies had murdered well over 10,000 civilians. After four such cynical certifications, President Reagan vetoed new legislation requiring further certifications.

The human rights situation in neighboring Nicaragua was hardly ideal. For example, the 1984–1985 Americas Watch annual report noted "prior censorship of the press, political jailings, the denial of due process of law by special tribunals, the mistreatment of prisoners by incommunicado detention, and forced relocation."[7] But torture and extrajudicial executions, which were commonplace in El Salvador, were rare in Nicaragua. Nonetheless, the United States helped to launch and aggressively supported a guerrilla war of terrorism against Nicaragua. As Americas Watch put it, "So consistent is this double standard that it can be fairly said [that] the Reagan administration has no true human rights policy."[8]

Human rights as an independent and immediate concern had virtually no place in the Reagan administration's Central America policy. Criticisms of the human rights practices of leftist regimes and the defense of the human rights practices of "friendly" governments were simply a continuation of the struggle with the Soviet Union by other means.

Nonetheless, the gap between the Carter and Reagan policies toward Central America was not as wide as their rhetoric suggested. Carter spoke of human rights as the "heart" of U.S. foreign policy, but in practice they were only a secondary goal. And Reagan's attempts to relegate human rights to the bottom of the list of U.S. foreign policy objectives were at least partially defeated by Congress. Carter did significantly elevate the place of human rights in U.S. policy toward Central America, but they never reached the top. Reagan did force human rights back down the list, but they never reached the bottom.[9]

The first Bush administration's Central America policy, both in word and in deed, lay between its predecessors. Bush generally supported the Salvadoran and Guatemalan governments, despite their lack of control over the military. For example, he strongly opposed congressional efforts to cut military aid to El Salvador after the November 1989 murder of six Jesuits. In January 1991, Bush even restored the aid Congress had cut in half just two months earlier, despite the continuing abuses and the absence of a single successful prosecution of anyone for these (or any other) human rights violations.

However, Bush did act to prevent further deterioration. For example, he suspended military aid to Guatemala in late 1990 after an upsurge in political violence. Vice President Dan Quayle was sent to El Salvador twice in 1989 to express the administration's concerns. Bush supported the implementation of the UN-mediated end to El Salvador's civil war. And in Nicaragua, he pursued a somewhat less belligerent strategy of opposition to the Sandinistas.

Although the Clinton administration was generally inclined to support human rights in the region, they were given low priority in his foreign policy. The most important accomplishment of the 1990s was the implementation of the peace agreement in El Salvador, with continuing American support, and a similar United Nations initiative in Guatemala in 1994. However, Clinton, like his predecessors, gave almost no serious attention to issues of economic, social, and cultural rights. The second Bush administration has pursued very similar policies.

3. THE UNITED STATES AND THE SOUTHERN CONE

As we saw in Chapter 4, Argentina, Chile, and Uruguay suffered under brutal military regimes in the 1970s and 1980s. What Argentineans call the Dirty War was a concerted campaign of violence directed against the political left, trade unions, intellectuals, mainstream autonomous social organizations, and dissidents of all sorts, as well as ordinary, apolitical citizens who were forced into or became accidentally enmeshed in the politics of torture and disappearances.

The United States played a significant supporting role in the rise to power of the Chilean military. The Nixon administration saw the 1970 election of Salvador Allende, an avowed Marxist, as an intolerable intrusion of communism in Latin America, despite Allende's fair and free election, strong democratic socialist background, and independence from Soviet and Cuban influence. Henry Kissinger, national security adviser and later secretary of state, crafted a campaign of economic sabotage. In addition, U.S. support encouraged dissident military officers (although the 1973 coup was largely a local Chilean initiative). Moreover, U.S. diplomacy supported the military regimes in all three countries.

Congress tried to distance the United States from the junta in Chile, limiting economic aid and banning new military assistance. Kissinger, however, did his best to circumvent Congress. For example, in 1976 he publicly reprimanded the U.S. ambassador to Chile for even raising the issue of human rights in private discussions. Even when human rights initiatives were undertaken, as in Argentina in 1976, they were low-key, private, and accompanied by public support for the military.

The Carter administration sharply reversed U.S. policy. President Carter, Secretary of State Cyrus Vance, and Assistant Secretary of State for Human Rights Patricia Derian all drew public attention to human rights violations in the Southern Cone. No head of a Southern Cone military regime was invited for a state visit to Washington. Human rights activists and major figures in the political opposition, by contrast, were received at the State Department and in local U.S. embassies.

During Carter's term, military aid to Southern Cone countries was halted (although Congress deserves much of the credit for this). The Carter administration voted against or abstained on twenty-three loans by international development banks to Argentina, eleven to Uruguay, and five to Chile (although the fact that all these loans were ultimately approved suggests that the votes were largely symbolic). The United States also supported UN and OAS activities directed against Argentina, Uruguay, and especially Chile.

These policies led to the release of several political prisoners, including prominent opposition journalist Jacobo Timerman and human rights activist (and future Nobel Peace Prize recipient) Adolfo Pérez Esquivel. Conditions of detention were eased for many others. The Carter administration also claimed credit for reductions in disappearances and political prisoners, although a much more important factor was probably the success of earlier efforts at terror and repression, which reduced the number of potential new victims.

The Carter policies, however, did not end military rule. Relations with Chile, Uruguay, and especially Argentina were strained. One may debate whether the achievements were significant enough or the costs sufficiently low to justify the policy. It is clear, though, that the Carter approach to the Southern Cone represented a major shift in U.S. policy. And unlike Central America, this new approach was sustained throughout the full four years of the Carter presidency.

In 1981, the Reagan administration abruptly returned to the policies of Nixon, Kissinger, and Ford. In fact, Argentina and Chile were principal examples in Jeane Kirkpatrick's criticism of the Carter administration for foolishly sacrificing more important U.S. interests to the quixotic pursuit of human rights.

Although Congress had explicitly prohibited economic or military aid to Chile, the Reagan administration did everything it could to foster cordial relations with the Pinochet government. In August 1981, Ambassador Kirkpatrick paid a formal visit to Chile and called for the full normalization of U.S.-Chilean relations. At the UN Commission on Human Rights, the United States voted against continuing the special rapporteur on Chile. Joint military exercises were reinstituted. Loans from the Inter-American Development Bank to Chile jumped from zero in 1980 to more than $180 million in 1981 and 1982. In 1983 alone, Chile received more than three times the total of multilateral loans it had obtained during the entire Carter administration.

For Argentina, the Reagan administration obtained the repeal of the 1978 Humphrey-Kennedy amendment that had banned U.S. military sales and security assistance. General Viola, the leader of Argentina's second junta, was one of the first foreign leaders invited by Reagan for a state visit, in March 1981. U.S. representatives to international financial institutions were instructed to cease abstaining on loan applications, despite a clear legal requirement that they do so. Ambassador Kirkpatrick did not even reply to a letter from the Mothers of the Plaza de Mayo asking for a meeting during her 1981 visit to Buenos Aires.

These signals of renewed U.S. support led directly to new human rights violations. Immediately after Kirkpatrick's visit, Chile expelled several political leaders, including centrist Christian Democrats, and arrested and tortured a number of human rights activists. The United States issued no public response. In Argentina, seven leading Argentine human rights activists were detained incommunicado immediately prior to General Viola's visit to Washington, to keep them from saying anything that might cloud Viola's reception. The Reagan administration made private efforts to obtain their release, but there was no public protest, and General Viola received a warm welcome at the White House.

Although the Reagan administration did engage in quiet diplomacy on behalf of individual victims in the Southern Cone, human rights violations were treated as a matter for private discussions between friends. The overriding priority was to maintain close relations. Other interests were considered far more important than pervasive human rights abuses.

Even after Argentina's Falklands disaster, which proved to be the prelude to the return of civilian rule, the Reagan administration did not publicly raise human rights concerns. Although the new civilian government was embraced in Washington, the United States had nothing to do with its creation. In Uruguay as well, civilian rule returned despite, rather than because of, U.S. policy.

In Chile, the Reagan administration did speak out against the intensified repression that led to the re-imposition of martial law in 1984. Assistant Secretary of State Elliott Abrams, previously a vocal supporter of the Chilean junta, publicly criticized the Pinochet government. The United States also abstained on some multilateral loans to Chile in February and March 1985. But soon after the state of siege was formally lifted in June 1985, the United States supported Chilean requests for $345 million in multilateral loans. And in December 1985, the United States cast the decisive vote in the OAS General Assembly that removed reference to Chile from a resolution on human rights violations. Even after Pinochet lost the 1988 plebiscite for another eight-year term as president, U.S. criticism of military rule remained low-key. Democracy returned to Chile largely in spite of U.S. policy.

4. U.S. POLICY TOWARD SOUTH AFRICA

The human rights situation in South Africa was discussed in §5.4.B. Here we are concerned with the response of the United States. Before the Sharpeville Massacre in 1960, the United States treated apartheid as an internal South African matter. The turmoil following Sharpeville, however, raised the specter of revolution and mobilized American fear of communism. The United States thus began to treat apartheid as a matter of international concern. The Eisenhower administration even agreed to put apartheid permanently on the agenda of the UN Security Council.

The new Kennedy administration initiated a policy review in 1961 (which dragged on until 1964). Kennedy also imposed a selective arms embargo even before the Security Council called for a voluntary embargo at the end of 1963. As the crisis receded, however, so did U.S. attention. Sanctions remained in effect, but they were modest and had no discernible impact.

When Henry Kissinger took over as national security adviser to President Nixon in 1969, he instituted a series of policy reviews for all areas of the world. The resulting document on South Africa, National Security Memorandum 39 (NSM 39), proposed closer association with South Africa in order to put the United States in a better position to press for reform. Relations were not fully normalized. For example, the arms embargo was loosened but not eliminated. The goal was to combine negative sanctions with more positive inducements to change and to use areas of mutual interest, such as regional security, as a wedge to open South Africa to U.S. pressure on apartheid.

This approach, however, had no more impact than the Kennedy-Johnson strategy of dissociation had. Part of the problem was weak and inconsistent implementation. For example, false certifications of the nonmilitary nature of certain arms were accepted. A 1978 U.S. Department of Justice study found that 178 of South Africa's 578 military aircraft had been purchased from the United States during the embargo.[10] Furthermore, U.S. concessions were tied to no particular demands on South Africa. In other words, there was no real policy on South Africa. NSM 39 was adopted but never seriously implemented.

There were also major conceptual flaws in both the Kennedy-Johnson and the Nixon-Kissinger approaches. The United States asked for changes that the South African government refused even to consider. Although willing to ease some elements of "petty apartheid" (for example, by desegregating some public facilities in large cities), the government was unwilling to end racial separation. Democratic majority rule was not even open for discussion. The negative sanctions and positive inducements the United States was willing to use fell far short of what would have been necessary to make the white government change its mind.

The other conceptual error in U.S. policy was an excessive reliance on economic change and private enterprise. Liberals and conservatives alike believed that South Africa's atavistic racial policies would inevitably be eroded by the "modernization" that accompanied economic development. Trade and investment thus appeared as instruments for change rather than as support for apartheid. In practice, however, reforms required by economic necessity were prevented from spilling over into social and political changes. South Africa's immense bureaucracy, which intervened with totalitarian thoroughness in all aspects of life, largely prevented unplanned changes in the fundamental character of apartheid from going unnoticed or unchecked.

After the Portuguese coup in April 1974, which led to the rapid decolonization of Angola and Mozambique, even these modest U.S. efforts were largely abandoned in favor of a focus on "regional security"; that is, containing expanding Soviet influence. South Africa now appeared as a pro-Western regional power. Kissinger even met Prime Minister Vorster twice in 1976, the first official meeting at this level in thirty years.

The Soweto riots of 1976 returned apartheid to the center of international attention. Soon afterward, the election of Jimmy Carter changed the U.S. approach. The arms embargo was restored to its pre-Nixon status. Outstanding Export-Import Bank credits to South Africa were cut in half. South Africa's October 1977 clampdown on nonviolent opposition even led to U.S. support in the Security Council for a mandatory arms embargo.

These actions, however, were largely symbolic. Furthermore, there were tensions within the Carter administration. National Security Adviser Zbigniew Brzezinski favored a policy that, like Kissinger's, emphasized regional security. As Brzezinski's influence grew in the second half of Carter's term, U.S. policy took on an increasingly cold war tone, stressing the Cuban presence in Angola and the Soviet naval threat in the South Atlantic and the Indian Ocean. Even more than in Central America, the end of the Carter administration is best seen as preparing the way for Reagan's policies.

Reagan's policy of "constructive engagement" returned to the Nixon-era strategy of pursuing closer relations in order to increase U.S. leverage. Assistant Secretary of State Chester Crocker, the principal architect of the policy, had been a staff member on Kissinger's National Security Council. In the 1980s, he tried to turn the idea behind NSM 39 into an effective policy.

Despite international calls for new sanctions, the United States eased many that were already in place. New Export-Import Bank credits were approved. Efforts to discourage private bank loans were halted. In 1982, the Reagan administration supported a $1 billion International Monetary Fund (IMF) credit to South Africa, the largest ever made through the fund's Compensatory Financing Facility. Restrictions on the sale of aircraft, computers, and nuclear-related equipment with dual military and civilian uses were eased. In fact, the United States became South Africa's largest trading partner. Total private investment and loans rose to $10 billion.

The justification for constructive engagement was a belief that the government of P. W. Botha was pragmatic and committed to managing an ongoing transition from apartheid. The U.S. role, therefore, was to foster change through enlightened private enterprise and support for moderate forces of social change, such as trade unions and education. But there was an immense gap between policy and practice. The United States actually devoted almost no resources to education or trade unions. The reforms introduced by U.S. corporations helped a small number of employees but had no systematic impact on apartheid.

As in the early 1970s, the United States did not insist on any concrete human rights improvements in return for closer relations. And South African intentions continued to be misjudged. The Botha government was willing to modernize apartheid but not to eliminate it.

Events in South Africa, however, again forced a reevaluation of U.S. policy. Violence erupted in August 1984 in protest over elections held under the new Constitution of 1983, which completely excluded blacks from direct political participation. When repression once more tightened rather than eased, constructive engagement lost any remaining credibility.

The decisive changes in U.S. policy came from Congress. Progress on a bipartisan compromise sanctions bill forced Reagan to issue an executive order in September 1985 imposing limited economic sanctions. As late as July 1986, however, Reagan still argued that "we and our allies cannot dictate to the government of a sovereign nation—nor should we try." Critics scoffed, noting that Reagan had for years been funding a war against Nicaragua and had imposed sanctions against Cuba, Libya, Nicaragua, and Poland. Soon afterward, Congress overrode a presidential veto of a new sanctions bill.

Such strong congressional action was the work of a bipartisan coalition. In November 1984, Republican Senators Richard Lugar, chair of the Foreign Relations Committee, and Nancy Kassebaum, chair of the African Affairs Subcommittee, who were early supporters of constructive engagement, called on the president to review the administration's South Africa policy. The following month, thirty-five conservative members of the House, including Newt Gingrich, also called for abandoning constructive engagement, citing it as an embarrassing political liability—a view shared by most congressional Democrats.

These changes mirrored changes in the electorate that had been prepared by extensive NGO work. Activity on South Africa by U.S. NGOs goes back to at least 1912, when the National Association for the Advancement of Colored People was involved in the initial formation of South Africa's African National Congress. The American Committee on Africa was formed in 1953 in response to the pass-law demonstrations. In the late 1970s and 1980s, groups like TransAfrica focused their efforts on apartheid. Other NGOs, such as the American Friends Service Committee, the Interfaith Council on Corporate Responsibility, and the Lawyers' Committee for Civil Rights Under Law, made South Africa a major priority. In addition, churches, state and local governments, colleges and universities, student organizations, unions, and black organizations divested assets in corporations that did business in South Africa.

These activities brought home to a local audience the concerns and activities of the international anti-apartheid regime (see §5.4.B). Some of these U.S. NGO activities were even coordinated with divestment campaigns in other countries, with international anti-apartheid groups such as the International Defense and Aid Fund, and with other international NGOs such as the World Council of Churches and the Lutheran World Fund. They were also facilitated by Bishop Desmond Tutu's Nobel Peace Prize and his well-publicized visit to the United States at the end of 1984.

It is important not to overestimate U.S. efforts or their impact. Reagan's 1985 executive order was so limited and full of loopholes that Bishop Tutu described it as "not even a flea bite." The 1986 sanctions were also limited and partial. Nonetheless, South Africa was losing access to international capital (although in the short run more from lender fear caused by the 1984–1986 township riots than from sanctions). And the loss of U.S. support, even if the Reagan administration never actively opposed the white government, created concern among many of South Africa's less-conservative leaders and citizens, particularly in light of the growing internal crisis.

Apartheid ultimately collapsed because of the inability of the white government to keep opposition repressed. Nonetheless, changes in U.S. policy, particularly in the context of the global anti-apartheid campaign, made a small contribution to the final demise of apartheid. And even though American sanctions were largely symbolic, it was a very different sort of symbolism than had been typical of U.S. policy in the preceding years.

5. OTHER WESTERN APPROACHES
TO INTERNATIONAL HUMAN RIGHTS

Although the United States led the way in the 1970s in introducing human rights into bilateral diplomacy, other countries also incorporated human rights into their foreign policies. Particularly notable have been the efforts of the **like-minded countries**, a dozen smaller Western countries that since the mid-1970s have attempted to act together in international diplomacy as intermediaries between the larger Western countries, with which they are formally or informally aligned, and the countries of the Third World, for whose aspirations they have considerable sympathy. Norway and the Netherlands, in particular, have emphasized human rights in their foreign policies, signaled by white papers on the subject in 1977 and 1979.

Even more than in U.S. policy, foreign aid has been a central instrument in the international human rights policies of the like-minded countries. Development assistance tends to be not only an important element of their foreign policies but a matter of consensus among the major political parties. In the Netherlands, there is even a separate minister for development cooperation within the foreign ministry. By contrast, in the United States, foreign aid is a relatively peripheral part of foreign policy, yet it is a subject of considerable political controversy.

Their approach to linking human rights and development assistance also differs. The United States tends to base initial foreign aid decisions on political and humanitarian factors, modifying allocations at a later stage in light of human rights concerns. The like-minded countries, which lack the resources to engage in a massive, global foreign aid program, target their development assistance at a small set of countries—variously called "core," "program," or "priority" countries—with which they seek to develop relatively intensive, long-term aid relations. The Dutch and Norwegians, in particular, have emphasized both civil and political rights and economic, social, and cultural rights in selecting program countries.

In Norway, selection criteria since 1972 have included a strong preference for countries in which "the authorities of the country concerned [are] following a development-oriented and socially just policy in the best interests of all sections of the community." The Norwegian Storting (parliament) in 1976 reiterated its desire to cooperate with countries that are pursuing a "socially just policy" and are committed to implementing the economic, social, and cultural rights laid out in the Universal Declaration and the Covenants. And in 1984, a center-right coalition government, using language more characteristic of left-wing liberals in the United States, declared that "development assistance is an extension to the international level of the efforts to create social justice, characteristic of the Norwegian welfare state" and that "all have the right to have their basic needs for food, water, clothing, education, and housing satisfied."[11] Social justice is given roughly equal priority with civil and political rights largely across the Norwegian political spectrum.

As early as 1973, the Dutch officially emphasized a "close relationship between peace, a just distribution of wealth, international legal order and respect for human rights."[12] Since the late 1970s, the Dutch have also stressed a desire to cooperate with countries that emphasize civil and political rights as well as economic, social, and cultural rights in their domestic politics and development strategies. In practice, the selection of priority countries only partially meets these noble statements of intent. Nonetheless, the overall human rights records of recipients of Dutch aid compare favorably with international averages and with the pattern of American aid.

Even more striking than the selection of priority countries has been the relatively rapid response of the like-minded countries to changes in human rights conditions. For example, Norway broke its aid relationship with Uganda in 1972, the year that Idi Amin overthrew the government of Milton Obote and embarked on a dictatorial career that made him one of the most notorious human rights violators of the decade. The Netherlands dropped Uganda from its list of program countries in 1974. The United States, by contrast, was Uganda's largest trading partner until October 1978, less than a year before Amin was overthrown.

Sweden stopped all assistance to Chile shortly after Pinochet's coup and was a significant international supporter of the work of the Vicaría. Canada was also a vocal critic of military rule in the Southern Cone. In the 1980s, as ethnic violence escalated in Sri Lanka, a country with which Norway had developed close ties in the 1970s, the Norwegians dramatically downgraded their relationship. Canada, the Netherlands, and the Nordic countries all increased their aid to Nicaragua in the 1980s, reflecting a radically different understanding of human rights than the Reagan administration.

The Dutch response to the deteriorating human rights situation in their former colony of Suriname is especially revealing. They strongly condemned the 1980 military coup. Following the execution of fifteen opposition figures in 1982, the Netherlands not only suspended all aid but refused to provide new aid for the remainder of the decade. The Dutch also led the effort to apply international pressure on Suriname, for example, by regularly raising the issue in annual UN discussions of human rights violations. The contrast to U.S. behavior toward its Caribbean Basin clients in Guatemala and El Salvador, who were guilty of much more severe human rights violations, is striking.

The Dutch even carried human rights into relations with Indonesia, a country of far greater importance. Although severe Indonesian abuses in the 1960s were not a major concern of Dutch foreign policy, "from 1977 on, the Dutch Government tried to raise informally the human rights issue" in aid consortium meetings.[13] In 1990, in response to new political executions, 27 million guilders in aid was withdrawn. When additional executions were announced, the Dutch took the issue to the Council of Ministers of the European Community. Throughout 1991, Minister for Development Cooperation Jan Pronk continued public criticisms of Indonesia. Following the Dili Massacre in November 1991, which brought ongoing human rights problems in Indonesian–occupied East Timor into the international spotlight, another 27 million guilders in aid was suspended. The Indonesian response was to terminate its aid relationship with the Netherlands in 1992.

These actions were not easy. The Dutch, as a former colonial power, were especially sensitive to Indonesian charges of paternalism. Substantial commercial interests also cut against acting on human rights concerns. Nonetheless, the government of the Netherlands took relatively forceful public actions that had real costs for their relations with Indonesia. And they did so despite the failure of other Western countries and Japan, Indonesia's largest source of aid, to follow their lead. The Dutch acted because they felt it was the right thing to do and because it was demanded by the precedents established by their previous actions and policy statements.

The like-minded countries also adopted an approach to South Africa very different from that of the United States in the 1970s and 1980s. Starting in 1969, Sweden and Norway provided both political support and development assistance funds to the ANC during its exile from South Africa. The Dutch adopted a similar policy in 1973. And in the 1980s, these efforts were expanded by the Nordic countries and the Netherlands alike into broad, high-priority programs for the whole region of Southern Africa. These countries also played a leading role in the international movement for sanctions against South Africa.

We should be careful not to romanticize the policies of the like-minded countries. Considerations other than human rights are central, sometimes even overriding, in their foreign policies. For example, Dutch aid sanctions against Indonesia did not extend to trade or other economic relations. Canada also pursued close relations with Indonesia for commercial reasons. Economic interests in South Africa seriously delayed Canada's decision to adopt sanctions and led Norway to exclude shipping from its initial sanctions. Nonetheless, the overall international human rights record of the like-minded countries is clearly superior to that of the United States, both in avoiding associations with severe violators and in responding to abuses in countries with which they have special relations. The like-minded countries have also given human rights a high priority in their multilateral foreign policies, in contrast to the, at best, secondary emphasis of the United States.

6. EXPLAINING DIFFERENCES IN HUMAN RIGHTS POLICIES

Jan Egeland, in comparing Norwegian and U.S. international human rights policies, argued that "small and big nations are differently disposed to undertaking coherent rights-oriented foreign policies." In fact, Egeland argued that the relatively meager international human rights accomplishments of the United States are "because of, rather than in spite of, her superpower status."[14] Small countries are not so much "better," in this analysis, as less constrained than large states. "The frequency and intensity of the conflict between self-interest and [international human rights] norms seems, in short, proportional to a nation's economic and military power, as well as to its foreign policy ambitions."[15] Large states have multiple interests and responsibilities that preclude the consistent pursuit of human rights objectives. Small states rarely have to choose between human rights and other foreign policy goals.

This explanation focuses on the structure of the international system. Large states are also more likely to pursue bilateral policies because they are more likely to have the power to achieve their aims without multilateral support. Small states, by contrast, tend to prefer international organizations because multilateral processes allow them greater opportunities to exert international influence. Such structural explanations would also seem to be supported by the fact that larger powers, such as Britain, France, Japan, and to a lesser extent, Germany, have international human rights policies closer to those of the United States than to Norway or the Netherlands.

Size alone, however, cannot explain even the differences that are influenced by relative power. For example, despite declining American power, the United States remains reluctant to operate through multilateral channels (unless it can control the organization). As the power of Germany and Japan grows, they continue to rely heavily on multilateral organizations. Britain has tended to pursue a much more unilateral foreign policy than France, Germany, or Japan. Among small states, Sweden, Austria, and especially Switzerland have emphasized a neutral foreign policy. Canada, Belgium, and the Netherlands have had a strong Western orientation in their foreign policies. Size or power at most inclines states in certain directions.

Furthermore, we should not overlook factors that have little or nothing to do with size. Why did the United States emphasize international human rights in the 1970s while other large powers did not, and Japan still does not? Why did Britain and France intervene in their spheres of influence so much less frequently than the United States? Why are human rights as a foreign policy issue so much more controversial in the United States than in most other Western countries? Why does Belgium have a much less active international human rights policy than the Netherlands? Such questions can be answered only if we take history, political culture, and institutions into account.

Throughout the cold war era, the United States viewed the world in East-West terms, reducing all foreign policy issues to U.S.-Soviet rivalry. Although part of this can be attributed to the size and power of the United States, the cold war was not simply a bipolar political rivalry between hegemonic states; it was a rivalry that placed immense emphasis on ideology. It was generally assumed that radical reformers and their programs were Soviet backed, inspired, or influenced. Without the ideological element, many actual or attempted political changes in the Third World would not have been deemed such a threat to the United States and thus would not have led to a conflict with human rights objectives. Ideology, however, has nothing to do with size. Many small states, especially in Latin America, were at least as anticommunist as the

United States. Conversely, it is historically rare for a large state to define its interests in ideological terms.

Consider also the tendency of the like-minded states to view international conflicts more in North-South than East-West terms. During the cold war, these countries saw the principal lines of international cleavage as dividing rich and poor, not liberal democratic and communist. For example, in 1982, Mark MacGuigan, the Canadian secretary of state for external affairs, argued: "Instability in Central America . . . is not a product of East-West rivalry. It is a product of poverty, the unfair distribution of wealth, and social injustice. Instability feeds poverty and injustice. East-West rivalries flow in its wake."[16] The Dutch and the Nordic countries shared this view.

Some part of this might be related to size. For example, it is not surprising that a country like Canada, which fears being overwhelmed by the United States, or the Netherlands, which borders on powerful Germany and France, is more sympathetic to a perspective that sees differences in power as no less important than differences in ideology. But size alone cannot explain the difference in ideological perspective.

We can see this even in Egeland's own analysis. In explaining the "strong moral impact" on Norwegian policy, he stressed four factors: (1) no legacy of imperialism and intervention, (2) a good domestic human rights record, (3) a high level of foreign aid and support for changes in the world economy to favor Third World countries, and (4) consistent support for decolonization and national liberation movements.[17] The first of these four factors is related to size—although Belgium, Portugal, and the Netherlands did have significant colonial holdings; German, Austrian, Russian, and American colonial holdings were small; and the Netherlands rapidly overcame its imperial legacy. The other three factors, however, have little or nothing to do with size.

Size explains almost nothing about internal human rights records, as comparison of pairs of similarly sized countries such as the United States and the Soviet Union, China and India, Japan and Indonesia, Belgium and Holland, and Costa Rica and Guatemala vividly illustrates. If small size were really central, we would expect unusually good human rights records in Latin America and Africa, when, for the most part, the opposite has been the case. Nor does size have much to do with levels of foreign aid. The United States chooses to be niggardly, whereas Norway and the Netherlands (and Japan) choose to be generous.[18] And the United States has had a better record on supporting decolonization than small states such as Portugal and Spain or second-tier powers such as Britain and France.

Much the same can be said of the role of consensus in Norwegian international human rights and foreign policy, another factor Egeland emphasizes. Foreign policy consensus is hardly characteristic of small states, as the varying policies of dozens of Third World countries indicate. In the Nordic countries, foreign policy consensus is a function of a parliamentary system, in which there is no sharp division between executive and legislative branches, a strong reliance on a professional foreign and civil service (in contrast to the extensive use of political appointees in the U.S. bureaucracy), and a political tradition that assures direct representation and special consideration for all major social groups.[19] Conversely, although multiple interests and the large size of the U.S. bureaucracy do create more arenas for foreign policy conflict, the lack of consensus is at least as much a function of a presidential system and the turnover of the leadership of most bureaucratic agencies with every election.

Size tells us little or nothing about whether or why a country will choose to emphasize human rights in its foreign policy. Certainly it is not size that explains why Norway and the Netherlands in the 1970s embarked on unusually active international human rights policies, whereas Austria, Belgium, and Greece did not. Likewise, size cannot explain either the active (if inconsistent) international human rights policy of the United States or the lack of an active international human rights policy in Japan, let alone China.

How a country defines its interests is constrained by its power and its position in the international system. But interests are not fixed by power or position. Most impediments to strong international human rights policies lie in the relatively free decisions of states to give higher weight to other foreign policy objectives. Most of the factors that contribute to aggressive efforts to pursue international human rights in a country's foreign policy have much more to do with its national political culture and contingent political facts (for example, the election of Jimmy Carter) than with its international political position. Consider a simple but telling example: On a per capita basis, Dutch membership in Amnesty International exceeds American membership in the National Rifle Association, one of the largest and most powerful interest groups in the United States.

National political culture is especially important in explaining the striking differences between the attitudes of the United States and the like-minded countries toward economic and social rights. American foreign aid has been used almost exclusively in the pursuit of civil and political rights objectives. Humanitarian objectives such as nutrition, literacy, and health care have been pursued, but in the United States these objectives simply are not perceived in terms of human rights. U.S. foreign aid and human rights policy are seen as two fundamentally separate issues that are tactically linked. The like-minded countries, by contrast, see development assistance as central to their international human rights policies. They also emphasize the intrinsic importance of economic, social, and cultural rights and their interdependence with civil and political rights.

Size, power, and the structure of the international system are of secondary significance. States have considerable latitude in formulating international human rights policies. Differences between the United States and the like-minded countries are largely matters of choice, of differing understandings of and priorities attached to internationally recognized human rights. Norway and the Netherlands place a relatively high value on international human rights not because they are small and weak but because their citizens feel a moral obligation to implement and protect human rights.

7. TRADE-OFFS AND THE CHOICE OF MEANS

In a world of sovereign states, foreign policy is principally concerned with the pursuit of the national interest, as each country sees it. The national interest may include respect for human rights in other countries, either as an intrinsic value or for instrumental reasons (such as the belief that rights-protective regimes are more likely to be dependable friends in international relations). In no country, however, can the national interest be reduced solely to international human rights.

The obvious question, then, is *what* place human rights occupy. The best way to tell is to look at what happens when there is a conflict of objectives. Talk about human rights is cheap—often not free, but usually relatively cheap. The decisive tests are the costs a country is willing to bear in pursuing human rights concerns and the competing objectives it is willing to sacrifice or subordinate.

The three principal means used by the United States (and other countries) on behalf of international human rights have been **quiet diplomacy** (private discussions with foreign governments), public statements, and granting or withholding foreign aid. This consistent use of only weak instruments of foreign policy is clear evidence of the low value placed on human rights.

Consider, for example, the Reagan administration's insistence on quiet diplomacy as the principal, and usually the sole, appropriate means to pursue human rights goals in foreign policy—at least with "friendly" (anticommunist) governments. Governments rarely engage in the sorts of human rights violations that provoke serious diplomatic concern unless they feel that something very important is at stake. Therefore, it is implausible to imagine that quiet diplomacy alone, without at least the threat of more forceful public or punitive action, will produce anything more than symbolic gestures.

Nonetheless, even symbolic gestures may improve the lot of individual victims. Quiet diplomacy, under both Carter and Reagan, helped free hundreds of political prisoners, and it ameliorated the conditions of detention for many more. However, it never significantly improved a country's general human rights situation.

The strongest means typically used to back international human rights policies has been the conditioning of aid on human rights practices. In the American case, however, although aid decisions were altered in some individual cases, there is no strong, clear general linkage between U.S. economic (let alone security) assistance and the human rights practices of recipient states. (The link is much stronger in the like-minded countries.)

The United States, like most other states, has been unwilling to pay very much to achieve its international human rights objectives. The Carter, Reagan, Bush, Clinton, and Bush administrations have all regularly taken various concrete steps ranging from private diplomatic expressions of concern to the suspension of foreign aid. Rarely, though, has the United States been willing to use stronger means or to accept significant costs to its other interests. Human rights have had a place in U.S. foreign policy since the mid-1970s, but that place has been peripheral, especially during the cold war.

8. SELECTIVITY AND CONSISTENCY

If human rights are moral values, how can they be appropriately or "consistently" sacrificed to non-moral interests? Such a question rests on a contentious conception of morality. For example, **utilitarianism** and other consequentialist moral theories see morality as centrally concerned with calculating relative costs and benefits rather than rigidly following a moral law. But even if we conceive of morality as a matter of **categorical imperatives**, challenges to the "consistency" of international human rights policies often confuse foreign policy and moral decision making.

Realists rightly remind us that foreign policy decision makers are required by their office to take into account the national interest, which is (at most) only partly defined by morality. Moral perfectionism certainly is an inappropriate standard for foreign policy. Many realists, however, go too far when they categorically denigrate morality in foreign policy. The national interest may—and today for many states does—include a moral dimension. Moral interests are as legitimate as economic or security interests. The task of the statesman is to balance competing national interests, whatever their character.

Nonetheless, the realist tendency to contrast material and moral interests does point to a significant problem. The difference between human rights and, say, national security involves matters of quality, not quantity. How then are we to treat like cases alike—that is, consistently—in the absence of a common metric? Staying with the balance metaphor, how much does one unit of national security (whatever that might mean) weigh relative to one unit of human rights?

However, the problem of balancing interests is not limited to human rights. How can we weigh the economic interests against the national security interests in the relationship between the United States and China?

Consider also the choice of means. How many American (or Pakistani, or Canadian) lives was it worth to save hundreds of thousands of Somalis from starvation in 1992? To save a smaller number of Somalis from factional warfare among their leaders in 1993? There is no apparent qualitative difference between such calculations and those involved in, for example, the Gulf War. How many American (or British, or Dutch) soldiers was it worth to expel Iraq from Kuwait? To overthrow Saddam Hussein? The problem of competing incommensurable interests is a general problem of foreign policy, not one restricted to human rights and other moral interests.

Issues of consistency do have a special force in moral reasoning. The "golden rule" of doing to others as one would have others do to oneself underscores the fact that morality in significant measure means not making an exception for oneself (or those one is allied with). But even from a purely moral point of view, only comparable human rights violations require comparable responses. Human rights may be "interdependent and indivisible," but that does not require an identical response to every violation of every right.

Even from a purely moral point of view, considerations of cost may be relevant. Few would consider the United States to be morally bound, all things considered, to risk nuclear war in order to remedy human rights violations in China simply because we acted strongly to remedy similar violations in, say, Guatemala. Conversely, the fact that no state is willing to threaten the use of force to free Tibet from Chinese domination, and thus risk nuclear war, does not mean that considerations of moral consistency should have precluded the use of force in, say, East Timor. Balancing competing values *requires* taking account of all the values involved. And consistency requires treating like cases alike *all things considered,* not just looking at human rights violations.

Furthermore, to address only moral (in)consistency is to address but one part of the relevant foreign policy. In addition to the authoritative international human rights standards of the Universal Declaration and the Covenants, which can be taken as a rough approximation of an international moral standard, states must consider their own, often much more limited, international human rights objectives, as well as other aspects of the national interest. Even if a state's actions or policies are morally inconsistent, they may be consistent from a foreign policy point of view.

For example, President George H. W. Bush extended most-favored-nation trading status to China in 1990 but denied it to the Soviet Union. Looking solely at human rights behaviors—Tiananmen Square versus perestroika, glasnost, new thinking, and the collapse of the Soviet empire—this seems wildly inconsistent. Considering all the interests involved, however, it is plausible, if controversial, to find no *foreign policy* inconsistency. Bush argued, not implausibly, that his actions properly balanced a complex set of competing security, economic, and human rights interests.

We can determine whether different responses to comparable human rights violations represent inconsistent foreign policy only if we know all the interests involved and the values (weights) attached to them. Alleged inconsistencies in international human rights policies may be—and I would suggest most often are—consistent policies based on a relatively low weighting of international human rights interests. Moreover, hypocrisy, error, and inattention are no less common in foreign policy than in other human endeavors. However, they must be distinguished from foreign policy actions that reflect a relatively low valuation of a state's international human rights interests.

In any case, human rights policies are only a part—most often, a rather modest part—of the foreign policy of most states. Therefore, even well-designed foreign policies will treat comparable human rights violations differently.

9. AIMS AND EFFECTS

The success or failure of international human rights initiatives is more complex than one might imagine. The obvious measure of success is the extent to which human rights practices in the target country change in response to foreign policy initiatives. The release of individual prisoners of conscience is a common occurrence in response to international pressure. Rarely, however, have major structural reforms in rights-abusive regimes been produced. In between these two extremes is a broad range of possible effects that vary not only with the means employed but also with the objectives sought and the particular conditions in the country in question.

It is important to note, though, that the effects of international human rights policies are often indirect and may even be felt outside of the immediate target country. For example, the limited pressures of the Reagan administration on El Salvador had little discernible immediate influence on military violations of human rights, but they may have reduced the level and intensity of future violations in El Salvador and elsewhere. In other words, deterrence and issues of credibility may be as important in human rights policy as they are in national security policy.

Human rights initiatives that bring no immediate change in a government's practices may nonetheless have positive effects by supporting local human rights advocates or delegitimating repressive regimes. By subtly altering the local human rights environment that a rights-abusive regime faces, human rights initiatives may have significant long-term effects. This is perhaps the greatest lesson of the Helsinki process in countries such as Czechoslovakia and Russia. South Africa is another prominent example.

Altering the broader normative environment is another possible impact for international human rights policies. For example, sanctions imposed in the late 1970s and 1980s on governments in Central and South America usually had little impact on the behavior of the target governments, but they were crucial elements in altering international expectations and giving new force to the norms of the Universal Declaration and other international instruments. Some of the most striking differences between cold war and post–cold war international human rights politics owe as much to normative change as to changes in the global balance of power.

Doing *a* at time *t* in country *x*, whatever its immediate effects, may create precedents that shape future responses to similar violations later or elsewhere. For example, the initial Carter decision to suspend aid to Guatemala in 1977 established a precedent that influenced policy in a number of later cases in the Americas and elsewhere.

International human rights policies may also be undertaken primarily to satisfy domestic constituencies. There certainly is something troubling in the notion of a "successful" policy that satisfies national political constituencies while having no international effect. If that is what it is designed to do, though, that reality must be acknowledged. For example, periodic changes in American support to the United Nations Fund for Population Activities seem driven more by the abortion debate in the United States than anything else.

We must also note that speaking out and acting against evil may be desirable, even demanded, whether or not there is a reasonable prospect of change. In personal relations we may appropriately chastise friends, colleagues, or relations over whose behavior we have no substantial influence. We may even be held in disrepute if we silently stand by in the face of their misbehavior. So too in international politics. This seems to have been central to the U.S. decision to intervene in Bosnia and Kosovo (see §§8.2., 8.4). Our values may demand that we speak and act even when it has no discernible effect, if only because failing to do so may undermine those values or our own identity and credibility.

Finally, in assessing impact, it is important to recognize that states rarely engage in serious human rights violations unless there are substantial (political, financial, or other) costs to respecting the rights in question. Target governments are not passive recipients of external initiatives. "What works" often is determined by the reaction of target governments to the ends sought, sometimes irrespective of the means applied on their behalf.

10. THE RESOURCES AND
ROLES OF NGOS AND STATES

Although we have focused on multilateral regimes and bilateral foreign policy, national and transnational human rights NGOs have appeared recurrently in all the cases we have examined. In addition to the international campaigns waged by Amnesty International (AI), such U.S. NGOs as Americas Watch, the American Civil Liberties Union, and several other organizations were important players in the struggles over Central American policy in the 1980s. And in both North America and Europe, NGOs played a major role in national debates over sanctions against South Africa during the 1980s.

The private status of NGOs allows them to operate free of the political control of states. In addition, as single-issue advocacy groups, human rights NGOs are not required to take into account other international or foreign policy objectives.

Human rights NGOs may also have a special advantage as national advocates of improved human rights practices. Because they are narrowly focused and generally nonpartisan, they sometimes can raise human rights issues within a country that no other actor can. Particularly where independent political activity is repressed and civil society is weak, as in the Soviet bloc or the Southern Cone of South America during the late 1970s and early 1980s, human rights NGOs may be the only national voice not completely silenced. In countries where democratization and political liberalization remain incomplete, partisan political activity often is far more dangerous than less directly partisan human rights activity. And both national and international human rights NGOs have a special role when political space begins to open, or threatens to close back down, because they act with a single-minded focus on human rights.

NGO lobbying helped to assure that human rights language was included in the United Nations Charter. Since then, NGOs have become regular, active, and occasionally influential participants in the human rights work of the UN. For example, national and international campaigns by Amnesty International played an important role in UN initiatives on torture in the 1970s and 1980s.

NGOs have also helped to incorporate concern for human rights into the foreign policies of individual states. For instance, Amnesty International's Dutch section contributed to the drafting of the 1979 white paper that made human rights a formal part of the foreign policy of the Netherlands. In the United States, AI has been especially active on Capitol Hill, lobbying, testifying, and providing information and support to sympathetic members of Congress and their staffs. In Australia, there is even an Amnesty International group in the parliament. And national human rights NGOs, such as the American Civil Liberties Union in the United States, have been actively involved in the domestic politics of numerous states.

However, NGOs must rely on the power of publicity and persuasion. They lack the resources of even weak states. States are free to remain unpersuaded. And many states have used their powers of coercion against the members of human rights NGOs, turning them into new victims.

Sovereign states have almost the opposite strengths and weaknesses of NGOs. States in their foreign policies must accommodate a wide range of interests. Foreign policy can never be reduced to or identical to human rights policy. Furthermore, foreign policy is by its nature directed toward the realization of the national interest, which rarely places human rights above material and political interests. However, when states do choose to pursue human rights objectives, they typically possess resources, channels of influence, and even publicity capabilities that are unavailable to NGOs.

The national role of states also needs to be emphasized. States, in addition to being the principal violators of human rights, are the principal mechanism for their protection and implementation in the contemporary world. The ultimate goal of most human rights advocacy is to alter national law and practice. The contribution of international actors—states, international organizations, and NGOs alike—is therefore almost always secondary to the national political struggles by which citizens force their own government to respect their rights. International action can help to quicken the pace, provide support for national human rights advocates, and add further incentives for regimes to respect the rights of their citizens. It is at the level of the nation-state, however, that human rights must ultimately be vindicated.

Finally, in thinking about international human rights pressures on states, one should not overlook the role of actors who are only episodically involved, or who may not even have an explicit human rights mandate. For example, the 1993 Vienna World Human Rights Conference, a one-time, ad hoc gathering, helped refocus international attention on human rights in the post–cold war world. The war crimes tribunals for the former Yugoslavia and Rwanda are ad hoc bodies that may help to shape the direction of international human rights activities. The 1995 United Nations Fourth World Conference on Women in Beijing attempted to introduce women's issues more explicitly into the mainstream of international human rights discussions. The World Bank in its recent emphasis on "good governance" has begun to touch on important human rights issues. In addition, both the Council of Europe and the European Union have stressed the importance of rights-protective policies for inclusion in "Europe."

11. A SYSTEM OF INTERNATIONAL ACCOUNTABILITY

We can summarize the general thrust of this and the preceding chapter by noting that although sovereign states retain a primary responsibility for implementing internationally recognized human rights in their territories, they no longer enjoy the protections of discreet diplomatic silence. Quite the contrary, persistent human rights violators increasingly must act in the light of embarrassing international publicity mobilized by public and private groups. Global, regional, national, and transnational actors have created a web of pressures that make it almost impossible today for states to avoid a public accounting of their human rights practices.

Admittedly, most of the current mechanisms of accountability rely principally on the power of public exposure and scrutiny. However, the value of publicizing violations and trying to shame states into better compliance should not be underestimated. Even vicious governments may care about their international reputation. For example, in the late 1970s and early 1980s, no less vile a government than the Argentine military regime devoted considerable diplomatic effort to thwart the investigations of the UN Commission on Human Rights. Furthermore, publicity often helps at least a few of the more prominent victims of repression.

The most important impact of all this (largely verbal) international human rights activity, however, probably lies less in its immediate achievements on behalf of victims than in the fact that national and international norms and expectations are being altered. The idea of human rights has a moral force and mobilizing power in the contemporary world that seems hard to resist. And as more and more citizens throughout the world come to think of themselves as endowed with inalienable rights, the demand for human rights continues to cause dictators to flee and their governments to crumble.

The sword often proves mightier than the word, at least in the short run. But the task of human rights advocates, wherever they may be, is the ancient and noble one of speaking the truth of justice to power. And far more often than so-called realists would ever allow, truth can triumph.

DISCUSSION QUESTIONS

1. Should we accept the description of post–World War II U.S. foreign policy as dominated by anticommunism? Suppose that we do. Was it a poor policy decision? Should anticommunism have been assigned a less-overriding priority? Or was the problem that anticommunism was pursued with unreasonable zeal? Is there an important lesson here about an ideological (or moralistic) foreign policy that leads to such excess? If so, should we reconsider the arguments of the realists?

2. Should the United States be able to define for itself which internationally recognized human rights it wishes to recognize or pursue? If so, why? How can we sustain and enforce an international human rights policy if states can pick and choose the parts they want to comply with? Why should the United States (or any other sovereign state) have to comply with international human rights norms, no matter how widely accepted they are?

3. The United States has a relatively active and aggressive bilateral international human rights policy but has been reluctant to participate in most multilateral international human rights regimes. (The United States did not ratify the International Covenant on Civil and Political Rights until April 1992, and even then it did not ratify the optional protocol.) Isn't this a double standard? Can it be justified? Why should other countries take U.S. international human rights policy seriously when the United States is so reluctant to open itself to international human rights scrutiny?

4. In reviewing the evidence of U.S. policy toward South Africa, Central America, and the Southern Cone, what strikes you more, the continuities or the changes between different U.S. administrations? When all is said and done, just how different was Carter's policy from that of either Ford or Reagan? Were the differences largely symbolic? If they were, how serious a criticism is that? How large a role does symbolic rhetoric play in foreign policy? In international human rights policy?

5. The same question might be asked about the differences between the international human rights policies of the United States and the policies of the like-minded countries. When it comes to making difficult choices, when it comes to sacrificing their own interests, just how different are Canada, Norway, and the Netherlands from the United States? Compare, for example, the Netherlands' policy toward Indonesia and its policy toward Suriname. Is the difference one of quality or merely a matter of degree?

6. Whether large or small, "real" or "symbolic," there are differences among the international human rights policies of the like-minded countries. How can these be explained? What are the factors considered in the chapter? What additional possible explanations can you advance?

7. Consider the emphasis of the like-minded countries on economic, social, and cultural rights. Is their approach better than or just different from that of the United States? Why? Does your answer change if you look at the issue from the perspectives of foreign policy, foreign aid policy, and international human rights policy?

8. What do you think of the distinction drawn in the chapter between human rights policy consistency and foreign policy consistency? Is it really appropriate to treat similar human rights situations differently because of other foreign policy interests? How does your answer to this question change if you adopt the perspectives of, say, a foreign policy decision maker, a human rights advocate, a concerned citizen of your own country, or someone who sees herself as a citizen of the world?

9. How can one justify trading off human rights? Are human rights really the kind of thing that is appropriately balanced against, say, the economic interests of corporations? How do your answers vary when the human rights in question are those of your fellow citizens versus those of foreign citizens?

10. Can a viable international human rights policy be constructed by responding to violations according to the principles of severity, trends, responsibility, and efficacy? Are there other principles that are equally important? Is this list too long?

11. The role of NGOs is presented here as largely supplementary to that of states. Is that accurate? Is that a good thing? What are the *problems* with NGOs?

12. The chapter closes with a discussion of a system of international accountability. Is there really accountability in any strong sense of that term? How good or bad is that?

SUGGESTED READINGS

Debra Liang-Fenton, ed., *Implementing U.S. Human Rights Policy* (Washington, D.C.: U.S. Institute of Peace Press, 2004) provides more than a dozen superb case studies of U.S. human rights policy toward a wide range of prominent countries, focusing on the post–cold war era. It is the single best source to get some sense of the texture and range of American international human rights policy in recent years. Kathryn Sikkink, *Mixed Signals: U.S. Human Rights Policy and Latin America* (Ithaca: Cornell University Press, 2005) provides a comprehensive overview of U.S. human rights policy toward Latin America, covering the entire post–World War II era. Michael Ignatieff, ed., *American Exceptionalism and Human Rights* (Princeton: Princeton University Press, 2005) is an excellent collection of essays covering a wide range of both domestic and international human rights issues. Harold Koh, "America's Jeckyll-and-Hyde Exceptionalism," and John Ruggie, "American, Exceptionalism, Exemptionalism, and Global Governance," are particularly good and especially relevant to the issues covered in this chapter. Taken together, these three books provide an excellent overview of the topic of human rights in American foreign policy. For a more critical assessment, see Julie Mertus, *Bait and Switch? Human Rights and U.S. Foreign Policy* (New York: Routledge, 2004). Harold Hongju Koh, "A United States Human Rights Policy for the 21st Century," *Saint Louis University Law Journal* 46 (Spring 2002): 293–344, is a powerful programmatic statement by Clinton's former assistant secretary of state. In my view, there is no single piece that does a better job of provoking serious thought about the appropriate contours of American international human rights policy.

On the general issue of human rights and foreign policy, Peter R. Baehr and Monique Castermans-Holleman, *The Role of Human Rights in Foreign Policy*, 3rd ed. (New York: Palgrave Macmillan, 2004) provides a useful and accessible general introduction. There are also several classic articles that, although somewhat dated, remain well worth reading. Stanley Hoffmann, "Reaching for the Most Difficult: Human Rights as a Foreign Policy Goal," *Daedalus* 112 (Fall 1983): 19–49, provides an excellent and subtle discussion of some of the fundamental problems and possibilities in pursuing human rights in foreign policy. A good, short introductory discussion, with an especially thorough presentation of the means available for use on behalf of human rights, is Evan Luard, *Human Rights and Foreign Policy* (Oxford: Pergamon Press, 1981). An abbreviated version of this essay is available in Richard Pierre Claude and Burns H. Weston, eds., *Human Rights in the World Community* (Philadelphia: University of Pennsylvania Press, 1992). Arthur Schlesinger Jr., "Human Rights and the American Tradition," *Foreign Affairs* 57, no. 3 (1979): 503–526, is again dated but presents a lively version of a standard, mainstream U.S. liberal approach. Jeane J. Kirkpatrick, "Dictatorships and Double Standards," *Commentary* 68 (November 1979): 34–45, is the authoritative presentation of the Reagan position. Hans Morgenthau's essay *Human Rights and Foreign Policy* (New York: Council on Religion and International Affairs, 1979) offers a classic statement of the realist perspective. For another classic realist analysis, see Henry A. Kissinger, "Continuity and Change in

American Foreign Policy," in *Human Rights and World Order,* ed. Abdul Aziz Said (New York: Praeger, 1978).

There has been very little written on human rights and foreign policy in countries other than the United States. The principal exception is David P. Forsythe, ed., *Human Rights and Comparative Foreign Policy* (Tokyo: United Nations University Press, 2000). Jan Egeland, *Impotent Superpower—Potent Small State: Potentialities and Limitations of Human Rights Objectives in the Foreign Policies of the United States and Norway* (Oslo: Norwegian University Press [distributed by Oxford University Press], 1988) is becoming dated but is still interesting. David Gillies, *Between Principle and Practice: Human Rights in North-South Relations* (Toronto: University of Toronto Press, 1997) has a Canadian focus.

Claude E. Welch Jr., ed., *NGOs and Human Rights: Promise and Performance* (Philadelphia: University of Pennsylvania Press, 2001) is an excellent, wide-ranging assessment of the contribution of NGOs. Philip Alston (ed.) *Non-State Actors and Human Rights* (Oxford: Oxford University Press, 2005) has a more legal focus but is excellent, especially on issues of corporate responsibility. Ann Marie Clark, *Diplomacy of Conscience: Amnesty International and Changing Human Rights Norms* (Princeton: Princeton University Press, 2001) is perhaps the best available study of the world's best-known human rights NGO. William F. Schulz, *In Our Own Best Interest: How Defending Human Rights Benefits Us All* (Boston: Beacon Press, 2001) is an impassioned argument by a longtime advocate. Cheryl Fisher Pibbs, ed., *Pioneers of Human Rights* (San Diego: Greenhaven Press, 2005) tells the story of several prominent activists. See also George W. Shepherd Jr., *They Are Us: Fifty Years of Human Rights Advocacy* (Philadelphia: Xlibris Press, 2002).

NGO activism, however, is not without its problems. David Kennedy, *The Dark Sides of Virtue: Reassessing International Humanitarianism* (Princeton: Princeton University Press, 2004) is a brilliant analysis of the pitfalls of advocacy that matches its powerful criticisms with a genuine sympathy and commitment to a more just and humane world. Michael Ignatieff's *Human Rights as Politics and Idolatry* (Princeton: Princeton University Press, 2001) offers a powerful warning about the dangers of excessive self-righteousness and rigidity, again from the perspective of a sympathetic scholar-activist.

7

◄○►

Responding to Tiananmen

The year 1989 was a decisive turning point in world history and in the international struggle for human rights. The remarkably quick and bloodless collapse of the Soviet empire, symbolized most dramatically by the opening of the Berlin Wall and by Czechoslovakia's Velvet Revolution, ushered in a new historical era. Combined with the steady progress of democratization in Latin America and accelerating liberalization in Africa and Asia, these changes suggest that it is not entirely wishful thinking to talk of a new world order, especially in human rights.

Understandable satisfaction with change, however, should not blind us to equally striking continuities, especially in *international* human rights policies. This first of four chapters on post–cold war human rights politics examines international responses to one of the most prominent setbacks, China's Tiananmen Square massacre—ironically, in June 1989, on the cusp of the new post–cold war era.

1. CHINA'S DEMOCRACY MOVEMENT

Students have been the heart of China's democracy movement since its symbolic beginning on May 4, 1919, when 3,000 students took to Tiananmen Square to protest concessions to Japan at the end of World War I. For over a thousand years, China's governing elite was composed of Confucian scholar-bureaucrats recruited through a national system of competitive examinations. Beyond their ordinary duties, these officials had an extraordinary right, even obligation, of political remonstrance: In difficult times, they were expected to call on the emperor to live up to the standards of good government that justified his rule.

The emperor's authority was seen to rest on a Mandate of Heaven. Remonstrances recalled to the emperor the duties to his people that accompanied the heavenly grant of power. This provided limited checks and balances in a political system without formal separation of powers. Remonstrances allowed the people, through intellectuals acting as their representatives, to press for reform when they were no longer able to tolerate injustice but were unwilling to resort to riots and rebellions (a recurrent feature of Chinese politics, especially in hard economic times). Widespread protests

149

by intellectuals have long been a recognized sign of political crisis in China. Student protests thus have unusually heavy cultural weight in China.

Human rights problems in contemporary China are rooted in the creation of the People's Republic of China on October 1, 1949, when Mao Zedong and his Communist Party installed a classic Leninist party-state totalitarian regime. Under Communist Party rule, all aspects of life have been controlled by a centralized bureaucracy that enforces rigid conformity with ideological directives. Most internationally recognized civil and political rights are regularly and systematically violated. Remarkable progress has been made in some areas of economic and social rights, especially by abolishing feudal land tenure and social relations. But tens of millions of people died in famines that resulted from state policy decisions in the 1950s. And over the past decade, housing, health care, and social services have become increasingly problematic for the bottom quarter of the population.

The most frightening systematic human rights violations in contemporary China, however, came during the Great Proletarian Cultural Revolution. On July 28, 1966, all universities and schools were closed. In August, the Chinese Communist Party (CCP) called upon the masses to form cultural revolutionary groups to attack "rightist" elements that had taken a "capitalist road." "Red Guards" spread an arbitrary reign of political intimidation and terror, dispensing "socialist justice" for offenses as minor as a casual critical comment, insufficient revolutionary fervor, or simply because a friend or relative's former job had branded that person a "class enemy."

Many millions of people were accused—and thus almost automatically found guilty—of ideological offenses. At minimum, this meant demeaning forced "reeducation." Most also lost jobs, school places, and housing. Literally millions suffered forced internal exile or imprisonment, usually accompanied by violent physical abuse during detention. An unknown number of people were executed.

Repression in contemporary China, however, has been punctuated with interludes of political opening. The best-known period followed a speech in May 1956 by Mao that called for letting a hundred flowers bloom—instead of the single path previously enforced by the CCP. But the party soon returned to its old ways, imprisoning many of the Hundred Flowers intellectuals.

Serious public stirrings of a new democracy movement began in April 1976 with national demonstrations in memory of Zhou Enlai, one of the leaders of the Chinese Revolution and through much of the Mao era the second most powerful man in China. Although these demonstrations were violently repressed, Mao's own death in September 1976 touched off an intense power struggle. The result was a new political opening at the end of 1978.

In Beijing, public political debate took place in "big-character" posters on what came to be known as Democracy Wall. Particularly noteworthy was Wei Jingsheng's call for a "fifth modernization"—democracy—to complete the officially proclaimed modernizations in industry, science and technology, agriculture, and defense. Wei called on China to think of progress as involving more than just power and prosperity, to recognize important human and political dimensions beyond economic and military development. But the Democracy Wall movement, like the Hundred Flowers opening, was short lived. Wei and other leading dissidents were sentenced to long prison terms in 1979.

In the 1980s, under the leadership of Deng Xiaoping, China did embark on sustained economic liberalization. A cheap and disciplined workforce made China a rapidly growing presence in world markets. Markets were also given an expanding role in domestic production and pricing decisions. A thriving industrial economy developed on China's south coast, and the government used its control over agricultural marketing to pay farmers more for their produce. Average farm incomes doubled during the decade.

Political reforms, however, continued to be resisted. In December 1986, demonstrations at more than 150 campuses in over twenty cities called for better living conditions, a free press, and democracy. In mid-January 1987, the authorities cracked down. Fang Lizhi, who was emerging as one of China's leading dissidents, was removed as vice rector of the University of Science and Technology in Hubei. At the same time, the CCP purged its leading advocate of reform, General Secretary Hu Yaobang. The ensuing campaign against "bourgeois liberalization," however, was mild and notably unsuccessful. Debate over democracy, although restricted to private discussions, continued through 1988.

In a country unusually attuned to historical symbolism, China's democracy movement eagerly anticipated the approach of 1989, a most portentous year: the two hundredth anniversary of the French Revolution, the seventieth anniversary of the May 4 movement, the fortieth anniversary of the Chinese Revolution, and the tenth anniversary of the repression of the Democracy Wall movement.

Fang Lizhi kicked off new protests in February 1989 with a letter calling for the release of Wei Jingsheng and other political prisoners. This in effect reopened the arguments of the Democracy Wall movement. Following the death of Hu Yaobang on April 15, 1989, students defied the government and held their own unofficial memorial, as they had with Zhou Enlai in 1976. Beginning with 10,000 students, their numbers grew to more than 100,000 on April 22, the day of the official funeral. This was the start of the Tiananmen democracy movement.

A statement drafted by Fang in December 1988, on the fortieth anniversary of the Universal Declaration of Human Rights, received wide endorsement as the movement developed. Its five proposals indicate the general tenor of demands.

1. Lift the ban on nonofficial publications . . . The government should not intervene as long as those publications do not advocate violence or spread pornography . . .
2. Guarantee the right of freedom of association . . . with a prerequisite of nonviolence, people, through organizations and parties not in power, have the right to openly criticize the policies of the party in office.
3. Direct elections of county and district leaders . . .
4. Release all political prisoners . . . Delete the words "crime of counterrevolution" from the code of criminal law. Declare that it is forbidden to charge anyone for reasons of ideology or politics.
5. Separation of party and government.[1]

In the spring of 1989, China's democracy movement was developing into a theoretically coherent call for political opening, focusing on freedom of speech and association. Practically, it was taking to the streets. And in a symbolic gesture, recalling Qing dynasty (1644–1922) remonstrances, student leaders knelt on the steps of the Great Hall of the People and asked Premier Li Peng to come out to talk. When he refused, they launched a massive boycott of classes on April 24.

The official response was complete rejection of all student demands. A private speech by Deng Xiaoping on April 25 set the tone: "This is not an ordinary student movement but a turmoil. We must take a clear-cut stance, carry out effective measures, and counteract quickly to stop this agitation . . . This entire episode is a planned, conspiratorial activity."[2] On April 26, the official *People's Daily* published an editorial titled, "We Must Oppose the Turmoil with a Clear-Cut Stance."

The protesters, however, seemed to be inspired rather than intimidated. Although the government would carry out its implied threats in less than six weeks, the surprising resolve of the students provided breathing room. On May 4, more than 100,000 students marched to Tiananmen Square. New petitions called for even greater reforms. And on May 13, 3,000 students began a hunger strike.

The hunger strike coincided with the visit of Mikhail Gorbachev, the first by a Soviet leader since 1959. For the government, Gorbachev's visit symbolized the end of the Sino-Soviet rift and China's new position in the world. To the students, however, Gorbachev symbolized dramatic reform from within. More broadly, the hunger strike, held in front of Mao's mausoleum, in the shadows of the monument to the martyrs of the Communist Revolution, was a gesture of self-sacrifice. It recalled, for example, Qu Yuan, a fourth-century functionary who, when his advice was rejected, committed suicide, demonstrating both loyalty and his inability to accept the emperor's decision.

Popular support continued to grow. By May 17, as a thousand hunger strikers were hospitalized, over 1 million protesters and onlookers jammed the streets in and around Tiananmen Square. Smaller demonstrations were being held in more than twenty cities. And the CCP was losing its monopoly over civil society.

Totalitarian states seek to maintain control not through direct force but by monopolizing public and private associations, preventing citizens from acting collectively outside of state control. By late spring, increasingly sophisticated and effective autonomous student organizations began to emerge. Press reports on Tiananmen were largely ignoring official controls. The students were also receiving growing support from workers, businessmen, bureaucrats, and even some soldiers.

China's rulers faced a decisive choice: accept structural political changes or crack down, with violence if necessary. In fall 1989, communist leaders in Eastern Europe did not have the heart or the stomach to shoot their own people. In late spring 1989, China's leaders did.

On May 20, 1989, martial law was declared in Beijing. Troops were summoned to remove the protesters. Demonstrators, however, still numbered over 1 million. The troops were slowed by mass passive resistance: "The people of [Beijing] took to the streets and erected makeshift barricades. They surrounded the army convoys, sometimes to let the air out of tires or stall engines but more often to argue with or cajole the troops, urging them not to enforce the martial-law restrictions and not to turn their guns on their fellow Chinese."[3]

With absolute party rule at stake, Deng called in new, hardened, and loyal troops. The students, sensing crisis, reduced their numbers in the square. But they did not go quietly. On May 29–30, a statue of the Goddess of Democracy was erected.[4] Defiant declarations and interviews continued, while an estimated 100,000 people attended what proved to be the final demonstrations on June 2–3.

The army's attack—as shocking as it was inescapable—came on June 3. The government admits killing three hundred unarmed protesters and bystanders. Outside estimates put the number at three times that figure, plus another three hundred killed in Chengdu. In the ensuing repression, thousands were arrested. Thousands more fled underground or overseas. At least dozens were executed. And hopes for human rights and democracy in China lay bulldozed beneath the treads of the tanks of the "People's Liberation Army."

2. INTERNATIONAL RESPONSES TO TIANANMEN

The international response was swift, strong, and coordinated. On June 5, the United States imposed an arms embargo, suspended high-level official contacts, and froze new aid. The European Community adopted similar sanctions on June 27, one day after the World Bank froze $780 million in loans to China. Japan suspended its new five-year aid program, valued at ¥810 billion (roughly $6 or $7 billion, depending on exchange rate fluctuations). The Group of Seven (G7) annual economic summit in Paris in July also condemned the massacre.

China's political costs are extremely difficult to measure. Its economic costs, however, were demonstrably significant. New commitments of bilateral foreign aid dropped from $3.4 billion in 1988 to $1.5 billion in 1989 and to $0.7 billion in 1990. Assuming a 20 percent annual increase in aid commitments without the disruption of Tiananmen (well below the average 50 percent annual growth for the period 1985–1988), China lost about $11 billion over four years in bilateral aid alone.[5]

Despite numerous small violations, sanctions were widely observed until July 1990, when Japan announced the end of its aid moratorium. Most other countries then began to relax their sanctions more or less rapidly. A series of visits by foreign ministers to Beijing in spring 1991 marked China's emergence from diplomatic isolation. The renewal of China's economic boom in late 1991 substantially increased the incentives to abandon sanctions. By 1993, most countries other than the United States had returned to business as usual—which included criticism of Chinese human rights practices (especially the treatment of dissidents) but not sanctions. Official bilateral aid committed in 1992 exceeded the previous record year of 1988. We can get a good sense of the politics involved by looking at the actions of the two principal bilateral actors, Japan and the United States, and the multilateral response at the United Nations.

A. Japan

Japan opposed more than guarded statements of disapproval, imposing sanctions only under pressure from its allies (especially the United States).[6] This position reflected strong economic interests, regional security concerns, and a genuine belief that isolating China was an inappropriate and unproductive strategy.

Within the limits set by U.S. pressure, Japan consistently advocated what amounted to Reagan-style quiet diplomacy and constructive engagement. On June 5, the day that U.S. sanctions were announced, Japan merely indicated that it was monitoring the situation, regretted the loss of life, and hoped for a quick end to the turmoil. On June 7, the Chinese ambassador was given a note indicating that Japan had no desire to interfere in China's internal affairs (which was China's description not only of sanctions but even of public criticism). Japanese lobbying before and during the Paris G7 summit succeeded in avoiding new collective sanctions. And after the G7 summit, Japan worked to end international sanctions as quickly as possible and in the interim to blunt their impact.

In September 1989, a Diet (parliament) delegation led by Foreign Minister Ito Masayoshi met with Deng Xiaoping and other top Chinese leaders. In December, Japan renewed cultural exchanges and donated a symbolic $3.5 million to modernize a hospital and a television station. Requests for political asylum were denied. Japanese authorities allowed Chinese embassy and consular officials to harass and intimidate Chinese students in Japan. Students were sent home against their will, despite official pledges made in June and July 1989 to extend lapsed student visas. And the resumption of foreign aid, along with a major new five-year $8 billion agreement at the end of 1990 to exchange oil and coal for technology and equipment, helped to buffer China from continuing Western sanctions.[7]

Much money was to be made in China, and both Japanese firms and their government wanted to make sure that Japan got at least its fair share. But economic engagement was also part of a broader strategy of tying China into cooperative bilateral and regional relationships to maximize regional stability, Japan's overriding geopolitical goal. Japan is deeply committed to the power of cooperative diplomatic engagement and the long-run transforming power of economic development, a topic addressed later in this chapter. As an Asian regional power, Japan also had security interests (for example, in Korea and the South China Sea) that could be compromised by Chinese hostility. The Japanese response to Tiananmen thus was a consistent part of a clear general strategy.

Peter Van Ness has aptly described Japan's policy as "nominal conditionality."[8] Without allowing Chinese brutality to pass unnoticed, Japanese officials tried to minimize its impact on their relations with China and focused their diplomatic effort on doing the least they possibly could to harm or even offend China.

B. The United States

The United States represents the other end of the spectrum of international responses. Americans were captivated by the Tiananmen protesters. Popular shock and disgust at the massacre produced an unusually strong and long-lasting reaction. As the rest of the world returned to business as usual with China, the United States maintained, and even considered expanding, its sanctions. But divided government—a Republican president who preferred engagement and a Democratic Congress that preferred sanctions—led to considerable inconsistency.

In July 1989, four aircraft were delivered to China with navigation systems covered by the arms embargo. Secretary of State James Baker met with Chinese Foreign Minister Qian Qichen in Paris to discuss the civil war in Cambodia, despite the embargo on high-level contacts. National Security Adviser Brent Scowcroft and Thomas Eagleburger, the number two official at the State Department, made a secret visit to Beijing. And Secretary Baker's speech at the annual meeting of the Association of Southeast Asian Nations (ASEAN) did not even mention China.

December 1989 was another month of multiple American concessions. Scowcroft and Eagleburger made a second visit to Beijing. Three communications satellites were sold. And President George Bush vetoed a bill to extend the expired visas of Chinese students.

Bush did criticize China, both publicly and privately. In December 1990, he devoted the bulk of his discussions with Foreign Minister Qian to human rights. In April 1991, Bush met with the Dalai Lama, thus raising the sensitive issue of human rights in Tibet.[9] There was even limited administration support for material sanctions. For example, Bush accepted November 1989 legislation that called for suspending new World Bank loans to China. In April 1991, the sale of U.S. parts for a Chinese communications satellite was blocked.

Conversely, Congress did not consistently demand stronger sanctions. Despite early tough talk, sanctions legislation did not receive a final vote in 1989 or 1990. Nonetheless, Congress, with support from and prodding by NGOs, was the driving force behind U.S. pressure on China. Representative Nancy Pelosi and Senate Majority Leader George Mitchell led an extended campaign against administration policy that came closest to success in March 1992, when Bush was forced to veto legislation that linked human rights to an extension of China's most-favored-nation (MFN) trading privileges in American markets.

Candidate Bill Clinton criticized Bush's position during the 1992 campaign. As president, on May 28, 1993, he issued an executive order listing seven human rights criteria (including a general provision on observance of the Universal Declaration of Human Rights) that China would be required to meet before he would recommend extending MFN privileges again in 1994. China now faced a credible threat of reduced access to the American market.

Nevertheless, delinkage of trade and human rights began almost immediately. A memorandum by Assistant Secretary of State Winston Lord in mid-July 1993 called for a new strategy of "comprehensive engagement." This became administration policy in September. As National Security Adviser Anthony Lake put it, "the successor to a doctrine of containment must be a strategy of enlargement—enlargement of the world's free community of market democracies."[10] Top officials from the Departments of State, Defense, Treasury, and Agriculture visited China. And in November 1993, Clinton met with Chinese president Jiang Zemin at the

Seattle summit of leaders from the Asia-Pacific Economic Cooperation forum. The United States was clearly preparing for China's return to full status in the international community.

Meanwhile, with George Bush no longer there to do the work (and take the heat), opponents of human rights conditions on MFN status began to organize. Business mobilized its considerable lobbying skills and power. A bipartisan group in Congress argued that blunt, blanket sanctions like withholding MFN privileges were not an appropriate tool—a view shared by former President Carter and former Secretary of State Cyrus Vance. As one administration official put it, the MFN designation was "an atomic bomb. And nobody drops a bomb. What we need is to get usable tools."[11] A growing number of people were also becoming convinced that rapid social change in China was making broad trade sanctions obsolete, even counterproductive. For example, Massachusetts Senator John Kerry returned from a trip to China in early 1994 a convert to ending linkage.

Aggressive Chinese diplomacy also had an impact. Protests and threats were effectively mixed with cooperative gestures. Strategically timed releases of prisoners were a standard tactic. China also made concessions on secondary human rights issues, such as prison labor, and on unrelated issues. For example, China signed the Nuclear Nonproliferation Treaty in 1992. Understandings were reached with both the Bush and Clinton administrations on transferring missiles and missile technology. Discussions were opened on piracy of music and software.

Few were surprised, then, when on May 26, 1994, Clinton announced that despite China's failure to meet the conditions of the 1993 executive order, MFN status would be extended unconditionally. "In the end, economics won the day. It wasn't really even close."[12] China's energy market alone was estimated to be worth as much as $150 billion over the coming decade. By the end of the century, $30 billion was to be spent for telephone modernization. Aircraft purchases over two decades were projected to be $40 billion. These were staggering opportunities for profits and jobs.

Trade and investment had never been included in American sanctions (except for military and "dual-use" products). Nonetheless, there was concern that continued human rights friction would harm the competitive position of American firms. For example, German Chancellor Helmut Kohl returned from a visit to China in November 1993 with nearly $3 billion in new contracts. And China did prove to be generous after linkage was buried. A business delegation led by Secretary of Commerce Ron Brown returned in September 1994 with over $5 billion in contracts. The following February, a visit by Energy Secretary Hazel O'Leary netted $2 billion in new contracts.

But there was more to the decision than simple greed. The collapse of allied support left the United States with little choice. Trade sanctions are vulnerable to "free riding" and "defection"; that is, some parties not abiding by sanctions take advantage of those who do. With limited defections (for example, Japan in 1990), sanctions may still affect the target, and the costs will remain spread across several cooperating parties. But by 1994, when everyone else had already defected, the United States, not China, was most likely to be harmed by sanctions.

Cooperation on security issues also counterbalanced China's human rights record. We have already noted the civil war in Cambodia, missile technology, and nonproliferation. China also acquiesced in the UN attack on Iraq after its invasion of Kuwait.

For all its limitations, though, the most striking feature of the U.S. response to Tiananmen was its sustained strength, especially given China's economic and military power. Only against South Africa in the 1980s had the United States ever pursued a comparably strong set of human rights initiatives. And never before (or since) has the United States been willing to accept such high political and economic costs on behalf of human rights violations short of genocide.

Some of this can be attributed to the particular details of the case. But part of the explanation lies in the maturing of human rights as an international issue and in the improved post–cold war environment for international human rights.

C. The United Nations

China's power largely insulated it from multilateral criticism. The massacre was never the subject of a UN General Assembly resolution. Even a mild resolution in the Commission on Human Rights was defeated in 1990. But the Commission's sub-commission did adopt a resolution in August 1989. And Geneva became the site of intensive diplomatic struggle.[13] The sub-commission is the only United Nations human rights body made up of (ostensibly, and often in fact) independent experts rather than instructed government delegates. It was thus the place where China was most vulnerable to multilateral criticism—especially because the sub-commission's scheduled annual meeting was in August, when the issue was fresh. Although they had little time to prepare, Chinese diplomats met unprecedented Western and Third World cooperation with intensive lobbying. "At times it seemed as if every table in the delegates' lounge had been commandeered by the Chinese mission, and there appeared to be no way in which a member of the Sub-Commission in need of a tea-break could escape."[14]

The focus of all this activity was a resolution that read, in its entirety:

The Sub-Commission on Prevention of Discrimination and Protection of Minorities,

Concerned about the events which took place recently in China and about their consequences in the field of human rights,

1. Requests the Secretary-General to transmit to the Commission on Human Rights information provided by the Government of China and by other reliable sources;
2. Makes an appeal for clemency, in particular in favor of persons deprived of their liberty as a result of the above-mentioned events.

Timid as this resolution may seem, Chinese Ambassador Fan Guoxiang responded that it "constituted interference in China's internal affairs . . . [was] incompatible

with the purposes and principles of the Charter of the United Nations, and contra-
vened the rules that regulated international relations."[15] China descended on the
Commission on Human Rights the following February with an entourage of forty
diplomats committed to preventing even such a mild reference to these "events."

Such exertion by a potential target of multilateral human rights criticism is perhaps the strongest evidence that it is not all just hot air and pointless words. If a government that calls up the army to shoot unarmed students is this concerned about
oblique criticism by a relatively obscure UN body, shame and reputation cannot be
entirely negligible considerations.

But in multilateral no less than national politics, power usually triumphs in a
struggle with justice. The resolution considered by the Commission on Human
Rights, although as mild as that of the sub-commission six months earlier, was defeated 17–15, with 11 abstentions. Even the sub-commission was not immune to
politics. At its August 1990 meeting, a resolution on Tibet was never introduced in
return for Chinese agreement not to oppose a resolution on Iraq.[16]

In August 1991, the sub-commission did narrowly adopt a resolution on human
rights in Tibet. This, though, was the final victory for China's critics in Geneva. At
the 1992 commission session, a resolution on Tibet was defeated 27–15 (with 10 abstentions). China managed to escape even a vote in the 1992 sub-commission. At the
1993 commission meeting, the resolution on China was defeated 22–17–12. And at
the August 1993 sub-commission meeting, a resolution on Tibet was defeated
17–6–2.

3. ASSESSING THE IMPACT OF
INTERNATIONAL ACTION

The "bottom line" is that China's communist dictators seem even more firmly entrenched today than they were in 1989. Despite looser controls on speech and publication, pleas for political reform remain rare and dangerous. For example,
Tiananmen activist Wang Dan was sentenced in November 1996 to eleven years in
prison for continuing to call for democracy. And repression continues today. In 2003,
Lizhi was sentenced to eight years in prison for criticizing corruption. In 2005, Shi
Tao was jailed for ten years for criticizing human rights abuses. The totals perhaps
will never be known because of continuing government secrecy. But one group, the
Dui Hua Foundation, based in San Francisco, has documented over 9,000 political
prisoners since 1980, and about 2,500 still in prison in 2005. And the total is certainly
much higher than that.

Nevertheless, international action did have an impact on China. Numerous individual prisoners were released, both in response to general pressure (for example,
573 detainees were released when martial law was lifted in January 1990) and in exchange for particular concessions. For example, in early May 1990, prior to Bush's
first MFN decision, China released two hundred detainees. In January 1994, in response to Clinton's moves toward engagement, some prominent Tibetan prisoners
were freed. Several thousand lives, perhaps even tens of thousands, were improved

because foreign governments were willing to exert political influence and expend political and financial resources on behalf of human rights. International pressure also seems to have been a modest deterrent to new acts of repression, some executions, and mistreatment of some prisoners.

China was also punished for its behavior. Several billion dollars were lost, and China's economic boom was delayed by a year or two. Furthermore, as was just mentioned, the Chinese acted as if they were stung by international criticisms.

Chinese concessions on security and economic issues were further costs. They were also a benefit to the United States, Japan, and Europe. Although human rights advocates may be reluctant to trumpet such indirect, non-rights benefits of international human rights policies, they cannot be ignored in a broader foreign policy assessment. Rights-abusive governments may be forced to make side payments to third parties even where direct benefits for victims cannot be obtained.

In passing, we should also note that sanctions were not cost free to the sanctioning states. Bilateral foreign aid is usually sufficiently "tied" to donor-country suppliers to produce substantial sales (and thus jobs). Suspending military sales even more clearly forgoes profits and jobs (which are usually well paid and, especially in the United States, often located in politically significant places). After Tiananmen, sanctioning countries did more than just talk. They accepted modest domestic economic costs to pursue international human rights objectives. Even talk created frictions that had costs for the pursuit of other objectives in relations with China. Human rights remained a serious irritant in Sino-American relations through 1996.

We should also consider the potential moral and political costs of inaction. One's own commitment to human rights requires some sort of action, even if there is scant chance to punish or transform the target state. To fail to act in the case of gross violations would be shameful. Furthermore, considerations of consistency may also require action that one knows is likely to be largely symbolic. Yet even symbolic action has symbolic value; rarely is it entirely futile.

Finally, I want to suggest that international action subtly but significantly transformed China's normative political environment, both nationally and internationally. Consider the changes in the regime's counteroffensive after Tiananmen.

China initially used "the big lie." For example, one Chinese diplomat claimed that "not a single person had been killed by the army or run over by military vehicles."[17] But even the Chinese leadership seems not to have expected many to accept this account.

Appeals to sovereignty were therefore central. For example, the first issue of *Beijing Review* published after the massacre described the U.S. response as "flagrant accusations against China regarding something which is exclusively China's affair."[18] But in 1989, few other countries saw criticism of human rights abuses as an interference in a country's internal affairs.

A more subtle Chinese argument allowed talk, but only talk. "The two countries may exchange criticisms on issues of human rights . . . but it is not advisable for one to use human rights as a tool to hurt the other."[19] However, all foreign policy manipulates negative and positive incentives, harms and benefits, to alter the behavior of others. In fact, by the late 1980s, diplomatic protests and military and economic sanctions had become an accepted, even an expected, means for expressing human rights disapproval. China was thus forced to back away from extreme claims of sovereign prerogative.

As a result of post-Tiananmen diplomacy, "China [came] to accept human rights as a legitimate part of the international agenda."[20] Chinese defenses thus increasingly emphasized arguments of cultural relativism. For example, China's 1991 Human Rights White Paper claimed that human rights were indeed being realized in China, particularly subsistence rights, the most important rights of all. The substance of such arguments are addressed in the final section of this chapter. Here I am interested only in the politics.

Although clearly intended as cynical manipulation of the language of human rights, this change in rhetoric has had subtle positive consequences. Less than twenty years ago, the very term *human rights* was dangerous. Even Chinese scholars of international law writing in English rarely touched on human rights. Today, however, the term is relatively widely used.

Although there are still severe limits on how human rights issues are addressed, those boundaries are not fixed. And arguing over the proper human rights strategy rather than the very use of international human rights norms is significant progress. The Chinese have been dragged beyond denial and forced to engage the international human rights regime—with consequences that are hard to predict.

Human rights have an internal logic that may escape state control, as Soviet bloc countries discovered with the Helsinki process. China now operates in a realm of national and international discourse in which human rights are legitimate grounds for argument and action. The result is implicit recognition of a new kind of accountability. That recognition is extremely limited and has been even more reluctantly tendered. But this conceptual opening may prove to be the principal contribution of international responses to the Tiananmen massacre.

4. CONSTRUCTIVE ENGAGEMENT REVISITED

Europe and the United States initially adopted a "classic" strategy of punishment, shame, and isolation. They came around, however, to Japan's strategy of engagement. Is there more to be said for constructive engagement in the 1990s and 2000s than its failure in South Africa in the 1980s would suggest?

Engagement has a broad foreign policy justification. Because countries have multiple, cross-cutting policy objectives, it would be self-defeating for them to let any one objective preempt efforts to pursue other objectives. Human rights is but one important issue in Sino-American relations. Therefore, human rights concerns must be integrated with interests such as trade and security into a general bilateral strategy. Comprehensive engagement attempts to maximize linkages and increase overall influence and achievements.

Engagement, however, also has a human rights justification, which is my focus here. Markets, it is argued, lead those whom they make prosperous to demand civil and political rights. Economic "freedom" leads to calls for political freedom that repressive governments cannot ultimately resist. Therefore, fostering economic development contributes to fundamental political change. Manipulating selfish economic interests thus becomes a way to realize civil and political rights. Economic support that appears to help stabilize repression actually undermines it.

This argument seems suspiciously convenient and a bit too clever. Reliance on automatic mechanisms, even if successful, fails to respond to the psychological and moral need to do what one can, here and now, to resist or at least respond to gross and systematic violations of human rights. Waiting for other processes to have a positive human rights impact also consigns those who face a moderately efficient state, unusually ruthless oppressors, or a highly underdeveloped economy to decades of suffering.

But public criticisms and sanctions have almost never caused structural political change. And in countries such as South Korea, prosperity does seem to have supported demands for political opening. Engagement thus deserves a hearing. However, there must be active engagement in the human rights struggle of people living today—*constructive* engagement rather than passive waiting.

Consider an analogy with peace. Democracies, understood as regimes that respect internationally recognized political rights, almost never fight wars with other democracies. Therefore, if markets produce civil and political rights, they will also produce peace. But no one would seriously suggest handing national security policy over to the Department of Commerce and the International Monetary Fund. While waiting for peace, immediate, concrete security interests and objectives must be addressed. Likewise, we cannot sit back and wait for markets to produce human rights—if we take human rights seriously as a foreign policy objective.

Long-term economic engagement may be a significant background force for human rights. But if engagement is to be a defensible human rights strategy, both sides must be at least minimally engaged in an active, ongoing process of change. For example, target governments must be expected to produce at least the symbolic gestures and incremental changes that public strategies of pressure regularly yield. This requires foreign states to retain and periodically use the reactive and punitive tactics of the 1970s and 1980s.

Likewise, if business involvement is justified in part because it helps human rights, we can legitimately ask for concrete evidence of that help. At the very least we can ask that firms avoid actively denying human rights—for example, that they try to avoid actively participating in state efforts to suppress free trade unions. During the MFN debate, however, American business opposed even voluntary codes of conduct for firms operating in China. Resisting even such modest measures of responsibility and accountability raises suspicions that profits, not human rights, lay behind the appeal for a return to business as usual in China.

Consider also a full-page ad by a major U.S. company under the title "Staying the Course Benefits Others."[21] The company argued that in the future as in the past, "rather than cut and run from trouble spots, we will work to change them." And this company explicitly pointed to civil and political rights. "Particularly in countries where attention is focused on civil and political reforms . . . great global companies can be a positive force for change." As Caiman J. Cohen of the Business Coalition for

U.S. China Trade put it during the 1994 MFN debate, trade is "part of the solution—not part of the problem."[22]

The ad's first example was Indonesia. The "bloodshed and months of turmoil" mentioned were in fact one of the most massive episodes of state terrorism anywhere in the world in the 1960s. But the "change" the company touted was new jobs and the transfer of skills and technology. This did not even address, let alone contribute to ending, systematic violations of civil and political rights. And the same government that murdered several hundred thousand Indonesians—estimates ranged up to a million when this ad appeared—remained in power for more than three decades afterward.

The ad also pointed to Nigeria, which suffered under a succession of military dictatorships over three decades and which became a prominent international concern when human rights and environmental activist Ken Saro-Wiwa was executed in 1995. Again, though, the "change" produced was jobs. Although these jobs were a significant benefit to the 1,500 Nigerian employees and their families, there was no connection between employment and civil and political reforms.

Multinational corporations that provide good jobs to local workers and are aware of the social consequences of their activities are indeed desirable. But the issue in engagement arguments is the link between the pursuit of profits and political change. Treating workers well is irrelevant—especially for firms that see human rights almost entirely as a matter of civil and political, not economic and social, rights. If the best advocates of engagement can point to are regimes that have for decades successfully resisted structural political change, the strategy would seem to be completely bankrupt.

My point is not to criticize business in general, let alone particular firms. Quite the contrary, taking business seriously as a human rights agent may open exciting avenues for thinking about implementing human rights. In reminding us that the transnational sector includes not just NGOs but also multinational corporations (MNCs), this perspective suggests largely unexplored responsibilities and opportunities. The question is whether business is committed to active constructive engagement or merely passive waiting and hoping.

If businesses are simply pursuing profits, let them argue for the single-minded pursuit of gain. Debate then would focus on when, where, or even whether firms should pursue human rights objectives. If they claim to be making a human rights contribution, though, it is fair to ask for the evidence.

Similar challenges must be posed to advocates of foreign policy engagement. "Engagement" may easily degenerate into inaction against, or even collusion with, human rights violators. In engaging others, we must not become disengaged from our own values and day-to-day efforts to realize them. Even where we cannot remove murderers from power, we must speak out against them and do what we can to make them pay for their crimes.

5. POSTSCRIPT: "ASIAN VALUES"

As I noted earlier, China claimed to be pursuing a distinctive and defensible human rights strategy emphasizing economic and social rights. This sort of argument has become associated with broader cultural relativist arguments based on "Asian values." Although often little more than a device by which repressive regimes try to cover their abuses, appeals to Asian values do tap a widespread concern. Human rights are based on autonomous individuals. Traditional Asian values, however, emphasize harmony and deference within a group, not individual assertion.

I readily grant the existence of cultural differences between East and West. Cultural facts, however, are only a starting point for moral argument. Traditional practices require political and moral, not antiquarian, justifications. That things used to be done this way ought to earn a hearing for any cultural practice. But it is a justification for only morally indifferent legal and political practices (for example, the attire of judges).

Many relativist arguments mistakenly assume that culture is constant and of timeless value. Are practices that evolved in small, static, agricultural communities relevant in anonymous urban societies with immense social and demographic mobility? How similar are traditional leaders and authoritarian leaders of intrusive modern states? Are traditional social sanctions legitimate when they are coercively enforced by modern states? What is the role of local autonomy, so much a part of traditional social and political relations, in the face of national, regional, and even global economic and political integration?

Most relativist arguments reflect a belief that because Asians did things a certain way in the past, they have no desire to do them differently today. "Popular pressures against East and Southeast Asian governments may not be so much for 'human rights' or 'democracy' but for good government: effective, efficient, and honest administrations able to provide security and basic needs with good opportunities for an improved standard of living."[23] Even if most ordinary Asians have traditionally expected (or hoped for) no more from their governments, I am skeptical that this remains true today.

Consider the pressures for democratization throughout the region, which have been relatively successful in South Korea and Taiwan but resisted by governments in, for example, China and Burma. These examples suggest that good government is not what Asians aspire to but the minimum they are willing to accept. And even good government, especially in the long run, seems unlikely in the absence of human rights.

Civil and political rights provide clear and powerful mechanisms to ascertain whether rulers' claims about popular preferences are true. For all their shortcomings—which I emphasize in §9.5—open and fair elections do provide a relatively reliable gauge of popular political preferences.

Furthermore, even if a country "enjoys" an efficient and relatively benevolent and incorruptible despot or ruling elite—for example, Lee Kuan Yew's relatively "soft" and clean authoritarianism made a small and resource-poor Singapore into an Asian "tiger"—maintaining that over time without civil and political rights seems unlikely, especially with the immense amounts of wealth made available by economic growth. Closed politics is a recipe for colossal corruption, as most countries in the region illustrate. There is an internal self-correcting logic to human rights that is absent in traditional mechanisms (at least when they operate in modern states rather than small and relatively static communities).

If such benefits of human rights could be purchased only at the cost of cultural suicide, the choice might boil down to that of the lesser evil. But international human rights norms no more ask Asians to give up their culture than John Locke or Thomas Paine asked the English, Americans, or French to give up theirs. In fact, they leave considerable space for distinctively Asian implementations.

In Chapter 3, I called this general position weak cultural relativism. Strong relativism, which I reject, allows significant variations from the list of rights specified in the Universal Declaration. Weak relativism holds that tradition is no excuse for violating internationally recognized human rights specified at the level of generality of torture, free speech, and health care. But that leaves much room for historical, cultural, and even idiosyncratic variations in implementing these rights.

For example, Article 5 of the Universal Declaration of Human Rights states, "No one shall be subjected to torture or to cruel, inhuman, or degrading treatment or punishment." A weak relativist position holds that because countries may not legitimately pick and choose among internationally recognized human rights, they must respect the prohibition on torture. No matter how deep the tradition of inquisitorial or punitive torture, locals should not be forced to continue to endure it, and outsiders should be free to condemn it.

The general prohibition of cruel and unusual punishment, however, leaves much room for legitimate variation. Consider the controversial punishment of Michael Fay in Singapore in 1994. For all the hoopla, caning someone who vandalized hundreds of thousands of dollars of private property is obviously permissible. It is probably less cruel than imprisonment in most of the world's jails. And a country like the United States, which executes children and warehouses criminals in unsafe and demeaning prisons, has no cause for indignation. What is universal is the overarching right, not the details of its implementation in any one country, no matter how highly that country thinks of itself.

Variations, however, are limited to the (relatively narrow) band specified by the core content of the right in question. Crucifying, drawing and quartering, or disemboweling a criminal are obvious examples of practices that today are by any reasonable standard inhumane. Amputation, no matter how "humanely" carried out, almost certainly exceeds the limits. Execution is a matter of intense controversy, although international opinion continues to move against it.

Should we be concerned about "imposing" such limits? Not, I would suggest, when we are talking at this high level of generality. And not when the "imposition" involves persuasion and modest forms of coercion such as reductions in aid. Invading a country that tortures convicts probably exceeds the moral bounds of proportionality and would undoubtedly violate the international legal prohibition of intervention. But it would be entirely proper for states and NGOs to raise the issue diplomatically and even forcefully pursue it in public.

Pornography is a subject often raised by proponents of strong relativism, especially in Asia. But free speech simply does not require licensing pornography. Most, and perhaps all, states limit some graphic sexual depictions, most notably those involving children. Most also restrict the depiction of certain acts and control the display of pornographic material.

Speech is no less appropriately limited by public morals than by public safety—although the meanings of these terms are themselves controversial, as are questions of how to strike a balance. Drawing the lines is always an appropriate matter for local controversy. Only in extreme cases, though, would it be an appropriate matter of international human rights concern. The effort of some Taliban members in Afghanistan to prohibit all pictures showing unveiled women is perhaps such a case. But even here, the central issues concern discrimination against women and wholesale restrictions of free expression, not pornography.

To take a very different example, the Asian preference for consensual decision making is likely to have an impact on party politics. Consider de facto one-party rule in postwar Japan. If peaceful political activity by opposition parties is unhindered and elections are carried out fairly and under more or less impartial rules, the choice of voters cannot be legitimately challenged by outsiders.

Gender equality, which touches everyday life for most people, is an unusually sensitive issue. International norms do require that all human rights be available equally to men and women. Therefore, to deny women the right to run for political office is to violate their human rights. They remain free, however, not to run. And voters are at liberty to treat sex as a relevant consideration in casting their ballots. Article 22 of the Universal Declaration recognizes the right of everyone to work and to free choice of employment. Therefore, women cannot be legitimately prevented from working outside the home. They are free, however, to choose not to.

I realize that discussion of free choice is somewhat forced. Women (everywhere) are under immense pressure to conform to traditional role models. But that is precisely why the right to choose is so crucial. Traditional roles must be protected by the state neither more nor less than nontraditional roles.

"Free" choice is rarely without costs in any domain. Human rights focus on assuring that the state is not directly or indirectly responsible for those costs. At the very least, acts that would be prohibited were they done by men to men must be treated as especially heinous offenses when they are done to women for acting "uppity." And no group can be allowed to use the apparatus of the state to impose rules and roles on any other group that they do not impose on themselves.

Human rights empower those individuals and groups who will bear the consequences to decide, within certain limits, how they will lead their lives. Differences across time and place are thus not merely justifiable but are to be expected. For example, we would anticipate that Asian children would give greater weight to the views and interests of their families than would North American children. Confrontational political tactics are likely to be less common (and less successful). There is likely to be less social tolerance of deviant behavior of all types.

These examples, however, illustrate individuals exercising the same human rights in different ways, not a different conception of human rights. And they do not suggest the legitimacy of prohibiting "Western" exercises of these rights. To prevent children who meet requirements such as minimum age and genetic distance from marrying their chosen partner is to deny the human right to marry and found a family. Families are free to ostracize rebellious children. The state, however, has no business enforcing family preferences on adult children.

A human rights approach rests on the idea that people are probably best suited, and in any case entitled, to choose the good life for themselves. If Asians value family over self, they will exercise personal rights with family consequences in mind. If they value harmony and order over liberty, they will exercise their civil liberties in a harmonious and orderly fashion. Such choices must be respected. But only so long as they remain matters of choice.

Cultural traditions are socially created legacies. Some are good, others bad. Many are morally indifferent. Some have become irrelevant. Traditions change with time. And in most cases, no group, either inside or outside that society, is entitled to impose on others its views of which traditions are (or deserve to be) living and which are dead.

The choices and opportunities guaranteed by human rights make people (co)creators of their traditions rather than passive subjects to them. If people accept traditions, they will reproduce them as valued parts of their life. If not, so much the worse for tradition—and those who would impose it on others. The necessity of massive state coercion is the clearest evidence that we are dealing with "traditions" that do not have the respect of local people and do not deserve ours.

DISCUSSION QUESTIONS

1. The evidence from Eastern Europe in late 1989 suggests that the Chinese government was basically right in its political assessment: substantial liberalization would have meant the end of Communist Party rule. Does this provide some justification for the Chinese crackdown? Why should some states but not others be allowed to preserve their social and political systems?

2. Why was there so much fuss over the Tiananmen massacre? China had for decades regularly engaged in massive repression and yet received only mild criticism. In the 1950s, tens of millions died as the direct and indirect results of China's "development" policy. And in the Great Proletarian Cultural Revolution of the 1960s, perhaps as many as hundreds of millions had their basic human rights aggressively assaulted. Why were these earlier abuses largely ignored? Why did Tiananmen receive extensive global condemnation?

3. Why should killing several hundred people in order to restore things to pretty much the way they were one year earlier make such a difference? Could one argue that the real failure in international human rights policies toward China lay not in responses to Tiananmen but in acquiescence to decades of massive totalitarian repression, not just before but also after Tiananmen?

4. Who was hurt by economic sanctions? To what extent do sanctions merely victimize innocent people a second time? Consider Iraq in the 1990s, an even more extreme case, where by some estimates thousands of children a month were dying from food shortages caused in significant part by international sanctions.

But if we don't impose economic sanctions, aren't we, in effect, giving in to regimes that use their people as hostages? If leading opposition figures request the imposition of sanctions, as was the case in South Africa in the 1980s, that may simplify our problem. But what about cases such as Iraq (or China), where the opposition has been silenced or eliminated?

5. What were the various motives in Japan's response to Tiananmen? In the U.S. response? How would you evaluate these priorities?

6. How long should a country be punished for even a shocking act such as the Tiananmen massacre? At some point, the past needs to be forgotten—not buried, but set aside in foreign policy. How do we know when that is? Are there general standards or guidelines that we might develop or draw on?

7. I suggested that the abandonment of sanctions by U.S. allies largely justified an American return to business as usual. Isn't this troubling? Should we really let others dictate to us when to lift (or impose) sanctions? Aren't we obliged to follow our own judgments? At what cost?

8. Which "bottom line" do you find most persuasive? Did China literally get away with murder? Or did it suffer unusually strong and sustained international punishment? Both?

9. Repressive regimes regularly release prisoners or improve their treatment in response to international pressure. This may make us feel that we have achieved something. But just how important is it? Does it amount to just treating symptoms while ignoring causes?

10. What, though, is the alternative? It is clear that outside actors can often make things a lot worse. But how often have they made things systematically better? Can outsiders really do much more than apply Band-Aids to wounds while they wait for deeper social, economic, and political forces to transform local people's tolerance for repression?

11. Should businesses be in the "business" of improving human rights? If you believe that individuals and governments have a responsibility to do something about international human rights, why shouldn't businesses have similar responsibilities? If businesses don't have any international human rights responsibilities, why should states or individuals?

12. If businesses have no human rights responsibilities overseas, why do we impose them on businesses operating domestically? Answer the same question for individual citizens. And then for governments.

13. *Do* international human rights standards leave enough room for incorporating Asian (or other foreign) values into national human rights practices? If you think not, what particular examples seem most compelling?

14. Why shouldn't a government be able to enforce long-established traditions? Does the fact that they have to be imposed by force really make that much difference? Don't laws that protect internationally recognized human rights also have to be enforced and thus in some important sense be imposed? What is the difference?

SUGGESTED READINGS

Readers interested in further information on international responses to Tiananmen ought to begin with Rosemary Foot, *Rights Beyond Borders: The Global Community and the Struggle over Human Rights in China* (Oxford: Oxford University Press, 2000). This almost perfect book covers foreign policy, the United Nations, and NGO activity carefully and subtly and gives a superb sense of the possibilities for and limits on international human rights action. It is also very readable. (Rosemary Foot, "Bush, China and Human Rights," *Survival* 45 [2003]: 167–186, extends the discussion into the post-9/11 era.) Those who want just a single chapter can do no better than Merle Goodman, "China," in *Implementing U.S. Human Rights Policy*, ed. Debra Liang-Fenton (Washington, D.C.: U.S. Institute of Peace Press, 2004).

Roberta Cohen, "People's Republic of China: The Human Rights Exception," *Human Rights Quarterly*, (November 1987): 447–549, provides essential background reading that demonstrates how the international responses to Tiananmen were a dramatic change. Elizabeth Economy and Michel Oksenberg, *China Joins the World* (New York: Council on Foreign Relations Press, 1999), and Alastair Iain Johnston and Robert S. Ross, eds., *Engaging China: The Management of an Emerging Power* (London: Routledge, 1999) examine broader changes in China's relations with the external world in the 1990s, focusing primarily on economic and security issues.

Perry Link's *Evening Chats in Beijing: Probing China's Predicament* (New York: W. W. Norton, 1992) is an immensely engaging attempt to capture the political climate of Tiananmen and the ideas and aspirations of many Chinese democrats. Zhang Liang, Andrew J. Nathan, and Perry Link, eds., *The Tiananmen Papers* (New York: Public Affairs, 2001) provides an inside account of high-level decision making. Stephen C. Angle and Marina Svensson, trans. and eds., *The Chinese Human Rights Reader: Documents and Commentary, 1900–2000* (Armonk, N.Y.: M. E. Sharpe, 2001) provides an excellent selection of primary source material for the whole twentieth century. Ann Kent, *Between Freedom and Subsistence: China and Human Rights* (Hong Kong: Oxford University Press, 1993) is a useful general discussion of human rights issues in China, although the book is beginning to show its age.

David M. Lampton, "America's China Policy in the Age of the Finance Minister: Clinton Ends Linkage," *China Quarterly*, no. 139 (1994): 597–621, provides an excellent, detailed, but brief review of Clinton's China policy, focusing on the 1994 MFN decision. The UN response is covered in detail in Ann Kent, "China and the International Human Rights Regime: A Case Study of Multilateral Monitoring, 1989–1994," *Human Rights Quarterly* 17 (February 1995): 1–47. David Arase, "Japanese Policy Toward Democracy and Human Rights in Asia," *Asian Survey* 33 (October 1993): 935–952, sets Japan's post-Tiananmen policy in a broader regional context. Michael A. Santoro, *Profits and Principles: Global Capitalism and Human Rights in China* (Ithaca: Cornell University Press, 2000) provides a good discussion of the highly contentious issue of the role of international business.

For an unusually subtle Chinese defense by the director of the Department of American Studies at the Shanghai Institute of International Studies, see Ding Xinghao, "Managing Sino-American Relations in a Changing World," *Asian Survey* 31

(December 1991): 1155–1169. More typically vitriolic and xenophobic official Chinese statements can be found in numerous issues of the *Beijing Review*. For 1989, for example, see the issues of June 12, p. 10; July 3, pp. 9–10; July 10, pp. 18–21; July 17, pp. 18–19; July 31, p. 10; and November 20, pp. 38–40. John F. Cooper, "Peking's Post-Tiananmen Foreign Policy: The Human Rights Factor," *Issues and Studies* 30 (October 1994): 49–73, reviews in detail the evolution of China's response. China's official White Paper is *Human Rights in China* (Beijing: Information Office of the State Council, 1991).

On Asian values, the best general reader is Joanne Bauer and Daniel Bell, eds., *The East Asian Challenge for Human Rights* (Cambridge: Cambridge University Press, 1999). Anthony J. Langlois, *The Politics of Justice and Human Rights* (Cambridge: Cambridge University Press, 2001) is an excellent sympathetic critique that takes the idea of Asian values seriously while strongly criticizing the manipulation of the idea by Asian autocrats. Chapters 1 and 2 provide perhaps the best overview of the nature of the debate available in a single place.

Two unusually clear and subtle presentations of the argument for distinctive Asian values are Bilahari Kausikan, "Asia's Different Standard," *Foreign Policy* 92 (1993): 24–41, and Fareed Zakaria, "Culture Is Destiny: A Conversation with Lee Kuan Yew," *Foreign Affairs* 73 (March/April 1994): 109–126. James T. H. Chang, ed., *Human Rights and International Relations in the Asia-Pacific Region* (London: Pinter, 1995) is another good reader. The essays by Joseph Chan ("The Asian Challenge to Universal Human Rights") and Yash Ghai ("Asian Perspectives on Human Rights") present subtle discussions that should appeal to readers who find my presentation extreme or one-sided. Although not focused explicitly on human rights, Daniel A. Bell and Hahm Chaibong, eds., *Confucianism for the Modern World* (Cambridge: Cambridge University Press, 2003) offers a series of thoughtful and creative efforts to apply Confucian ideas to the social and political problems of modernity.

8

◄○►

Humanitarian Intervention
Against Genocide

As we saw in Chapter 1, the Convention on the Prevention and Punishment of the Crime of Genocide was adopted by the UN General Assembly on December 9, 1948, the day before the Universal Declaration was adopted. This reflected the central role of the Holocaust in crystallizing international concern with human rights. It also marked the separation of **genocide** from human rights as an international issue. A separate legal regime was developed for genocide, largely divorced from the global human rights regime (see §5.4.C). Genocide is not mentioned in either the Universal Declaration or the Covenants.

The 1990s reintegrated—or more accurately, finally integrated—genocide into the international human rights mainstream. The development of a practice of armed **humanitarian intervention** was driven by a combination of a new geopolitical environment, in which rivalry between the superpowers no longer prevented humanitarian action, and the unusually brutal character of the "new wars" of the 1990s. These were largely wars within, rather than between, states, often in failing or failed states. They also largely ignored the traditional distinction between civilians and soldiers, often intentionally targeting the civilian population of the other side, even defining those civilians as "the enemy."

Here I will focus on the former Yugoslavia, particularly Bosnia-Herzegovina and Kosovo, which introduced **ethnic cleansing** to the world's vocabulary. I will also discuss more briefly the dramatically contrasting examples of Rwanda and East Timor.

1. THE BREAKUP OF
YUGOSLAVIA AND ETHNIC CLEANSING

Yugoslavia was created at the end of World War I, an assemblage of the previously independent states of Serbia and Montenegro; the former Austro-Hungarian territories of Slovenia, Istria, Dalmatia, Croatia-Slavonia, Vojvodina, and Bosnia-Herzegovina;

and Macedonia, taken from the Ottoman Empire's last European holdings. Although the dominant Serbs actively discriminated against other ethnic groups, different groups lived together more or less harmoniously (except under Nazi occupation during World War II, when Serbs were targets of genocide by the Ustasha, a local fascist group operating a puppet regime in Croatia).

After World War II, the communists, the strongest force in the resistance to Nazi rule, reorganized Yugoslavia under the leadership of Josip Broz Tito. In a country in which every ethnic group was a minority (roughly two-fifths were Serbs and a fifth Croats), a federal political system granted substantial power to six republics (Serbia, Croatia, Slovenia, Bosnia-Herzegovina, Macedonia, and Montenegro) and two autonomous regions within Serbia (Kosovo and Vojvodina).

For three decades, the system worked tolerably well. In fact, the considerable repressive apparatus of the totalitarian Yugoslav state was used to discourage, and when necessary suppress, claims of superiority by Serbs or separatist demands by non-Serbs. The principal exception was the treatment of ethnic Albanians in the Kosovo region of Serbia, who faced far more discrimination than other ethnic groups in Yugoslavia and were denied the recognition and self-rule that went with federal republic status.

Tito's death in 1980 removed the final arbiter from a system with immense potential for squabbling and deadlock. The accumulated inefficiencies of decades of control by nine separate communist bureaucracies (six republics, two autonomous regions, and the federal government) ended the economic growth that had greased the system. Yugoslavia by the mid-1980s faced a political and economic crisis well beyond the capabilities of its ruling communist functionaries.

In 1987, Slobodan Milosevic in the Serbian republic seized on Serbian nationalism to consolidate his rapid rise to power. Milosevic skillfully manipulated memories of Ustasha brutality, fostering hatred of Croats. He also invoked the quasi-mythic grandeur of Serbia's fourteenth-century Nemanjid dynasty. He aimed to paint Muslims, who made up about one-sixth of the country's population, as enemies, successors of the Turks who had defeated medieval Serbia. Milosevic also revived and cleverly manipulated the Serbian Orthodox Church to further mobilize hostility toward Croats, most of whom are Roman Catholics or Muslims.

Using tactics made famous by Hitler, Milosevic and his front group, the Committee for the Protection of Kosovo Serbs and Montenegrins, organized over one hundred mass protest demonstrations with average turnouts of over 50,000 people. By February 1989, the last vestiges of regional autonomy in Vojvodina and Kosovo were eliminated, and Milosevic allies had been installed in Montenegro, leaving him in firm control of half the country.

Kosovo, whose population was 90 percent ethnic Albanian, was particularly severely repressed. Milosevic abolished the regional government, imposed Serbo-Croatian as the official language, banned Albanian-language media, and fired 6,000 teachers after prohibiting Albanian-language secondary schooling. All of this was presented as "liberating" Serbs from the remnants of the "Turkish yoke." In

July 1991, he even confiscated 6,000 hectares of land for distribution to Serbian colonists.

The other republics, especially Slovenia and Croatia, had the legal and political power to block this proto-fascist Serbian imperialism. But this only led Milosevic to rely increasingly on extralegal means. For example, arms shipments for the Yugoslav National Army (JNA) "inexplicably" began appearing in Knin, Croatia's principal Serbian city, in the fall of 1990. After negotiations to maintain a loose federal system failed, Slovenia and Croatia, fearing the worst, declared independence on June 25, 1991.

Slovenia was ethnically homogeneous, prosperous, and did not share a border with Serbia. Although it was invaded by Serbia the day after it declared independence, by early July a cease-fire negotiated by the European Community effectively secured Slovenian independence.

The conflict thus shifted to Croatia, where violence had been escalating since the ethnically Serb region of Krajina had not only declared autonomy in March 1991 but asked for union with Serbia. Both Croats and Serbs manipulated memories of past discrimination and atrocities—and prepared to inflict new ones.

In the last four months of 1991, Serbs and Croats fought a brutal war that targeted "opposition" civilians no less than opposing armies. The fifteenth cease-fire, reached on January 2, 1992, and supported by 14,000 peacekeepers of the United Nations Protection Force in the former Yugoslavia (UNPROFOR), lasted about a year. Serbian separatists, however, controlled one-third of Croatia's territory, which remained under (sporadically violent) dispute until a successful Croatian offensive in summer 1995.

With the stalemate in Croatia, international attention turned to an even more brutal conflict in Bosnia-Herzegovina (hereafter referred to as simply Bosnia). Bosnia was in many ways a microcosm of Yugoslavia, itself a republic of minorities. In the 1991 census, 44 percent identified themselves as "ethnic Muslims," 32 percent as Serbs, 17 percent as Croats, and 7 percent as "Yugoslavs" or other. In fact, Bosnia was the only Yugoslav republic without an ethnic majority.

Although Bosnia had been a place of considerable ethnic tolerance, especially in the capital of Sarajevo, when war did come it hit with unprecedented ferocity. And Bosnia's Muslims were particularly vulnerable because they lacked the support of neighboring co-nationals.

Separatist Serbs gained control of two-thirds of the territory of Bosnia. They perfected and popularized the strategy of ethnic cleansing, introduced by Croatian Serbs the preceding year, which aimed to rid "Serbian" territory of Muslim (and Croat) residents through systematic terror and sporadic murder. Serbian military action was directed as much at innocent civilians as at opposing soldiers. Relief supplies were blocked. Villages and cities were shelled from a distance when they could not be shot up and burned at close range. Captured men were routinely tortured or murdered, often en masse. Women, children, and the elderly were sometimes shot, often physically abused, but more typically "merely" forced to flee. And Serbian soldiers systematically, on orders from superiors, raped young Muslim women, to degrade them and shame their families.

2. RESPONDING TO THE BOSNIAN GENOCIDE

Out of a pre-war Yugoslav population of 23 million, about 250,000 people died and 2.5 million were left homeless in the various Yugoslav wars of the early 1990s. The international community was often, and in many ways justly, criticized for doing too little, too late. However, it did not sit by and idly watch the genocide, as it had during the cold war in places like Uganda and Cambodia.

The UN Security Council "experiment[ed] with about every available form of coercion short of war."[1] An arms embargo was imposed on all parties. Serbia was both suspended by the Conference on Security and Co-operation in Europe (CSCE) (see §5.5.D) and placed under a comprehensive UN economic embargo. Intensive and extended multilateral diplomatic efforts sought an end to the conflict. Peacekeepers were sent to protect civilians and facilitate the delivery of humanitarian assistance. A special war crimes tribunal was established. When a peace agreement was finally signed at Dayton in December 1995, there were 50,000 UN peacekeepers in the former Yugoslavia, at an annual cost of about $2 billion. Three thousand humanitarian workers were in the field. The United Nations High Commissioner for Refugees alone was spending $500 million a year on humanitarian assistance.

Initial responses, however, were timid and largely reflected geopolitical concerns. The principal goal of the West, especially the United States, was to keep Yugoslavia intact. The Bush administration was willing to allow immense suffering to prevent Yugoslavia from becoming a precedent for an even more catastrophic breakup of the Soviet Union—which, it must be remembered, had not yet dissolved. (At that time, there was no way of knowing that its breakup would be anywhere near as peaceful as it ultimately proved to be.) Thus, even Slovenia, despite its democratic credentials and westward-leaning orientation, was pressured into formally remaining within the increasingly imaginary federal Yugoslavia.

By the time the war entered its Bosnian phase, however, the Soviet Union had already broken up. The EC had already recognized the independence of Croatia and Slovenia, and the United States followed suit in April 1992. Although geopolitical concerns continued to intrude—for example, politics within NATO, the problem of defining the post–cold war role of Russia, and Russia's political ties to Serbia complicated diplomatic and peacekeeping activities—for the remainder of the conflict, the United States, Europe, the United Nations, and even Russia maintained sustained efforts in human rights, humanitarian assistance, peacekeeping, and diplomacy that were without parallel during the cold war.

A. Multilateral Human Rights Agencies

In August 1992, at the first special session in its history, the UN Commission on Human Rights appointed Tadeusz Mazowiecki, former prime minister of Poland, as special rapporteur. Mazowiecki visited Bosnia on August 21–26 and confirmed "massive and grave violations of human rights" throughout Bosnia. A second mission in October concluded that "the Muslim population are the principal victims and are virtually threatened with extermination." A second special session of the Commission, held November 30 and December 1, 1992, condemned Serbia, the JNA, and leaders of Serb-controlled areas. Never before had the Commission responded with anything even close to such speed. The vigor of its response was also striking.

The Security Council also acted quickly and with resolve, beginning with an embargo on arms to all parties in the former Yugoslavia. At the end of May 1992, the council imposed trade sanctions on Serbia, to pressure Milosevic to end his support of the Bosnian Serbs. In August 1992, it condemned the violations of humanitarian law. In February 1993, the Security Council created a war crimes tribunal for the former Yugoslavia, which by 1996 was actively prosecuting war criminals.

The CSCE also acted rapidly and firmly, suspending Serbia's membership in July 1992. The condemnation of Serbia by the CSCE at its ministers' meeting in Stockholm in December 1992 was particularly important in creating momentum for establishing a war crimes tribunal.

All of these initiatives responded to, rather than stopped, the genocide. As we have seen, though, the international community has never seriously discussed giving coercive enforcement powers to multilateral human rights institutions. Multilateral human rights diplomacy must rely primarily on international public opinion, which, at least in the short run, has little effect on shameless butchers like the Bosnian Serbs. The UN Commission on Human Rights and the CSCE did everything they could do within their legal constraints. And the war crimes tribunal, the first since Nuremberg, was a major innovation. The "problem" was the refusal of states to confer greater power on multilateral human rights institutions, which most states considered preferable to the "solution" of transferring authority to an international agency that might force them to act more strongly.

B. Humanitarian Assistance

Humanitarian assistance aims to cope with some of war's most pressing human consequences. Humanitarian workers seek not to prevent violence but to ease the burden on civilian victims. Even these limited tasks, though, undercut the Serbian strategies of pursuing ethnic cleansing in the countryside and strangling Sarajevo. The Bosnian Serbs therefore saw humanitarian assistance as intensely political— which it was, given their strategy—and consistently used all means in their power, including force, to stop international relief from reaching its targets. Muslim and Croat forces also prevented aid deliveries, although much more irregularly.

Forcing recalcitrant parties to permit delivery of humanitarian assistance, however, must remain a task for other actors if the integrity and safety of humanitarian operations are to be assured. For reasons of both cost and sovereignty, the international community has only rarely used force to protect the flow of aid. In comparison to similar cases, the international humanitarian response in Bosnia was swift, sustained, and relatively effective. All the external parties pressed both the Bosnian

Serbs and the Milosevic government to allow humanitarian aid to flow. The United Nations used strong diplomatic pressure and (limited) force to deliver aid to more than 2 million people. UNPROFOR provided intelligence, occasional armed convoys, and a visible, vigilant presence that reduced attacks on civilians.

I do not mean to minimize the horrible suffering in Bosnia. More than one-third of Bosnia's people were forced to flee their homes, and most of the Bosnian Muslims who did not flee were forced to endure extended Serbian sieges. The more than 200,000 deaths in Croatia and Bosnia were proportionally equivalent to the deaths of about 5 million Americans.

Nonetheless, to have achieved more, those providing assistance would have had to issue a credible military threat to enter the conflict on the side of Bosnia's Muslims. Leading states simply were not willing to endorse such an option, preferring instead to rely on diplomacy, humanitarian assistance, and sanctions short of the punitive use of force.

C. Peacekeeping

UNPROFOR was a **peacekeeping** force. Peacekeeping involves interposing neutral forces *with the permission of the belligerents* in order to monitor or maintain a truce or settlement. Peacekeepers are lightly armed and are authorized to use force only for self-defense. The aim of peacekeeping is not to repulse or punish an aggressor. That is a job for collective security enforcement, as in the Gulf War of 1991.

UNPROFOR's mandate was restricted to limiting the extent and severity of the fighting. The international community condemned ethnic cleansing, and it was willing to prosecute those responsible once the fighting ended, but it would not take the military steps necessary to end the conflict. Genocide occurred in Bosnia because outside powers were unwilling to fight a war to stop it.

The task of UNPROFOR was less to prevent war (soldiers shooting soldiers) than to prevent war crimes (soldiers massacring civilians). To the Serbs, UNPROFOR represented a hostile external world frustrating their objectives, which they were well on their way to achieving when the UN intervened. They thus focused their efforts on subverting UNPROFOR and completing the ethnic cleansing of "their" country. This was a near-certain recipe for disaster.

The compromised mission of UNPROFOR came to be embodied in the institution of United Nations Protected Areas (UNPAs) or "safe areas." First established in 1992 in Croatia, they were extended to Bosnia in 1993. UN strategy increasingly came to focus on excluding the Bosnian Serbs from UNPAs in Srebenica, Goradze, Tuzla, Zepa, and Bihac (as well as Sarajevo, which had been under siege since March 1992).

These enclaves were intended to provide: (1) humanitarian refuge for victims of the fighting; (2) temporary frontiers across which "peace" was to be kept; and (3) barriers to ethnic cleansing. Although the Serbs showed some tolerance for the first of these objectives, they rejected the second and third. The "safe areas" thus were under constant pressure and sporadic attack. In the summer 1995, they collapsed.

Serbs resumed heavy shelling of Sarajevo at the end of May 1995, provoking retaliatory NATO air strikes near Pale. The Serbs counter-retaliated by shelling the safe areas. For example, 65 children were killed in a single artillery barrage on the center of Tuzla. In addition, 325 UN peacekeepers were taken hostage. NATO responding by sending 12,500 new troops armed not merely for self-defense but with significant air- and ground-fighting capabilities. The Serbian response was to transform the "safe areas" into killing zones.

In July 1995, Srebenica was overrun, as an appalled and ashamed UN contingent found itself able only to stand by and watch. Adult men were separated from the rest of the refugees, who were sent fleeing. Of the total "protected" population of about 40,000, more than 7,000 were slaughtered and buried in mass graves.

With people now dying as an unintended but very real consequence of the "best efforts" of the international community, the West, and particularly the United States, finally intervened. NATO air strikes increased in number and severity. Political pressure built up to end the arms embargo, which had helped the Serbs (who received Serbian and JNA weapons) and harmed the Muslims (who had access only to modest quantities of primarily small arms smuggled in with difficulty). NATO's intensified air strikes, coupled with the Croatian victories in Krajina and renewed pressure applied to Milosevic (who was being increasingly squeezed by the West), forced the Bosnian Serbs to the negotiating table.

In November 1995, a marathon three-week session at Wright Patterson Air Force Base in Dayton, Ohio, backed by immense U.S. pressure, produced a peace agreement on December 14, 1995. Throughout 1996, a 60,000-person multilateral Implementation Force (IFOR) supervised the military disengagement. This was followed by a 30,000-person Stabilization Force (SFOR), which was replaced at the end of 2004 by the European Union Force (EUFOR). Fragile political institutions for a federal Bosnia-Herzegovina were created, although even a decade after the Dayton peace agreement they still operate only with considerable direct international involvement. Ethnic violence, however, has been largely eliminated, and massive quantities of Western aid have contributed to significant reconstruction of the country.

D. Assessing the Bosnian Intervention

Bosnia in many ways represents a failure of international action. The international community waited three and a half years to meet Serb force with force. Although earlier military engagement might have had high human and financial costs, it almost certainly could have prevented much of the suffering of Bosnia's civilians and probably could have also reduced the total human, financial, and political costs.

Nonetheless, Bosnia and its people were, quite literally, kept alive. More than 2 million people received humanitarian assistance. International action helped to keep Sarajevo from falling, thus averting an even greater disaster. The arms embargo prevented an even larger bloodbath (especially if one attributes part of the relatively good record of the Bosnian Muslims to their lack of opportunities to exact revenge). UN peacekeepers sent to the border of Macedonia in December 1992 stopped the fighting from moving east and south. And for all its inadequacies, international action was relatively rapid and was much greater in scope than in any previous undertaking. Bosnia represented, and marked a crucial step in bringing about, a significant transformation in international responses to genocide.

Precedents, however, are made by later actions that treat them as constraining. They do not automatically cause comparable action in the future. Furthermore, their meaning changes as they become embedded in streams of action. The meaning of Bosnia emerged only as the international community confronted new genocides in Rwanda, Kosovo, and East Timor.

3. RWANDA

If Bosnia is the "success story" of the early 1990s, Rwanda was the great, and horribly tragic, failure.

Ethnic conflict in Rwanda was in large measure the creation of Belgian colonial rule. After receiving control over Rwanda from Germany after World War I, the Belgians exacerbated the tensions between the two main groups in the territory, the majority Hutu and the minority Tutsi. After having purged Hutus from the largely Tutsi elite, the Belgians used the Tutsi elite as an instrument of colonial domination, provoking understandable resentment from the Hutu majority.

In 1959, as independence was approaching, Hutu resentment turned into the violent assertion of political dominance. Some 20,000 Tutsis were massacred and another 200,000 were forced to flee. In the ensuing years, sporadic ethnic violence, with short bursts of genocidal killing (particularly in 1964 and 1974) marked politics in Rwanda, as well as in neighboring Burundi. The staggering scope of the violence that occurred in 1994, however, was unprecedented.

The prelude to genocide began in October 1990 when the Rwandan Patriotic Front, made up primarily of Tutsis living in refugee camps, invaded Rwanda from their bases in Uganda. The Hutu-dominated military government of Juvénal Habyarimana portrayed this as an attempt to (re)impose Tutsi domination and responded with increased repression. A cease-fire to this inconclusive conflict was finally negotiated in the summer of 1992. In August 1993, a fragile peace agreement was signed in Arusha, Tanzania.

Meanwhile, the Habyarimana government and its radical Hutu supporters established a network of Hutu militias *(interahamwe)*, which by the spring of 1994 numbered about 30,000. Radio stations, especially the government-controlled Radio Mille Collines, spread increasingly virulent anti-Tutsi propaganda. From the national cabinet down to local mayors, preparations were laid for a massive, organized campaign of violence against Tutsis and political opponents of the regime. The killings began on the night of April 6, 1994, after the plane carrying the presidents of both Rwanda and Burundi was shot down. (Responsibility remains a matter of considerable controversy.)

Individual contingents of the United Nations Assistance Mission in Rwanda (UNAMIR), a peacekeeping forcing observing implementation of the Arusha

Accords, tried to shelter some civilians. The formal mandate of UNAMIR, however, restricted the troops to monitoring. In any case, United Nations peacekeepers themselves quickly became targets. Ten Belgian soldiers were captured on April 7, tortured, and murdered.

Two weeks later, the Security Council unanimously agreed to cut the UNAMIR force from 2,500 to 270, despite estimates that more than 100,000 civilians had already been massacred. Not until April 30, when perhaps as many as half a million had been killed, did the Security Council even condemn the violence. Even then it pointedly refused to call it a genocide, admitting only that "acts of genocide" had been committed. The United States, as late as June, also continued to refer only to "acts of genocide," wary of the international legal obligation under the genocide convention to respond.

The world stood by and watched while more than 750,000 Rwandans out of a prewar population of about 6,750,000 (proportionally the equivalent of roughly 30 million deaths in the United States) were butchered in a little more than three months. And butchered is a brutally accurate term: The weapon of choice of many of the *génocidaires* was a simple machete. Another 2 million Rwandans fled to Zaire (now the Democratic Republic of the Congo).

All of this was particularly troubling because information was available—in the media, at the United Nations, and in the major governments involved (France, the United States, and Belgium)—that genocide was imminent. In January 1994 the commander of the UN force, General Roméo Dallaire, asked for, but was denied, permission to confiscate the weapons of the *interahamwe*. Throughout February and March, General Dallaire pled, with increasing desperation, for reinforcements and a more robust mandate, but the Security Council refused.

As we have noted, the United Nations is an intergovernmental organization, made up of and controlled by its member states. The Security Council is dominated by its five permanent members (China, France, Russia, the U.S., and U.K.), each of whom can veto Security Council action. In the case of Rwanda, four of the permanent powers actively opposed UN action. The United States had recently been forced to make a humiliating withdrawal from Somalia and was unwilling to consider involvement in another small, fractious African country. France, which considered itself to have special geopolitical interests in Central Africa, was wary of weakening its regional influence. Russia and China had "principled" objections, insisting that the conflict was an internal Rwandan matter. (Britain appeared not unwilling to consider stronger action but had no desire to lead on the issue of Rwanda.) All these political forces conspired against UN intervention. And in a cruel irony, Rwanda happened to occupy one of the ten rotating seats on the Security Council and used this position to minimize the scope and severity of the problem.

Because of the low-tech nature of the genocide, even as few as several thousand troops could have stopped much, probably even most, of the killing. However, those states with the knowledge and power to do something chose inaction, or worse. In their "defense," few expected anything like the scope of violence that occurred— although a willingness to tolerate tens of thousands of deaths is still shameful. As the tragedy unfolded, though, and appreciation grew of the opportunity for humanitarian action that had been forfeited, a deep sense of shame spread through the international community.

4. KOSOVO

When the next major humanitarian crisis arose, in Kosovo in 1998 and 1999, the contrasting lessons of Bosnia and Rwanda weighed heavily on the minds of decision makers and affected public opinion in many countries. In Bosnia, limited but real success had been achieved, despite rather difficult conditions. In Rwanda, relatively modest measures undertaken at modest costs almost certainly would have had immense humanitarian payoffs. Nonetheless, the worst genocide since World War II had been permitted to proceed, largely without international resistance. When the Kosovo crisis presented itself, key international actors, led by the Clinton administration in the United States and the Blair government in Britain, seem to have "learned" from Bosnia and Rwanda that successful humanitarian intervention was both (politically and logistically) possible and (morally, perhaps even politically) necessary.

Kosovo, as noted above, had been a region of Serbia, not a republic of Yugoslavia. This was crucial because when Yugoslavia, and then the Soviet Union, broke up, it did so according to the old internal boundaries. The model was the decolonization of the Western empires, where new states were created by following old colonial boundaries. Absurd as many of those boundaries were, they had the inestimable virtue of being long established. Anything else would have been a recipe for border wars. The breakup of Yugoslavia was treated as analogous to the dissolution of the Serbian empire, just as the breakup of the Soviet Union was treated as analogous to the dissolution of the Russian empire. Thus federal republics such as Serbia, Bosnia, and Slovenia, and Russia, Kazakhstan, and Georgia rather easily received local and international recognition of their independence. Other internal units, such as Kosovo in Serbia/Yugoslavia and Chechnya in Russia/USSR, did not.

As discussed above, this left Kosovo's ethnically Albanian population under the increasingly brutal domination of Serbia. Although the Milosevic government regularly hinted at its goal of "cleansing" Kosovo, it was not included in the Dayton settlement because Kosovo was neither independent nor a site of widespread fighting. Western leaders would soon regret this calculated concession to Serbia.

Throughout the mid-1990s, the Kosovo Liberation Army carried out sporadic, quite ineffective guerrilla operations that appear to have had very little popular support. The Serbian government, however, responded with increasingly brutal repression, including attacks on civilians. The Serb massacre of fifty-eight people in Perkazi in February 1998 initiated a spiral of escalation. In the following twelve months, about 1,000 people, mostly Kosovar civilians, were killed. Perhaps even more ominously, more than 400,000 were forced to flee their homes.

Some debate remains about the intent of the Milosevic government. The prevailing opinion in much of the West by early 1999 was that ethnic cleansing had begun in earnest. Efforts to get the Security Council to act were nonetheless blocked, primarily by Russia.

The Clinton administration, however, continued to argue forcefully that the lessons of Bosnia and Rwanda proved that early action was necessary. Britain and some other European states agreed. The problem was determining who would act, on what rationale, in the absence of Security Council authorization. Rather than act unilaterally, or create an ad hoc coalition, they decided to use NATO, the old cold war alliance against the Soviet Union that had for the past several years been trying to reinvent itself as a new kind of regional security organization.

A land invasion was ruled out, as the costs, in terms of troops mobilized and lives lost, were anticipated to be more than the public would accept. This left only air power. From March 24 to June 19, 1999, NATO forces carried out an increasingly punishing campaign of aerial bombardments, including repeated attacks on the Serbian capital of Belgrade.

The Serbian authorities took advantage of the attacks to put into action a well-coordinated campaign of ethnic cleansing. About 10,000 people were killed, and close to 1.5 million people were forced to flee their homes. Although it is not clear whether full-scale ethnic cleansing had begun before the bombing, it most certainly took place, on a massive scale, during the NATO attacks. And its speed and efficiency clearly indicated that Milosevic had, at the very least, a rather elaborate plan waiting to be implemented at the "right" moment.

Three features of the Kosovo intervention deserve special mention. First, it was undertaken as genocide began, or perhaps even before. In Bosnia, intervention occurred when genocide was well under way. In Rwanda, genocide was pretty much over when the international community finally intervened. The intervention in Kosovo marked the first time that international action came early, perhaps even pre-emptively.

Second, the intervention was undertaken despite the fact that the number of deaths was *relatively* low. The Serbian strategy of ethnic cleansing used targeted, largely exemplary violence to coerce people into fleeing the territory to be cleansed. Part of the motivation seems to have been a calculated attempt to stay under a perceived killing threshold for an international response. The international response, however, recognized and responded to genuine genocide—a violent attack against a people because of who they are—even though perhaps only several hundred, and certainly less than several thousand, people had been killed when the bombings began.

Third, regional powers acted on humanitarian grounds, in the absence of Security Council authorization or any other particularly powerful legal justification. In effect, the "negative precedent" of Rwanda—something has to be done—took priority over the usual requirements of authorization and legality.

5. THE AUTHORITY TO INTERVENE

Who is entitled to intervene on behalf of (potential) victims of genocide? Figure 8.1 distinguishes interveners by their mode of action (bilateral[2] or multilateral) and the scope of the community within or for which they act (global or regional).

FIGURE 8.1   Types of Interveners

	Global	Regional
Multilateral	United Nations	ECOWAS, NATO (?)
Bilateral	United States	India

The authority of multilateral interveners arises from legal, political, or moral recognition by the political communities that the organization or its members represent. Multilateral intervention necessitates the building of political coalitions across states. Although the requirement of multilateral consent does not entirely eliminate the influence of national selfishness, it does increase the likelihood of genuinely humanitarian motivation. At the very least, it makes the political self-interests involved somewhat less narrow. When the multilateral forum is the Security Council, any use of force that is authorized is likely to have a very central humanitarian dimension to it.

Bilateral actors may or may not have comparable recognition by broader political communities. It is an empirical question whether a great power acting bilaterally intervenes with authority or merely as a result of its superior power. The historical record clearly indicates that great powers have engaged in far more *anti*-humanitarian than humanitarian interventions, making multilateral intervention in general the preferred alternative for practical, let alone theoretical, reasons. Nonetheless, bilateral action by a great power with highly mixed motives may save lives that would be lost while waiting for a more "pure" multilateral intervention that never comes. Classic cold war examples include the conflict between India and East Pakistan (Bangladesh) and that of Vietnam in Cambodia (see also §9 below). Furthermore, bilateral actors, being politically autonomous, may be able to intervene when multilateral action is blocked.

Sometimes bilateral great power intervention rests almost entirely on selfish national interests, with little broader support among other states or in the target country. In such cases, the "authority" of the intervening state is much like that of the highwayman. But when bilateral actors intervene as de facto representatives of both victims and broader regional or international political communities, their actions may be more characteristic of the policeman.

The second dimension of this typology, the distinction between regional and global interveners, concerns the appropriate "level" for action within the international system. Regional and global actors, whether bilateral or multilateral, may have different capacities and authorities. For example, regional multilateral action may be easier because of greater common interests within the region. Regional actors may also have the advantage of superior knowledge or authority because they are "closer" to the problem. But if a regional organization is dominated by a regional hegemon (for example, Nigeria in ECOWAS or the United States in the OAS), it may be (perceived as) a captive of that state, undermining its legitimacy.[3]

Let us apply this typology to Kosovo. Global multilateral action was effectively blocked. China and Russia had a deep and relatively "principled" opposition to multilateral intervention. In addition, Russia had a much more selfish political interest in its relationship with Serbia.

The Organization for Security and Co-operation in Europe (OSCE, formerly the CSCE), the most obvious regional actor, lacked the unified political will needed to act in this particular case. Even if that will had been present, the OSCE has no legal authority to use force, and its leading members remain unwilling even to consider expanding its authority in that direction. A similar political situation also precluded action through either the European Union (EU) or the Council of Europe. Furthermore, bilateral action by the United States was definitely unacceptable to most, if not all, the states of the EU, as well as most states outside of Europe.

Nonetheless, the states of the EU were unwilling—at least after a lot of political lobbying—to stand by and allow genocide to occur in Kosovo. NATO provided a convenient organizational forum for an action that was needed but for institutional reasons could not be authorized in other fora. Faced with a genuine dilemma, the members of NATO decided that intervention was the lesser of two evils.

Assuming that pre-emptive humanitarian intervention will generally be blocked at the global level, concerned states seem to be left with the uncomfortable alternatives of inaction, bilateral action, or regional multilateral action. This is a recipe for uneven and "selective" responses to humanitarian crises. There are large parts of the world where there is neither a viable regional actor nor a bilateral actor that has the necessary power, legitimacy, and commitment. Selectivity is further increased by the effective exemption of the permanent members of the Security Council from United Nations action, and a comparable regional exemption of leading local powers such as Nigeria and India.[4] Furthermore, the 2005 intervention of the African Union in Sudan suggests that relying on regional multilateral intervention can be a way for global actors to avoid taking difficult or costly action. In addition, regional interveners are likely to be more focused on genuine humanitarian needs than bilateral interveners.

So long as we retain an international system structured around sovereign states—that is, for the foreseeable future—we are not likely to be able to evade these problems of authority and inequality. But the humanitarian interventions in Kosovo and especially in East Timor, to which we turn next, suggest that we are finally beginning to grapple with them.

6. EAST TIMOR

The absence of Security Council authorization made Kosovo a problematic precedent for an emerging international legal right to humanitarian intervention. However, the UN-authorized intervention in East Timor later that year largely removed doubts that a right to humanitarian intervention was being established as a matter of positive international law.

The island of Timor was divided during the colonial era into East Timor and West Timor, held respectively by Portugal and the Netherlands. When Indonesia achieved independence, it received (only) the Dutch holdings in the East Indies (including West Timor, but not East Timor). Neither then, nor in 1960, when the United Nations reorganized its decolonization machinery and classified East Timor as a Portuguese colony, did Indonesia claim East Timor.

In 1974, a coup removed the military government in Portugal, the only Western state still holding a substantial colonial empire (most notably Angola and Mozambique). The new government was both much more sympathetic to decolonization and distracted from, if not positively disinterested in, its tiny holding in the East Indies. Taking advantage of the situation, East Timor declared independence. Indonesia, however, had other ideas and invaded East Timor on October 16, 1975. Although Indonesian rule was viewed as illegal by most countries and rejected by most of the local population, the government in Jakarta attempted to consolidate its rule through often brutal repression punctuated by special regional development assistance that suggested material benefits would follow from compliance.

Particularly striking was the Dili Massacre of November 12, 1991. Indonesian troops opened fire on peaceful pro-independence demonstrators killing at least 271 and wounding at least another 275. In addition, more than 250 people disappeared. Besides being unusually brutal, the Dili Massacre was widely publicized, mobilizing public opinion in Portugal, where there was still considerable unease over allowing Indonesia to take control so easily, and in Australia, where the government's strong support for Indonesia came under increasing public pressure. No less importantly, the initial news coverage, followed by a British television documentary in January 1992 using graphic video footage of the massacre, galvanized international attention in many countries previously uninterested in East Timor's plight, in much the same way (although on a smaller scale) as the Sharpeville Massacre did in South Africa (see §5.4.B).

Eventually, international pressure induced Indonesia to permit a UN-sponsored referendum on independence. In the election, held on August 30, 1999, more than three-quarters of the votes favored independence. Indonesia, however, balked. Local "militias," which were already operating with the acquiescence, and often the active assistance, of local Indonesian military authorities, went on a sustained rampage that increasingly appeared to have genocidal aspirations. Perhaps a fifth to a quarter of the population was forced to flee their homes, with thousands tracked down and killed in churches, schools, and public buildings where they sought refuge.

On September 15, 1999, the Security Council unanimously created the International Force for East Timor (INTERFET), an Australian-led force that, in combination with intensive international political pressure and diplomatic activity, restored order and produced Indonesian acquiescence in Timorese independence. On October 25, 1999, the Security Council established the United Nations Transitional Administration in East Timor (UNTAET). On November 1, 1999, the last Indonesian troops left East Timor. On May 20, 2002, East Timor achieved full independence. Accurate figures are difficult to come by, but it is likely that at least 100,000 people, and perhaps substantially more, were killed during the quarter century of Indonesian rule; that is, something on the order of one in every eight, or perhaps even one in every six, persons perished in the struggle for Timorese independence.

The technical illegality of Indonesia's occupation of East Timor certainly facilitated such a strong response. Many countries that would have otherwise been reluctant to accept a UN military operation were able to view this as a decolonization issue more than a humanitarian intervention. It is clear, though, that leading international actors had Kosovo (and Rwanda) very much in mind. East Timor was widely understood as a turning point, completing the transformation of Bosnia from an isolated exception to a precedent in a continuing stream of customary law formation that in some complex way also included Kosovo.

The power of the emerging norm of humanitarian intervention against genocide is illustrated by the fact that almost all the conventional political and material considerations counseled inaction. Indonesia is a large, strategically located country (the world's largest Muslim country) with considerable oil resources and a strong record of support for the West. In addition, there were well-founded fears, both within and outside Indonesia, about the susceptibility of the country to secessionist movements, some of which have been carrying on armed struggles for decades. East Timor, by contrast, is small, poor—whatever its oil resources, they are dwarfed by those of Indonesia—and of little material interest to anyone except its own people. Nonetheless, in the end, and with surprisingly little controversy, the major Western powers and the rest of the Security Council agreed to send in military force to protect the Timorese people and enforce their decision to attain independence.

7. A RIGHT TO HUMANITARIAN
INTERVENTION AGAINST GENOCIDE

The 1990s witnessed a dramatic transformation. At the beginning of the decade, positive international law clearly did not authorize armed humanitarian intervention, even in response to massive genocide. No interventions against genocide had been widely endorsed as legal. The Security Council had the authority to determine that genocide represented a threat to international peace and security. In principle, therefore, it could authorize international enforcement action. In practice, it had never exercised such theoretical authority. The standard pattern, right through the end of the cold war, was for the international community to wring its hands in anguish as genocide played itself out in Cambodia, Uganda, East Pakistan, and elsewhere. Neighboring states, usually with powerful geopolitical interests, sometimes intervened, but none of these interventions was accepted as legal, and most were not even justified as primarily humanitarian by the interveners.

By the end of the decade/century/millennium, however, the Security Council had authorized not only humanitarian interventions in Bosnia and East Timor but also peacekeeping operations in Sierra Leone, Liberia, and the Democratic Republic of the Congo that had a central humanitarian component. In the early 2000s, additional operations were approved for Côte d'Ivoire, Burundi, and Sudan. Today we have both a well-established norm and a surprisingly clear pattern of practice of Security Council–authorized humanitarian intervention against genocide. And the example of Kosovo suggests that there might even be considerable international toleration for genuinely humanitarian interventions taken in response to Security Council inaction.

The genocide in Darfur, which is continuing as I write this (at the beginning of 2006), clearly shows that needed UN action is not always forthcoming or adequate. Nonetheless, today, in sharp contrast to just fifteen years ago, humanitarian intervention is not merely accepted as legitimate but expected. When, as in Darfur, the international humanitarian response is inadequate, the burden of justification now lies principally with the UN, the United States, and regionally powerful actors that permit or impose inaction. The refusal to intervene against genocide, rather than intervention, requires special justification today.

Nonetheless, at least two limits on the existing right to humanitarian intervention deserve mention. First, it applies only in cases of genocide. There is no evidence to suggest that it is spilling over into other, more common, human rights violations. Even in cases of torture and slavery, where international human rights norms are increasingly being applied in national courts in Europe, North America, and elsewhere, the use of force has never been authorized and is rarely even suggested.

This poses a moral paradox. We seem willing to respond to certain kinds of graphic and concentrated suffering but to tolerate substantially greater suffering so long as it remains more diffuse.

This paradox is by no means restricted to genocide. Consider, for example, the contrast between the relatively strong international reaction to the Tiananmen massacre, where hundreds of people died in a relatively telegenic way, and the weak reactions to the systematic and severe daily violations of the human rights of hundreds of millions of Chinese citizens. Even more striking is the substantial international willingness to respond to famines but a parallel unwillingness to deal with the far more serious problem of malnutrition.

If we take seriously the interdependence of all human rights, and if we take seriously the idea that human rights are about a life of dignity, not mere life, then the restriction of humanitarian intervention to genocide is highly problematic. In the following section I suggest that it can be morally defended as a reflection of the limits of the extent of overlapping international consensus. Here I want to underscore the way in which this indicates the continuing centrality of state sovereignty. States may have renounced their traditional immunity from coercive international action in the case of genocide. They most definitely have not done so in the case of human rights more broadly.

Psychologically, the restriction to genocide acknowledges the realities of mobilizing an international response adequate to consider bearing the considerable costs associated with military humanitarian intervention—especially if that intervention is not to be restricted to high-altitude bombing. More broadly, the restriction to genocide reflects the continuing priority of local and national communities. It remains rare—but no longer unheard of—for states and citizens to be willing to bear the costs of rescuing foreigners from the depredations of "their own" governments. An active sense of cosmopolitan moral community remains very, very thin.

The second major limitation of the contemporary right to humanitarian intervention is that it is (only) a right, not a duty. Although the report of the Secretary-General's Independent International Commission on Intervention and State Sovereignty was titled *The Responsibility to Protect,* no such responsibility is recognized in international law.

There may be a strong moral case for claiming that the international community has an obligation to protect victims of genocide. Beyond the simple humanitarian justification, it might be argued that such a duty is implied by the very structure of the global human rights regime. National implementation of internationally recognized human rights, which is a basic principal of the regime, if it is more than a political compromise with the reality of state power, must assume that states are capable and not unwilling to protect the human rights of their citizens. But this is patently absurd in the case of genocidal regimes, and it would be a cruel hoax to continue to act on such an assumption. In such cases, it might be argued, residual responsibility reverts to the international community.

Regardless of the moral arguments, international law recognizes only a right to humanitarian intervention, and then only when authorized by the Security Council. As with any right, the Security Council may choose not to exercise it. It is free to intervene, or not, as it sees fit. And the grounds for both acting and not acting may legitimately appeal to a variety of non-moral considerations.

8. JUSTIFYING HUMANITARIAN INTERVENTION

The preceding discussion points to the complexities of justifying humanitarian intervention in contemporary international politics. Morality, law, and politics all are involved, often in conflicting ways.

The moral case for humanitarian intervention against genocide is relatively unproblematic. In §3.6 I used John Rawls's notion of overlapping consensus to circumvent disputes over foundational theories of human rights. In much the same way, we can see today an overlapping consensus on the use of armed force against genocide. Whatever their differences, most contemporary moral and religious doctrines agree that genocide is the kind of international crime that in principle justifies armed humanitarian intervention. Whatever one's moral theory—or at least across a very wide range of common theories and principles—*this* kind of suffering cannot be permitted.

Yet, states and international organizations are not unencumbered moral agents. They are also subjects of international law and deeply political actors, and international law and politics impose their own standards of justification.

As we have seen, the principles of sovereignty and nonintervention provide a strong prima facie case against armed intervention. In addition, the principle that force can be used only for self-defense also poses a powerful prima facie constraint. Whatever the force of moral justifications, questions of legality are also of vital importance in determining whether any particular humanitarian intervention is "justified."

Throughout the cold war, morality justified humanitarian intervention, but international law prohibited it. Today, in the case of genocide, law and morality largely converge. But as we saw in the cases of Rwanda and Kosovo, states still face a problem when the substantive standard of protecting victims of genocide conflicts with the international legal requirement of UN Security Council authorization.

"Justification" becomes even more complicated when we recognize that states, in addition to being moral and legal agents, are also political actors. National leaders are *supposed* to take into account the political standard of the national interest. In addition to acting in accordance with the demands of law, morality, and humanity, they should consult the interests of their own state (and perhaps the interests of international society).

States, as noted above, are (at most) entitled, not obliged, to intervene. Political interests may justify inaction that is morally demanded and legally warranted. In fact, it is essential that potential interveners consider the material and political costs, to themselves and others, of undertaking a morally and legally justifiable intervention. No less importantly, political interests—or at least the absence of competing political interests—may be a crucial final element in reaching a decision to act on moral and legal justifications. And there is nothing wrong with this.

How we balance these competing standards is, of course, a matter of intense controversy, both in general and in any particular case. But justifying humanitarian intervention requires that we take into account the full range of relevant moral, legal, and political principles—making "justification" a remarkably complex matter in many cases.

9. TYPES OF JUSTIFIABILITY

At least six senses of "justification" are regularly appealed to in cases of humanitarian intervention. The intervention may be what I call authorized, permitted, contested, excusable, tolerable, or justified but failed.

The simplest case is full *authorization*: The intervention fully meets the substantive demands of all the relevant legal and moral standards. East Timor is an example.

An intervention is *permitted* when it is neither authorized nor prohibited. Most standard understandings of the principle of nonintervention suggest that humanitarian intervention would rarely, if ever, fall into this category. Sovereignty is a foundational legal concept of the society of states. In the absence of clear legal authority to contravene prima facie sovereign rights, we have, at best, a case of competing standards.

Such cases involve what I call *contested* justifications: Different standards point in different directions.[5] Positive authorization, as I have defined it, requires that *all* relevant standards be satisfied. Where *a* prohibits action but *b* permits it, *a* is treated as trumping *b*. It is no less plausible, though, to see *a* and *b* as offsetting one another, either completely (thus leaving the actor at liberty) or partially. In such cases, intervention is *both* (positively) "justified" and (positively) "unjustified." Kosovo provides an excellent illustration. As the Independent International Commission on Kosovo put it, the intervention was illegal but legitimate.

Two kinds of contested cases deserve special mention. The first arises where the intervention is judged "unjustified," all things considered, but is nonetheless *excusable*. Typically, the excuse appeals to a conflicting but subordinate standard. Consider stealing food to feed one's family. Although the law clearly prohibits theft, the moral obligation to one's family may bear considerable weight as a mitigating factor even in a court of law, especially at the time of sentencing. Competing standards make us disinclined to say that the action is simply unjustified, even if it is appropriately punished.

The second case is an intervention that may be judged "justified," but in a significantly weaker sense of the term, which I call (merely) *tolerable*. An excusable intervention involves *intentionally* producing some positively desirable state of affairs through the use of unacceptable means. In contrast, a tolerable intervention either produces a good result largely unintentionally or is simply the lesser of two evils. For example, if we interpret the Vietnamese intervention that removed Pol Pot and the Khmer Rouge from power in Cambodia as an effort to impose a quasi-imperial regional hegemony through force, it was, at best, merely tolerable.

Compare this to the Tanzanian intervention that overthrew Idi Amin in Uganda in 1979. Although clearly unjustifiable according to positive international and regional law, it did remove a barbarous regime, at relatively modest cost (assuming that we need not attribute the later atrocities of the second Obote regime to the Tanzanians). Furthermore, narrow self-interest seems to have played a relatively small part in the decision to intervene. As a result, Tanzania was not sanctioned, except verbally (and even that rather lightly). In fact, it received considerable informal and popular support. Its behavior was treated as excusable, and in some sense perhaps even commendable. Many people interpreted the NATO intervention in Kosovo in these terms, especially after it succeeded.

With merely tolerable acts, though, the underlying principle (for example, conquest of a neighbor) cannot be widely endorsed. Although we should not deny their positive humanitarian consequences, neither should we give much credit to those who produced these results. They are very much like fortunate accidents.

This points to still another set of competing standards, namely, intentions and consequences. The rationale for undertaking an action is important to our evaluation. Results, however, also carry some weight. In the best of all worlds, humanitarian aims will underlie an intervention that has positive humanitarian consequences.

But, as we have already noted, good results need not arise from good intentions. And good intentions are no guarantee of humanitarian consequences.

Results that are both seriously bad and due to the negligence of the intervener may even overwhelm the initial justification for intervention. In other cases, however, the intervener will do everything "right" and yet still fail to achieve humanitarian results. To hold that failure alone makes an intervention unjustified would hold interveners up to second guessing that not only is unfair but would tend to deter desirable justifications. Therefore, I suggest that such interventions be classed as *justified failures*.

Another sort of conflict of standards arises when interveners have mixed motives. Humanitarian interventions typically are costly, both financially and in the risks to which they expose soldiers. States may occasionally accept such risks for purely humanitarian reasons. There is even growing evidence that a number of states are coming to see preventing or stopping systematic gross human rights violations as part of their national interest. But purely moral motives have been, and are likely to remain, rare.

Although the extent of humanitarian motivation certainly should be taken into account, nonhumanitarian motives do not necessarily reduce the justifiability of an intervention. Some political motives do not conflict with either humanitarian norms or international law. Even when particular political motives do conflict with important international norms, we need to *balance* the competing motives. So long as there are significant humanitarian motivations, interventions undertaken with mixed motives often will be contested or excusable, even where they are not authorized or permitted.

The standard charge of inconsistency raises the final conflict of standards that I consider here. Critics often present the impure as trumping the pure: Because one did not intervene in A, which is in all essential ways similar to B, intervening in B is somehow unjustified, or at least suspect. Such an argument, however, reflects an absurd perfectionism that would paralyze states not just in cases of humanitarian intervention but in almost all areas of endeavor.

Inconsistency arguments do have real force when they point to blatant partisanship: for example, supporting a practice among friends but intervening when an enemy does the same thing. Consistency per se certainly is desirable, for all kinds of political, psychological, and perhaps even moral reasons. But as Peter Baehr nicely put it, "One act of commission is not invalidated by many acts of omission."[6] Inconsistent need not mean unjustified.

10. CHANGING CONCEPTIONS OF SECURITY

The developing international practice of humanitarian intervention reflects not only the growing spread and deepening penetration of international human rights norms but also new post–cold war conceptions of security. Traditionally, "security" in international relations has referred to *national* security, and in particular the security of the state. National security has typically been seen as having primarily military and economic dimensions: protecting one's own territory from attack, projecting power abroad in the pursuit of other vital interests, protecting jobs, incomes, and production capabilities at home, and pursuing economic objectives overseas.

Thus understood, there is no necessary or even obvious connection between security and human rights. Indeed, ruling regimes have frequently seen (national) security and human rights as competing concerns. Consider, for example, the Southern Cone in the 1970s (see Chapter 4), the Soviet bloc during the cold war, and the United States during the McCarthy era.

Scholars and activists in peace studies, conflict resolution, and human rights have long challenged this understanding. In the past two decades, states and international organizations have also begun to consider new visions of security that are much more complementary to human rights.

A crucial international turning point was the Conference on Security and Co-operation in Europe (CSCE) and the Helsinki Final Act of 1975 (see §5.5.D). Although the human rights dimension of the Helsinki process ultimately proved to be of greatest importance, it was primarily a *security* agreement. Human rights were not merely explicitly addressed within the context of a major security agreement between the superpowers and their allies, but indirectly presented as a security issue in their own right.

A national security focus certainly was not abandoned. Security, however, was given a *personal* dimension as well. In a series of CSCE follow-up conferences, a number of Western states increasingly pushed the notion that in addition to the security of states, the security of individuals must be a central international political concern. Security, in other words, could be threatened not only by forces outside the state but by the state itself.

The Helsinki process, however, provided no significant direct role for foreign states in implementing human rights. The periodic Helsinki review conferences were diplomatic forums where sanctions were restricted to verbal shaming. The Helsinki process thus continued to reflect a hard and rigid conception of state sovereignty.

Nonetheless, this changing conception of security appears to be central to the emerging practice of humanitarian intervention. "Security" that leaves citizens subject to massacre by their own government no longer passes the "straight face" test.[7] Our conception of security has been expanded to include a minimal level of personal security against one's government, at least in the case of genocide.

DISCUSSION QUESTIONS

1. How do you interpret the rapid switch from ethnic tolerance to violent ethnic mobilization in the former Yugoslavia? Clearly we are not dealing with "primordial" animosities, especially in the case of Serbs and Croats, who had no significant political contact with one another until the twentieth century. But what do you imagine the relative mix was between deep but repressed animosities and the opportunistic manipulation of differences that lead to social and political discrimination? Which explanation is more frightening?

2. The evidence of the post–cold war era suggests a new willingness to act in response to genocide and humanitarian crises. How do you interpret its significance for the future? What are the prospects for "spillover" into either action to prevent (not merely respond to) genocide or coercive action against other, more "ordinary" types of human rights violations?

3. Is there any moral or theoretical significance in the sharp discrepancy in responses to genocide and responses to other kinds of human rights violations? What *dangers* are posed to international human rights policies when we respond forcefully only to unusually photogenic suffering? In thinking about this issue, consider the analogy of relatively strong international responses to famine but much more modest responses to the more serious problem of malnutrition.

4. In recent years there has been much talk of a clash of civilizations and the development of anti-Islamic attitudes in the West, especially in the United States. How does Bosnia fit into such arguments? Some have charged that the West did not do more because the Bosnians were Muslims. Others have pointed to the responses in Bosnia and in Kosovo to show how the West was able to distinguish between politicized Islamists and ordinary adherents of one of the world's great religions. Which reading seems more correct?

5. The former Yugoslavia has been used in arguments about the place of race in contemporary Western foreign policies. Here the comparison is with Rwanda. Did the West do more to stop genocide in Croatia and Bosnia because the victims were white, than in Rwanda, where the victims were black? What other explanations might there be? Is it as simple as the fact that the killing in Rwanda was over quickly? Remember the length of time it took to get the West seriously involved in Bosnia.

6. Bosnia and Rwanda illustrate a willingness to respond to genocide *after* it has occurred. Why is there no comparable international willingness to respond to *prevent* genocide? Is Kosovo the exception that proves the rule?

7. The war crimes tribunal for the former Yugoslavia, the parallel process for war crimes in Rwanda, and the creation of the International Criminal Court have finally introduced an element of personal international legal responsibility to human rights violations, at least in the case of genocidal warfare. This is obviously of great symbolic significance. But what is its practical value? In the particular cases? In the future? In answering these questions, try to recall the earlier discussions of the role of normative transformation and the relative strengths and weaknesses of individual petition procedures.

8. Do I present an unfair treatment of nationalism? What about the "good" side, embodied in values such as patriotism? More generally, aren't there values in groups and group loyalties that I have systematically undervalued in the highly individualistic account in both this and the preceding chapter?

9. Isn't there a paradox, or worse, in my criticism of nationalism and my acceptance of states as the basis of the international human rights system?
10. Why isn't the principle of humanitarian intervention spilling over to human rights violations other than genocide? Is this good or bad?
11. Would the world be a better place if there were a responsibility to protect victims of genocide? What about victims of other human rights violations?
12. Is justification for humanitarian intervention really as complex as suggested in this chapter? Isn't it more a simple case of choosing between the obvious moral obligation to act against genocide and the unwillingness to pay the costs of discharging that obligation?
13. Is the linkage between humanitarian intervention and changing conceptions of security as clear as suggested at the end of this chapter? As significant? How much of a difference does it make to say that a government cannot massacre its own citizens in great numbers, while pretty much anything else it does is overlooked? Isn't that the lesson not just of the cases considered in this chapter but of China as well? And even of the leading cold war cases? As long as you can repress your people without resorting to mass murder, doesn't sovereignty still protect even incredibly vicious states? Consider, for example, North Korea. Is it any less deserving of humanitarian intervention than Serbia or Indonesia? Consider the question again, taking nuclear weapons out of the picture.

SUGGESTED READINGS

Although this chapter focuses its attention narrowly on international responses to genocide, readers are likely to be interested in further sources on the broader issue. Dinah L. Shelton, ed., *Encyclopedia of Genocide and Crimes Against Humanity* (Detroit: Macmillan Reference, 2005) is an authoritative three-volume reference work. Good recent works with wide coverage include Benjamin A. Valentino, *Final Solutions: Mass Killing and Genocide in the Twentieth Century* (Ithaca: Cornell University Press, 2004), Martin Shaw, *War and Genocide: Organized Killing in Modern Society* (Cambridge: Polity Press, 2003), and Patricia Marchak, *Reigns of Terror* (Montreal: McGill-Queens University Press, 2003). For broad historical perspectives, see Robert Gellately and Ben Kiernan, eds., *The Specter of Genocide: Mass Murder in Historical Perspective* (Cambridge: Cambridge University Press, 2003), and William L. Hewitt, ed., *Defining the Horrific: Readings on Genocide and Holocaust in the 20th Century* (Upper Saddle River, N.J.: Pearson Education, 2004).

William A. Schabas, *Genocide in International Law: The Crime of Crimes* (Cambridge: Cambridge University Press, 2000) is authoritative on the international law of genocide. Adam Jones, ed., *Gendercide and Genocide* (Nashville, Tenn.: Vanderbilt University Press, 2004) provides a good introduction to some of the gendered dimensions of genocide. Jane Stromseth, ed., *Accountability for Atrocities: National and International Responses* (Ardsley, N.Y.: Transnational, 2003) provides a good overview of the problems of and possibilities for legal remedies. (See also the readings on transitional justice and reconciliation in the last three paragraphs of the suggested readings for Chapter 4.) James Waller, *Becoming Evil: How Ordinary People Commit Genocide and Mass Killing* (Oxford: Oxford University Press, 2002) offers an interesting perspective on how genocide becomes possible.

Three relatively brief readings stand out for thinking about the broad issue of humanitarian intervention. The essential starting point is Michael Walzer, *Just and Unjust Wars* (New York: Basic Books, 1977), pp. 53–63, 101–108. This classic book lays out a strong ethical-legal defense of sovereignty (as a reflection of the rights of individual and communal self-determination) and then argues no less powerfully for a limited right to humanitarian intervention in cases of enslavement or massacre that shock the moral conscience of mankind. Terry Nardin, "The Moral Basis of Humanitarian Intervention," *Ethics and International Affairs* 16 (2002): 57–70 is also essential reading, contrasting more statist defenses such as Walzer's with an alternative tradition that makes direct appeals to substantive principles of natural law and justice. Much recent debate has been structured around *The Responsibility to Protect*, the report of the International Commission on Intervention and State Sovereignty (available online at http://www.iciss.ca/members-en.asp), which can be read as an effort both to codify the normative progress of the 1990s and to begin a conversation over a more robust doctrine of armed humanitarian intervention.

There is now an immense international legal and political literature on the topic. J. L. Holzgref and Robert O. Keohane, eds., *Humanitarian Intervention: Ethical, Legal, and Political Dilemmas* (Cambridge: Cambridge University Press, 2003) and Jennifer M. Welsh, ed., *Humanitarian Intervention and International Relations* (Oxford: Oxford University Press, 2004) provide excellent statements of most leading mainstream perspectives. Nick Wheeler's *Saving Strangers: Humanitarian Intervention in International Society* (Oxford: Oxford University Press, 2000) is perhaps the best single book on the topic considered as an issue in international relations. It is particularly strong on cold war–era practice and its transformation in the 1990s. Two other valuable and often cited works with a more legal focus are Sean D. Murphy, *Humanitarian Intervention: The United Nations in an Evolving World Order* (Philadelphia: University of Pennsylvania Press, 1996), and Fernando R. Teson, *Humanitarian Intervention: An Inquiry into Law and Morality*, 2nd ed. (Irvington-on-Hudson, N.Y.: Transnational, 1997). Watanabe Koji, ed., *Humanitarian Intervention: The Evolving Asian Debate* (Tokyo and Washington, D.C.: Japan Center for International Exchange and Brookings Institution Press, 2003) is useful for its non-Western focus.

Among more critical perspectives, David Chandler's *From Kosovo to Kabul: Human Rights and International Intervention* (London: Pluto Press, 2002) is particularly notable. He offers a spirited reading of the rise of so-called humanitarian interventions as an expression of American hegemony. David Rieff is a prolific journalist who has long been an insightful critic of armed humanitarianism. Two good examples of his work are *At the Point of a Gun: Democratic Dreams and Armed Intervention* (New York: Simon & Schuster, 2005), and *A Bed for the Night: Humanitarianism in Crisis* (New York: Simon & Schuster, 2002). See also, Roberto Belloni, "Is Humanitarianism

Part of the Problem? Nine Theses," http://bcsia.ksg.harvard.edu/BCSIA_content/documents/Belloni.pdf.

Among article-length pieces, the following four cover much of the spectrum of views—and all are quite readable: Mohammed Ayoob, "Humanitarian Intervention and State Sovereignty," *International Journal of Human Rights* 6 (2002): 81–102; Jarat Chopra and Thomas G. Weiss, "Sovereignty Under Siege: From Intervention to Humanitarian Space," in *Beyond Westphalia? State Sovereignty and International Intervention*, ed. G. M. Lyons and M. Mastanduno (Baltimore: Johns Hopkins University Press, 1995); Kelly Kate Pease and David P. Forsythe, "Human Rights, Humanitarian Intervention, and World Politics," *Human Rights Quarterly* 15 (May 1993): 290–314; Ved P. Nanda, Thomas F. Muther Jr., and Amy E. Eckert, "Tragedies in Somalia, Yugoslavia, Haiti, Rwanda and Liberia: Revisiting the Validity of Humanitarian Intervention Under International Law, Part II," *Denver Journal of International Law and Policy* 26 (Winter 1998): 827–869. Although there is little support for the claim that humanitarian intervention has become legal for severe human rights violations other than genocide, Julie Mertus, "Reconsidering the Legality of Humanitarian Intervention: Lessons from Kosovo," *William and Mary Law Review* 41 (May 2000): 1743–1787, attempts to argue to this conclusion.

Samantha Power, '*A Problem from Hell': America and the Age of Genocide* (New York: Basic Books, 2002) is a well-written, thoughtful, and engaging, even gripping, account that includes extended case studies of Bosnia, Rwanda, and Kosovo. Peter Ronayne, *Never Again? The United States and the Prevention and Punishment of Genocide Since the Holocaust* (Lanham, Md.: Rowman & Littlefield, 2001) tells a similar story, with less verve but greater economy, and includes good case studies of Bosnia and Rwanda. John Shattuck, *Freedom on Fire: Human Rights Wars and America's Response* (Cambridge: Harvard University Press, 2003) is a thoughtful account by a former assistant secretary of state.

On the Kosovo intervention, there is no better starting point than Albrecht Schnabel and Ramesh Thakur, eds., *Kosovo and the Challenge of Humanitarian Intervention: Selective Indignation, Collective Action, and International Citizenship* (Tokyo: United Nations University Press, 2000). This remarkable volume not only covers broad issues such as sovereignty, citizenship, and responsibility but includes a dozen excellent brief chapters on the foreign policies of the great powers as well as many smaller powers. The other essential source is the report of the Independent International Commission on Kosovo, available online at http://www.reliefweb.int/library/documents/thekosovoreport.htm. Ken Booth, ed., *The Kosovo Tragedy: The Human Rights Dimensions* (London: Frank Cass, 2001) is a good collection of (largely critical) analyses. Florian Bieber and Zidas Daskalovski, eds., *Understanding the War in Kosovo* (London: Frank Cass, 2003) usefully explores both internal and international dimensions of the conflict.

The literature on Bosnia is much more extensive, but there is no obvious place to start, as with the volume on Kosovo by Schnabel and Thakur. Among the more useful books are Sabrina P. Ramet, *Balkan Babel: The Disintegration of Yugoslavia from the Death of Tito to the Fall of Milosevic*, 4th ed. (Boulder: Westview, 2002), Tom Gallagher, *The Balkans After the Cold War: From Tyranny to Tragedy* (London:

Routledge, 2003), and Jeffrey S. Morton, ed., *Reflections on the Balkan Wars: Ten Years after the Break Up of Yugoslavia* (Houndmills, U.K.: Palgrave Macmillan, 2004). Misha Glenny, *The Balkans: Nationalism, War, and the Great Powers, 1804–1999* (New York: Viking, 2000) is a very readable volume that places the conflict in a broad historical setting. Jon Western, "Bosnia," in *Implementing U.S. Human Rights Policy,* ed. Debra Liang-Fenton (Washington, D.C.: U.S. Institute of Peace Press, 2004) is a good brief account of the American response. See also "Bosnia: No More Than Witnesses at a Funeral," in the Powers and Ronayne books cited above. Peter Siani-Davies, ed., *International Intervention in the Balkans Since 1995* (London: Routledge, 2003) is useful for considering post-Dayton Bosnia and Kosovo together.

On Rwanda, Michael Barnett, *Eyewitness to a Genocide: The United Nations and Rwanda* (Ithaca: Cornell University Press, 2002) is excellent on the role of the United Nations. Bruce D. Jones, *Peacemaking in Rwanda: The Dynamics of Failure* (Boulder: Lynne Rienner, 2001) focuses on the failure of peacemaking. Christian P. Scherrer, *Genocide and Crisis in Central Africa* (Westport, Conn.: Praeger, 2002) places the genocide in a broader regional context. Mahmood Mamdani, *When Victims Become Killers: Colonialism, Nativism, and the Genocide in Rwanda* (Princeton: Princeton University Press, 2001) provides an excellent account of the development of ethnic conflict, showing very clearly that there was nothing "primordial" about it. Other useful volumes include Nigel Eltringham, *Accounting for Horror: Post-Genocide Debates In Rwanda* (London: Pluto Press, 2004), Alan J. Kuperman, *The Limits of Humanitarian Intervention: Genocide in Rwanda* (Washington, D.C.: Brookings Institution Press, 2001), Kingsley Moghalu, *Rwanda's Genocide: The Politics of Global Justice* (London: Palgrave Macmillan, 2005), and Linda Malvern, *Conspiracy to Murder: The Rwanda Genocide* (London: Verso, 2004). For a good brief account of American (in)action, see Alison Desforges, "Rwanda," in *Implementing U.S. Human Rights Policy,* ed. Debra Liang-Fenton (Washington, D.C.: U.S. Institute of Peace Press, 2004). Once again, the chapters in the Power (Chapter 10) and Roynane (Chapter 4) books cited above are also useful.

The recently released Final Report of the Commission for Reception, Truth and Reconciliation in East Timor (available online at http://www.easttimor-reconciliation.org/ and http://www.ictj.org/cavr.report.asp) is perhaps the best place to start for further reading on that conflict. See also Joseph Nevins, *A Not-So-Distant Horror: Mass Violence in East Timor* (Ithaca: Cornell University Press, 2005). Michael G. Smith and Moreen Dee, *Peacekeeping in East Timor: The Path to Independence* (Boulder: Lynne Rienner, 2003) provides one of the few book-length discussions of the international response.

9

Globalization, the State, and Human Rights

It is difficult today to talk about international relations for more than a few minutes without at least raising the issue of globalization. (The other unavoidable issue is terrorism, the subject of the next chapter.) What are the implications of globalization for human rights? I focus here on globalization as a set of processes that challenges the political, economic, and cultural primacy of the state. Because the global human rights regime, as we have seen, relies primarily on the national implementation of internationally recognized human rights, this suggests that globalization is undermining the principal mechanism for implementing and enforcing human rights. This chapter focuses in particular on the challenge that globalization poses to economic and social rights.

1. GLOBALIZATION

Globalization is generally understood literally to mean the creation of structures and processes that span the entire globe. People, goods, and ideas increasingly move and interact across—even irrespective of—national territorial boundaries. Politics, markets, and culture become transnational and even global rather than national.

Most prominently, globalization has involved the spread of capitalist markets and the growing transnational integration of market-based systems of production and distribution into the farthest reaches of the globe. Understood in this sense, though, globalization goes back at least to the maritime expansion of the West that began in the late fifteenth century. Karl Marx provided the classic analysis of globalization thus understood. His account of colonialism emphasized the progressive economic and social changes introduced by capitalist markets no less than the brutalities of capitalist imperialism. Marx also emphasized the internationalist perspective of the working-class movement, which he saw as a response to the transnational logic of capital accumulation.

Other aspects of globalization also have roots running back centuries. For example, today's telecommunications revolution, involving high-speed digital networks with ever growing bandwidth, has a lineage that stretches back not just through television, radio, telephone, and telegraph but to steamships, railroads, and clipper ships. The globalizing spread of ideas and practices of electoral democracy and individual human rights builds on the centuries-old spread of sovereign territorial states and the incorporation of the entire globe into what was originally the European states system.

Nonetheless, it is plausible to suggest that the pace of change has accelerated, with important qualitative differences that have become evident in the decades on either side of the year 2000. Political action above, below, outside, around, and even without much concern for the state is much more of a practical reality for a much greater number of individuals and groups, in a much greater number of arenas and areas of concern, than it has been for at least the preceding century and a half—which in many ways looks like the era of the nation-state.

Globalization today increasingly involves truly global, as opposed to merely international, processes and issues. Although international relations certainly remain central, supranational, transnational, subnational, and global issues, actors, and identities are much more prominent now than in the past.

This is particularly striking when we look beyond global flows of goods and services to globalizing changes in ideas and identities. The growing transnational consolidation of capitalist markets has been accompanied by the spread of neoliberal market ideology and its enforcement by multilateral agencies and multinational banks and corporations. The spread of American or Western economic and political power has been matched by the spread of Western economic and political ideas and models—including human rights. Revolutions in communication and transportation have even begun to alter our understandings of space and time, how we conceive of ourselves and the communities in which our lives are embedded, and how we relate to government.

The sovereign nation-state, which in the nineteenth and twentieth centuries typically appeared to be the optimal size for economic, political, and social organization, today often appears too small. Faced with ever larger and stronger business enterprises that are adopting a truly global perspective, even powerful states are losing control over aspects of their economies and polities that they had grown accustomed to dominating. Regional and international organizations increasingly influence, and sometimes even make, decisions that once were unquestionably the province of states. Transnational nongovernmental organizations now exert powerful and sophisticated pressures on states (and businesses) on issues such as human rights and the environment.

At the same time, globalization often makes the state appear too large. Local and regional autonomy has become a common theme, especially (but not only) in Europe. Spain has perhaps gone the farthest among nonfederal states in devolving spending and decision making to regional authorities, not just in the Basque and Catalan regions but throughout the country. Consider also the creation of the Scottish and Welsh parliaments in the United Kingdom, the emergence of the Northern

League as a powerful political force in Italy, and the revival of regional languages such as Breton in France and Frisian in the Netherlands. In many Third World countries as well, demands for greater autonomy are often focused on an intrastate region rather than creating a separate state. "Localization" has become another dimension of globalization.

In fact, the local and the global are increasingly linked without the intermediation of the state. Multinational business provides the most obvious example. But new information and transportation technologies also allow the disenfranchised to leap over their own (often hostile or indifferent) states. For example, Alison Brysk has shown how indigenous peoples in the Americas are able to interact with their colleagues and allies across the globe, dramatically improving their bargaining position vis-à-vis their own state.[1] This is a striking example of what Margaret Keck and Kathryn Sikkink call the "boomerang" model of transnational advocacy: Local actors direct information and appeals to transnational colleagues, foreign states, and regional and international organizations, who respond by mobilizing external pressure on resistant states.[2]

Some of these new flows of structures, processes, and opportunities are empowering. The spread of human rights ideas, and their rise to global preeminence in the post–cold war era, can be seen as an element of globalization. More prosaically, individuals and groups with shared interests increasingly are able to interact, in real time, over immense distances, without regard to the boundaries between, or the interests of, states. The Internet and modern transportation networks have allowed a growing number of Third World communities to exploit the benefits of agricultural and craft cooperatives, fair-trade products, and alternative crops such as miniature vegetables for high-profit markets in developed countries. Cell phones allow even small entrepreneurs in poor countries to make connections with customers and suppliers that open up previously unimagined possibilities for business and a better life for themselves and their families. Even the anti-globalization protests that have become a regular part of international politics over the past decade have been significantly facilitated by new communications and transportation technologies.

However, other global flows that circumvent the state have a much darker side. Consider, for example, burgeoning transnational criminal enterprises, sex tourism in Southeast Asia and the Caribbean, and the growing market in mercenaries and private "security" services. There is also an ominous side to the ability of large global firms to accumulate wealth and power that escapes national or international regulation.

No single chapter can even begin to approach anything close to the full range of human rights issues posed by globalization. Here I focus in depth on one, namely, the challenge that economic globalization poses to the liberal democratic welfare state and to economic and social human rights.

2. STATES AND HUMAN RIGHTS

As we saw in §§3.1–3.2, the conceptual universality of human rights—they are held universally by all people simply because they are human—has been paired with a highly relativist system of national implementation. International human rights treaties create obligations for states to respect, protect, and implement the rights of *their own* citizens (and foreigners under their jurisdiction). International human rights norms have made a state's national human rights practices a legitimate area of *noncoercive* international action. International enforcement of these obligations, however, remains largely prohibited. The human rights of non-nationals are largely matters for "their own" states to secure. States have neither a right nor a responsibility to implement or enforce the human rights of foreigners on foreign territory, with extremely limited exceptions such as genocide (and perhaps torture and slavery). Even international supervision of national human rights practices is extremely restricted, as we saw in Chapter 5.

States can do, have done, and will continue to do many nasty, even horrible, things to their citizens. During the cold war era, such abuses were the focus of most human rights advocates. National, transnational, and international human rights advocacy emphasized the state as a violator of human rights. Although that made considerable sense in the cold war political environment, today we might do well to focus more on the essential role that states play in implementing and protecting human rights.

Most people enjoy their internationally recognized human rights, particularly when they require coercive enforcement, as a result of action taken by "their own" state. Even Europe's strong and effective regional human rights regime is largely a supplement and spur to national action (see §5.5.A). In fact, the struggle of dispossessed groups has typically been a struggle for full legal and political recognition by the state, and thus inclusion among those whose rights are protected by the state. Human rights advocacy is in may ways aimed at transforming the state from a predator into a protector of rights.

This is no less true of economic and social rights than civil and political rights. Classical economists across the full range of the political spectrum, from Adam Smith to Karl Marx, acutely understood that market systems of production and distribution, by freeing productive forces from political constraints, have immensely liberating potential. They also recognized, though, that these same productive forces (and those who control them) are typically indifferent to the fates of individuals unable to compete successfully in the predatory world of capitalist competition. Historically, the only mechanism that has been able to protect individual rights in market systems has been the state.

Thus, a human rights perspective on the state is neither statist nor anti-statist. Rather, human rights advocates seek to promote a particular type of state. The struggle for economic and social rights has in many ways been a struggle to transform the state from the protector of a dominant economic and political elite into a guarantor of basic rights and equal concern and respect for all.

Globalization threatens "good" states as well as "bad" states. If liberal democratic welfare states are undermined by globalization, and we fail to create alternative mechanisms for implementing and enforcing human rights, the substantial achievements of the human rights movement since the end of World War II will be at risk.

3. THE WELFARE STATE, GLOBALIZATION, AND HUMAN RIGHTS

The state envisioned by contemporary international human rights norms is liberal; that is, its legitimacy rests on protecting the human rights of its citizens. It is democratic, in the sense that it is committed to universal political participation and, within the limits of the human rights of all, vests political power in "the people." It is also a welfare state, with extensive economic and social obligations to all citizens.

One of the great human rights achievements of the past century has been the humanization of capitalist markets by welfare states. State regulation of hours, wages, and working conditions are widely accepted (in theory at least) in most countries throughout the world. Furthermore, most states—not simply those with developed market economies—are widely considered to be obliged to provide minimum levels of subsistence, housing, health care, and social services to those unable to acquire them through family or market mechanisms.

The welfare state today, however, is under assault from economic globalization. As an international division of labor continues to develop, leading to a growing separation between locales of production and consumption, firms are increasingly free to move "offshore," in whole or in part, in order to escape the higher costs imposed by welfare state guarantees of economic and social rights. States, by contrast, for all their power, remain largely tied to and limited by a particular territory. The resulting threats to economic and social rights are perhaps most evident in the developed market economies of Western Europe, where benefits have already begun to erode.

But are such concerns anything more than the worries of a privileged few? The transfer of production to less-developed economies may produce (direct and indirect) benefits to citizens of those countries, allowing them to better realize *their* economic and social rights. One might even argue that relatively poor workers and their families gain more than relatively well-to-do workers lose.

Such outcomes are unlikely, however, especially in the short and medium run, without strong welfare states. For example, to the extent that firms are fleeing health and safety regulations, they simply relocate dangerous production and continue to threaten the rights of workers and their communities. Governments in new countries of production are also understandably reluctant to establish strong systems of labor protection, for fear of losing their competitive advantage to other, less scrupulous, countries.

Economic globalization has tended to shift the balance of power toward business, which is becoming increasingly global in its perspective and reach, and away from workers and the state, which remain much more national. In developed market economies, firms can use threats to relocate not only to press for relaxed health and safety standards but to deflate wages and obtain tax breaks or other subsidies that effectively transfer resources from labor to capital. This reallocation of resources is even more dramatic when production actually moves in pursuit of lower costs or a more "friendly" business environment.

Unless the additional profits generated by globalization are eliminated by competition or are reallocated through redistributive taxation and social welfare policies—

both of which are unlikely within the next few decades—the net consequences for economic and social rights are likely to be negative. Thus, even if globalization takes from relatively privileged Western workers and gives to less-privileged workers elsewhere, the biggest beneficiaries of globalization are likely to be even more privileged capitalists, managers, bureaucrats, and investors.

4. MARKETS AND ECONOMIC AND SOCIAL RIGHTS

The preceding should not be read as a blanket attack on national and international markets. The international community, and most states as well, have become well aware of the costs of command economies. The inefficiencies of central planning almost always swamp any equity benefits, at least in the medium and long run. Although countries such as Cuba and Sri Lanka did achieve notable short- and medium-run success, in the long run neither growth nor equity has proved to be possible within a command economy. A considerable degree of economic efficiency, and thus reliance on markets, is necessary for *sustainable* progress in implementing economic and social rights.

This important lesson, though, does not justify excluding or even dramatically restricting the role of the state in the economy. Rather, it means that the state's economic role should be primarily *re*distributive. States must not only facilitate the operation of markets, in order to create growth, but also redistribute resources and opportunities, to assure that growth contributes to the enjoyment of economic and social rights by all.

Markets, by design, distribute the benefits of growth without regard for individual needs and rights (other than property rights). Markets seek economic efficiency, maximizing the total quantity of goods and services produced with a given quantity of resources. Markets promise to produce more overall, not more for all.

Market distributions take into account only economic value added, which varies sharply across individuals and social groups. Free markets thus *necessarily* produce gross economic inequalities. The poor tend to be "less efficient"; as a class, they have fewer of the skills valued highly by markets. Their plight is then exacerbated when political disadvantage reinforces a vicious rights-abusive cycle. Efficient markets improve the lot of some—ideally even many—at the cost of (relative and perhaps even absolute) deprivation of others. And that suffering is concentrated among society's most vulnerable elements.

Without welfare states (or other comparable redistributive mechanisms) there is no necessary connection between market-led growth and development and the enjoyment of economic and social rights. This fact is now fully accepted; it is the basis of the welfare states that Westerners take for granted. All existing liberal democracies use the welfare state to compensate (some of) those who fare less well in the market.

Individuals who are harmed by the operation of social institutions (markets and private property rights) that benefit the whole are entitled to a fair share of the social product their participation has helped to produce. The collectivity that benefits in the aggregate has an obligation to look after individual members who are disadvantaged in or harmed by markets. The welfare state guarantees *all* individuals certain economic and social goods, services, and opportunities, irrespective of the market value of their labor.

Advocates of markets admit that some are harmed in the short run. Everyone, though, is supposed to benefit in the long run from the greater supply of goods and services. "Everyone," however, does not mean each and every individual. Rather, economists refer to the *average* individual, an entirely abstract entity. And even the average person is assured of significant gain only at some point in the future. In the here and now, and in the near future, many real, flesh and blood, individual human beings and families suffer. Even worse, because markets distribute the benefits of growth without regard to short-term deprivations, those who suffer "adjustment costs"—lost jobs, higher food prices, inferior health care—acquire no special claim to a future share of the collective benefits of efficient markets.

Markets, for all the talk of individual initiative, ground a collectivist, "utilitarian" political theory. Markets are justified by arguments of collective good and aggregate benefit, not individual rights (other than, perhaps, the right to economic accumulation). Free markets are an economic analogue to a political system of majority rule without minority rights. The welfare state, from this perspective, is a device to assure that a minority that is disadvantaged in or deprived by markets still is treated with minimum economic concern and respect. Only when the pursuit of prosperity is tamed by economic and social rights—when markets are embedded in a welfare state—does a market-based economy merit our respect.

Welfare states, though, are under assault in all countries as a result of competitive forces unleashed by globalization. This is exacerbated by the ideological hegemony of a market ideology that is directed rather indiscriminately at states in general. In much of the developing world, welfare states face additional attacks from internationally mandated and managed structural adjustment programs, which in addition to targeting waste and inefficiency also typically target social welfare expenditures.

Consider the changing role of the International Monetary Fund (IMF). Originally created to supervise a global financial regime based on fixed exchange rates—which were intended to *increase* national economic control in order to better realize welfare state policies—the IMF today serves principally to enforce the ever widening penetration of market mechanisms, with little concern for social welfare. Thus, where John Ruggie aptly described the postwar international economic order as "embedded liberalism"[3]—market mechanisms embedded within a political commitment to liberal democratic welfare states—the reigning ideology today is more (neo)classically liberal, that is, simply pursuing market efficiencies without regard to welfare.

5. MARKET DEMOCRACY AND
AMERICAN FOREIGN POLICY

Since the end of the cold war there has been a powerful convergence of markets, human rights ideas, and political power behind the idea of "market democracy," a vision of national and international political legitimacy that is arguably a central part of the process of globalization in the early twenty-first century. Markets and democracy certainly are "good things," especially when contrasted to the alternatives of command economies and authoritarian or totalitarian rule. They are not, however, the same good things as human rights. We have already seen that in the case of markets. The same is true of democracy.

A. *The Democratic Idea*

"Democracy" is derived from the ancient Greek *demokratia,* literally, the rule or power *(kratos)* of the people *(demos).* Democratic regimes are those in which the people rule.

It is conventional to distinguish substantive and procedural democracy. In a substantively democratic regime, goods, services, and real opportunities are enjoyed "democratically," that is, by the masses on an egalitarian basis. The people are beneficiaries of a regime that rules in their interest. A procedurally democratic regime fills its political offices through fair and open periodic elections. Such polities may or may not pursue egalitarian policies. Their democratic credentials rest on the authority of the government deriving from the sovereign choice of the people.

Jefferson's familiar formula—government of the people, by the people, and for the people—suggests a similar distinction. All democracies are governments *of* the people. Procedural conceptions of democracy, however, emphasize government *by* the people. Substantive conceptions stress government *for* the people.

Americans seem particularly inclined to think of democracy in procedural terms, assuming that fair and open elections will produce governments that pursue the popular will and the general good. Although often true, it is always legitimate to "test" democratic procedures by their substantive outputs. For example, a standard complaint about elected governments in much of Central America has been that in practice they protect the interests of a privileged minority. A procedurally democratic government may still systematically violate human rights.

Democracy answers the question of *who* should rule. Democracy empowers the people and seeks to realize their collective good. Human rights, by contrast, addresses *how* governments should rule. Human rights empower autonomous individuals. They seek to assure that personal and societal goals, including democratically defined goals, are pursued within the confines of guaranteeing every individual certain minimum goods, services, and opportunities.

Protected individual interests often conflict with the wishes of the majority. Many people, both individually and in groups, want to use their political power to harm their enemies or to gain (often unfair) advantage for themselves. "The people," understood as the substantial majority of the population, often want to do some very nasty things to some of their "fellow" citizens. For example, racial discrimination was for almost two centuries popular with the majority in the United States.

What students of comparative politics usually call liberal democracy seeks to resolve the conflicts between democracy and human rights by allowing democracy to operate only within the constraints imposed by the liberal commitment to the individual rights of each and every citizen. One standard civics text formula is "majority rule with minority rights." It is essential to note, though, that there is nothing distinctively "democratic" about minority rights. Quite the contrary, "minority rights"—the individual human rights of every citizen—are prior and superior to the democratic rights of the majority.

Human rights define the range within which democratic decision making is allowed to operate. Human rights are fundamentally nonmajoritarian. They are concerned with each, rather than all. They aim to protect every person, against majorities no less than against minorities. Human rights ordinarily take precedence over the wishes of the people, no matter how intensely even the vast majority of society desires to abuse some individual or group. In fact, in procedurally democratic states, where the majority is relatively well positioned to care for its own rights and interests, the principal function of human rights is to limit democratic decision making.

Contemporary liberal democracies are liberal (rights-protective) before they are democratic. Citizens' rights provide the government's authority and the standard by which its legitimacy is judged. And the sovereignty of the people derives from the individual rights of each person.

Electoral or procedural democracy is almost always preferable to the realistic alternatives. Only liberal democracy, though, is centrally and inherently committed to human rights. And that is because it is "liberal" (rights-based), not because it is "democratic" (based on the will of the people).

B. Democratization and Human Rights

The post–cold war world has seen the continued spread and deepening of electoral democracy. For the first time in history the majority of people on this planet live under democratically elected governments. This momentous achievement is a source of legitimate satisfaction. We must not, however, overestimate its human rights significance. In particular, we must not confuse decreased tolerance for old forms of repressive rule with support for, let alone institutionalization of, rights-protective regimes.

We can distinguish three levels of political progress toward respect for internationally recognized human rights.

Liberalization involves a decrease in human rights violations and an opening of political space for at least some previously excluded groups—roughly, progress in civil and political rights short of democratization. China has undergone periodic limited liberalizations. Poland liberalized in the 1980s, initially under the pressure of Solidarity, before it democratized in 1990. South Korea liberalized in the 1980s before establishing electoral democracy in the 1990s.

By *democratization,* I mean the process of establishing electoral democracy, which involves a qualitative leap beyond liberalization. When "soft" authoritarian regimes allow truly fair and open elections (not just once, or if they win), the political system is fundamentally transformed.

A *rights-protective regime* both makes the protection of internationally recognized human rights a central element of its mission, and through extensive, intense, and sustained effort, has achieved considerable success in realizing this aspiration. This is *liberal* democracy. If one insists on using the language of democratization to describe transitions from electoral to liberal democracy, one might talk about the "deepening" of democratization—although it is respect for human rights, rather than for the will of the people, that deepens.

Note that only the second of these three processes is centrally connected with democracy understood in the core sense of rule of the people. The distinction between electoral and liberal democracy concerns not who rules but how (within what limits). Liberalization, too, is concerned with the limits on government rather than who rules.

Nonetheless, "democratization" is often used to cover all three kinds of change, on the assumption that they are phases of a single, largely linear process of development. Political development, however, is not "naturally" driven toward a single end. Resistance to authoritarian rule is often not a transition to democracy, or anything else, but a reaction against injustice. Regimes that have liberalized often resist democratization. Even fair and moderately open elections may produce governments that violate human rights.

One of the most disturbing lessons of democratization in countries such as Belarus, Uzbekistan, Slovakia, and Bulgaria in the 1990s, as in much of Africa in the 1960s, is that voting often appears to people to be primarily a device for acquiring prosperity and a sense of control rather than a way to assure widespread protection of human rights. Even more disturbing are the cases where the majority seeks electoral power to oppress a minority.

Electoral democracy may be a necessary condition for liberal democracy. Liberalization and electoral democracy may even foster liberal democracy by allowing human rights advocates political space and opportunities. But there is no natural, inescapable evolution. Electorally democratic governments may use their power in ways that violate, threaten, or fail to defend internationally recognized human rights. Especially in times of crisis or disillusionment, electoral democracy may even be prone to populist, proto-fascist demagoguery.

Elections are only a device. They may have very different meanings in different political contexts. All other things being equal, it is a good thing if leaders are freely chosen and speak for the people. What is most important, though, is whether human rights are secure. Only when supported by rights-protective political attitudes and institutions will elections lead toward deeply liberal democratic regimes.

The danger, especially in U.S. foreign policy, is that we will forget that democratization is, at best, a good start on realizing human rights. Americans seem inclined to the convenient but dangerous illusion that once elections have been held, the struggle for human rights—or at least our part in the struggle—is largely over. In fact, as recent events in Iraq have shown, the struggle really begins then.

C. Market Democracy and Economic Rights

Turning to questions related to market democracy, Americans too often forget how heavily the U.S. government is involved in regulating markets and attempting to counteract the social inequities they produce. Not even Ronald Reagan proposed returning to anything even approximating a true free market economy. Twentieth-century liberal democracies are distinguished from "free market capitalism" by redistributive policies that protect individual rights and seek social justice.

Despite all the gaps in its coverage, the United States is a huge welfare state. For example, workers and employers together are taxed one-seventh of an employee's income just to fund a single social welfare program: state-supported old age pensions (Social Security). Even Americans, who are more individualistic and anti-statist than most Europeans, see their welfare state as an essential part of the American political ideal.

In American foreign policy, however, all one hears about is markets. When dealing with countries still shaped by the legacy of command economies, the allure of the market is perhaps understandable. However, American advocacy of markets in the former Soviet bloc and the Third World ignores their significant human costs. There is a disturbing parallel with cold war anticommunism: Excessive focus on the "problem" (communism; command economies) yields inattention to the "unintended" consequences of the "solution" (dictators; markets).

This is particularly true for American support of IMF-imposed structural adjustment programs. Structural adjustment almost always has immediate and detrimental short-term effects on the enjoyment of economic rights by large segments of the population. Reductions in state spending on education and health, retrenchments in public-sector employment, reductions in real wages, and programs to privatize land leave the poor even more vulnerable than they were before. In addition, the political unpopularity of often punitive cuts in social services may disrupt the pace and process of political liberalization and democratization.

I do not want to either belittle the problems faced in implementing economic and social rights or the contribution of properly regulated markets. I do not even want to deny that some countries may face a tragic choice between growth and equity. But where victims of market-driven growth truly cannot be prevented (at a reasonable cost), they must be acknowledged, and mourned. Instead, in their enthusiasm for sweeping away the old, Americans too often seem not to see, let alone be troubled by, the problems in the new.

6. AN ALLIANCE OF STATES AND HUMAN RIGHTS ADVOCATES?

If the welfare state is increasingly unable to assure economic and social rights for all, regional or global institutions present an obvious "solution." The problem, of course, is that there is little evidence of the imminent emergence of global redistributive institutions. Virtually all states, including even relatively well-to-do and committed liberal democratic welfare states, remain extremely reluctant to transfer substantial authority to global political institutions.

Nonetheless, inter-state mechanisms are not necessarily doomed to failure. For example, the harmonization of social policies in the European Union can be viewed as a collective regional effort to reduce the incentives of individual states to compete for jobs by dismantling the welfare state. Europe, however, looks very much like the exception that proves the rule. And even the Europeans seem uninterested in using the Organisation for Economic Co-operation and Development, or some new institution, to spread cooperation on social policy across a wider range of developed market economies.

Transnational actors offer another potential mechanism for revitalizing economic and social rights. Human rights NGOs, trade unions, women's groups, environmentalists, indigenous peoples, and a host of other groups in "civil society" share a common interest in (re-)asserting welfare state control over global markets and multinational business. Civil society actors, however, are at an extreme disadvantage, both because of their relative lack of economic and political resources and because they face far greater problems in forming national and transnational alliances. In addition, although not as territorially bound as states, they are usually less mobile than the businesses against whom they are pitted.

The current international situation with respect to economic and social rights is similar to conditions in Western Europe in the mid-nineteenth century, where business had the upper hand and skillfully used its resources to protect its interests. Contemporary multinational businesses also have the advantage of being able to play country against country. Whereas those seeking to strengthen the welfare state face the daunting task of (re-)establishing control, multinational businesses need only evade regulation.

Advocates of economic and social rights, however, have resources of their own, including national electoral power and advanced communications technologies that increase their capabilities for national and transnational organization. Furthermore, unlike in the nineteenth century, they can draw on the moral force of authoritative international human rights norms and the accumulated experience of many decades of welfare state policies.

In addition, advocates of internationally recognized economic and social rights share a common interest with at least some government elites in controlling transnational business. Especially in highly institutionalized liberal democratic welfare states, human rights advocates and states share a deeply rooted desire to temper the efficiency of markets with rights-based concerns for at least minimally equitable distributions of social goods, services, and opportunities. Of course, state elites often seek control over business for their own selfish, even predatory, purposes. But even then their shared desire to gain greater control over corporate practices and profits provides the basis for at least tactical political alliances with human rights advocates.

Once again, the issue is not the state per se but the *type* of state. Transnational business is using economic globalization to press for a state that gives greater emphasis to markets, the domain of social action where their power and skills are greatest. Human rights advocates and allied elements of civil society are seeking to use their electoral, organizational, and moral power on behalf of welfare states. Thus, the fate of human rights is likely to depend, in the early twenty-first century as in the late nineteenth and early twentieth centuries, on who controls the state and how they use that control. In those countries where human rights advocates are maintaining or strengthening their position, an alliance with the state may prove the best way to re-establish the social control over markets necessary to assure economic and social rights for all.

In the era of globalization, however, no individual state acting alone is able to impose new regulations, or even hold on to its former ability to control "its own" firms. They must cooperate, regionally and internationally, if they are to have a chance of humanizing global markets. And they must forge new alliances with national and transnational civil society actors. Whether this proves practically possible, however, is by no means clear.

My enemy's enemy is my friend, the old rule of realist international politics, applies today as well to states and human rights advocates. Whatever their past animosities, today they face a new common enemy. The future of human rights just might be determined by their ability to develop new forms of cooperation that protect the state as an essential mechanism for realizing human rights—at least until new mechanisms are created, which still seems, at best, very far off in an extremely speculative future.

A central purpose of human rights advocacy has always been to empower people to force "their" state to treat them as they deserve to be treated. This has meant shaping states into instruments to protect, rather than ignore or even trample on, the human rights of their citizens. Today, this increasingly requires states and citizens to stand up to, and attempt to exert control over, transnational and global, not merely national, forces. If not, then much of the hard-won human rights progress of the twentieth century is at risk.

DISCUSSION QUESTIONS

1. What exactly do you mean by globalization when you use the term? Is it a recent or a long-standing process? What are its dimensions? Is the global spread of human rights itself an phenomenon of globalization?

2. Human rights advocates typically focus on states as a threat to human rights. This chapter suggests that globalization is forcing human rights advocates to emphasize the role of the state as protector. Has there really been a change? Hasn't the role of the state as protector always been central?

3. Is the welfare state really such a wonderful achievement? Is globalization making a positive contribution by freeing economic initiative from the shackles of excessive welfare state regulation? Can't we see the shift in the balance of power away from states produced by globalization as basically a positive trend? Why do advocates of liberal democratic welfare states want the state in our lives economically but out of our lives in other domains?

4. How would you evaluate the distinction drawn between liberalization, democratization, and creating a rights-protective regime? Applying this distinction and the post–cold war history of the former Soviet bloc, what does it say about Iraq? About the broader process of "democratization" that the war in Iraq allegedly has triggered? Am I correct that this distinction is especially important for Americans, who tend to focus on the formalities of democratization, often to the exclusion of the real substance of protecting human rights?

5. Are markets, from a human rights point of view, really just the lesser evil? Am I correct in suggesting that questions of economic, social, and cultural rights have in recent years often gotten lost in the rush toward market-oriented economic reforms? Even if that is true, is this a necessary first step toward sustained progress on economic, social, and cultural rights? If so, how can we assure that progress continues?
6. Why are Americans, who claim to be so individualistic, so attracted to democracy and markets, which as I have argued are fundamentally collective systems of political justification? What kind of individualism is it that Americans really value?
7. Which is the biggest threat to human rights: globalization (markets), states, or terrorism? Does you answer depend on where you live? On which rights you are considering?

SUGGESTED READINGS

Although the literature on globalization is immense, a surprisingly small percentage focuses on human rights. Four good readers, however, are Alison Brysk, ed., *Globalization and Human Rights* (Berkeley: University of California Press, 2002), Jean-Marc Coicaud, Michael W. Doyle, and Anne-Marie Gardner, eds., *The Globalization of Human Rights* (Tokyo: United Nations University Press, 2003), Koen de Feyter, ed., *Human Rights: Social Justice in the Age of the Market* (London: Zed Books, 2005), and Mahmood Monshipouri et al., eds., *Constructing Human Rights in the Age of Globalization* (Armonk, N.Y.: M. E. Sharpe, 2003). Slightly broader in focus, but including many good essays with a specific human rights focus, is Pablo De Greiff and Ciaran Cronin, eds., *Global Justice and Transnational Politics: Essays on the Moral and Political Challenges of Globalization* (Cambridge: MIT Press, 2002). For a perspective explicitly focused on the margins of national and international societies, see Neve Gordon, ed., *From the Margins of Globalization: Critical Perspectives on Human Rights* (Lanham, Md.: Lexington Books, 2004).

An interesting and important topic not explored in the chapter is the movement to establish human rights obligations for corporations. Chapter 3 of Allison Brysk, *Human Rights, Private Wrongs* (New York: Routledge, 2005), and Chapter 8 of David P. Forsythe, *Human Rights and International Relations* (Cambridge: Cambridge University Press, 2000) provide good, largely complementary, introductions to the issue. For illustrative, creative attempts to address the issue by lawyers, see, for example, Lissett Ferreira, "Access to Affordable HIV/AIDS Drugs: The Human Rights Obligations of Multinational Pharmaceutical Corporations," *Fordham Law Review* 71 (2002): 1133–1179, Jordan Paust, "Human Rights Responsibilities of Private Corporations," *Vanderbilt Journal of Transnational Law* 35 (2002): 801–825, and David Weissbrodt and Muria Kruger, "Norms on the Responsibilities of Transnational Corporations and Other Business Enterprises with Regard to Human Rights," *American Journal of International Law* 97 (2003): 901–922.

10

Terrorism and Human Rights

The tragedy of September 11 has led to a substantial redirection of American foreign policy. This chapter explores the consequences of these changes for U.S. international human rights and democratization policies. It is difficult to make assessments in the midst of changes that are typically described as fundamental. Nonetheless, I will argue that the American "war on terrorism," whatever its justifications and achievements, has provoked a one-dimensional ideological campaign that has marginalized human rights in much the same way, although somewhat less intensely, as the crusade against communism did during the cold war. In other words, my focus is not on terrorism or antiterrorism per se but on their consequences for international human rights. I will also focus on American foreign policy, which has been the driving force behind international responses to terrorism.

1. HUMAN RIGHTS IN POST–COLD WAR AMERICAN FOREIGN POLICY

Assessing the impact of 9/11 requires a baseline of comparison. The preceding dozen years had witnessed a significant increase in the priority accorded to democracy and human rights objectives. In addition, as we saw in Chapter 8, a stream of unilateral and multilateral practice in the 1990s established an international right to humanitarian intervention against genocide.

Although there is little controversy about the existence of these changes, their cause is a matter of contention. How much was due to their rise in the hierarchy of U.S. foreign policy interests? How much was due instead to the demise of (anti) communism, which opened space for the pursuit of other interests? The evidence since September 11 suggests that it was much more the latter.

Consider a simple three-interest model of foreign policy. Let us assume that foreign policy comprises security interests, economic interests, and "other" interests. In general, security trumps everything else. Economic interests usually (though not always) take priority over "other" interests. Occasionally, economic interests may even compete with (secondary) security concerns. "Other" interests generally come last.

This, I would suggest, is a pretty good first approximation of the outlines of the foreign policy priorities of the United States (and most other countries as well).

The place of an interest within this hierarchy (and within the hierarchy of "other" interests) may change either absolutely or relatively; that is, the (absolute) value attributed to it may change or the (absolute) value of another interest above or below it may change. I suggest that the increased attention to human rights and democracy in post–cold war American foreign policy was largely relative rather than absolute. Although there may have been a modest absolute increase in the value attributed to human rights, the most important change was a dramatic contraction in the scope of security concerns, which opened space for increased attention to human rights.

Compare this to the absolute change in the place of human rights in American foreign policy that took place a decade earlier. As we saw in Chapter 6, throughout the Carter presidency, there was considerable (and often intense) debate over whether human rights were an appropriate foreign policy concern. A decade later, however, debate focused not on whether the United States should be pursuing international human rights objectives but on what place human rights should be given in particular cases and their importance relative to other foreign policy interests. By the late 1980s, human rights had become entrenched on the American foreign policy agenda as a largely nonpartisan objective. Across the entire mainstream of the political spectrum, which had shifted clearly to the right throughout the decade, human rights had become an accepted, and valued, objective of American foreign policy.

Although Ronald Reagan, during his early years in office, worked aggressively to turn his campaign criticisms of Jimmy Carter's human rights policies into action, these efforts largely failed. In fact, in its second term the Reagan administration largely adopted the language of human rights—often rather cynically, but sometimes, especially when anticommunism did not get in the way, with apparent sincerity. And when Reagan's vice president, George Bush, ran successfully in 1988, he regularly and freely used the language of human rights.

The post–cold war changes in American international human rights policy built on this entrenchment of human rights on the American foreign policy agenda. The geopolitical impediments to the pursuit of human rights objectives dramatically receded. In what has often been referred to as a unipolar world there were many fewer security concerns to interfere with the pursuit of human rights objectives. The American (and international) reaction against the Tiananmen massacre in June 1989, discussed in Chapter 7, is perhaps the clearest indication of the new geopolitical space for international human rights concerns.

No less important than the changes in the international power structure was the ideological space opened by the demise of communism. During the cold war, protecting "democracy" and "the free world" regularly was deemed to require tolerating or even actively supporting human rights violations directed against the "enemies of freedom." With the end of ideological rivalry, which had been at the heart of much of the American support for repressive regimes of the right, the "threat" posed to "friendly" dictators largely evaporated (in places such as Guatemala and El Salvador) or, when we looked more carefully, could no longer be found (in places like Uruguay and Zaire).

With the definition of democracy liberated from the tyranny of anticommunism, the United States not only developed a renewed emphasis on elections but increasingly came to see that real democracy required an active and effective independent civil society. As civil society promotion programs expanded, important conceptual and practical linkages were forged between human rights and democratization agendas. Whatever the shortcomings in program design, and for all the restrictions imposed by competing interests, this was a major advance in the sophistication and potential impact of U.S. human rights diplomacy.[1]

These progressive trends were significantly reinforced by the collapse of dictatorships of the right and left alike. Attention shifted, in part, from the largely reactive and remedial emphasis on stopping, and aiding victims of, systematic and often brutal repression toward a more positive emphasis on helping to build a human rights culture. Once the old dictators were gone, it became increasingly clear that the work of building rights-respecting societies and rights-protective regimes had only begun. This new attitude tended to be expressed primarily in the language of democracy and democratization.[2]

In its least attractive dimensions, this sometimes led to a fetishistic pursuit of elections. American policy has also often confused political liberalization (that is, reductions in or even elimination of old forms of repression) with democratization, in a naive belief that all progressive political change lies on a path that leads to democracy (see also §9.5). But in its more attractive dimensions—which were not entirely lacking during the Clinton years, and even during the first Bush administration—it involved a vision of human rights that went well beyond the simplistic cold war–era vision of stopping torture, freeing political prisoners, and "throwing the rascals out."

As these last paragraphs have suggested, in the 1990s there was genuine rethinking and learning that contributed to redesigned international human rights policies in the United States (and other countries as well). The crucial change, however, was less in the substance or absolute intensity of American human rights and democracy promotion interests than the space opened for such initiatives by the end of geopolitical and ideological rivalry with the Soviet Union.

2. THE RETREAT OF HUMAN RIGHTS

Some of the changes discussed in the preceding section have become deeply entrenched, most notably the acceptance throughout the political mainstream of human rights as a legitimate concern of American foreign policy. The relative priority attached to international human rights objectives, however, remains a matter of controversy. The argument above suggests that the post–cold war rise of human rights and democracy as objectives of American foreign policy was vulnerable to a re-inflation of security concerns. In this section, I suggest that since September 11 we have indeed seen democracy and human rights pushed back toward the margins of American foreign policy by a new geopolitical vision and a new ideological crusade that have striking analogies to their cold war predecessors.

Perhaps most striking was the transformation of Pakistan, in the official American representation, from a retrograde military dictatorship—and one that, in addition, was a major supporter of international terrorism, the preceding decade's most flagrant violator of the nonproliferation regime, and a bellicose threat to regional security in South Asia—to a leading American ally. And despite the lack of any substantial human rights improvements or any progress toward real democracy in Pakistan, the American embrace has continued, long after the war in Afghanistan. For example, on his visit to the United States in the summer of 2003, Pakistani strongman Pervez Musharraf was lavishly praised by the Bush administration.

Much more generally, governments have taken advantage of the rhetoric of antiterrorism to intensify their attacks on domestic and international enemies. "Particularly troubling, and common, have been the pretextual use of counter-terrorism laws as new weapons against old political foes."[3] Russia and Israel provide perhaps the most tragic examples of the war on terrorism run amok.

In Chechnya, intensified Russian military action certainly owed much to the seemingly interminable nature of that terrible conflict.[4] Russia, however, has been emboldened by the language and logic of a global war on terrorism, calculating, correctly, that appeals to antiterrorism today provide partial insulation from international criticism.[5] The muting and partial disabling of humanitarian criticism has certainly not caused Russian brutality, but it has facilitated it.

In Israel, the Sharon government responded to the flood of vicious terror bombings with a vengeance that reflected not only its own inclinations but also American toleration for a most brutal war on terrorism.[6] Assassination and collective punishment have become standard operating procedure. The indignities and human rights violations that have long characterized military occupation have intensified in number and severity. Perhaps most brutal have been policies consciously aimed at destroying the Palestinian economy and making every Palestinian civilian suffer, both economically and through the denial of personal liberties,[7] for the actions of a tiny group of extremists and the unwillingness or inability of the Palestinian Authority to control them.

The terrorist threats faced by Russia and Israel are very real. But that is no justification for a response that itself relies on systematic human rights violations and terrorist tactics.[8] The United States and its allies, however, have backed off of its criticism of Russia—the words are still there, but they lack much conviction any more.[9] And the United States, Israel's principal ally, has done little to impede its slide into policies that can only accurately be described as state terrorism. All this suffering inflicted upon innocent civilians has perhaps brought some of the satisfactions of retribution. But it has not made its perpetrators more secure. Quite the contrary, it has plunged them even deeper into a cycle of violence and despair.

Like anticommunism during the cold war, antiterrorism has become less a material interest of foreign policy than a crusade against evil to be pursued without too much concern for the ordinary restraints of law and conventional limits on the use of force. Where the conflict has been militarized, the classic just-war restrictions have eroded or been ignored: Noncombatants are directly targeted, proportionality is ignored, and the very idea of innocent civilians is undermined by direct and indirect attributions of collective responsibility and guilt. Where the struggle is carried out through the institutions of "law and order" and the internal security forces, human rights are the price exacted not just from terrorists but from peaceful political opponents, members of groups that are feared or despised, and ordinary individuals accidentally or arbitrarily caught up in the security apparatus.

These relatively dramatic examples, which involve the positive enabling of rights-abusive policies, are matched by a general decline in American attention to human rights and democracy promotion. The United States remains committed to human rights and democracy, but they have moved toward the background in a growing number of cases. Although the decline has been substantially less dramatic in the past few years than during the cold war—an analogy with the impact of the war on drugs on U.S. policy in the Andean region is closer to the mark—American support for human rights and democracy has been among the more prominent casualties of the war on terrorism.

Support for these changes has by no means been restricted to the political right. In fact, the most striking fact has been the participation in or tolerance for this shift in policy by moderates and liberals, who are generally inclined toward pursuing international human rights objectives. The Bush administration's antiterrorism policy has strong bipartisan support. Although its domestic dimensions have provoked sustained (although limited) criticism from prominent mainstream political figures, criticism of its international dimensions has been restricted primarily to human rights NGOs and figures on the fringes of the political mainstream.

Nevertheless, within the administration and its allies, there has been no attack on human rights and democracy objectives. They remain rhetorically important goals of American foreign policy. One need not be overly charitable to suggest that this reflects genuine commitment to these values. At the very least, it indicates that other important domestic and international constituencies continue to take them seriously. Hypocrisy is effective only to the extent that it taps into widely and genuinely held values.

In an important sense, then, the relative decline of human rights in American foreign policy has been largely unintended. The explicit aim has been not to harm or even slight human rights but rather to pursue security objectives that are deemed to be more important.

This is not to suggest that American responsibility for the decline is in any way lessened. Although "unintended," the negative human rights consequences have been very real, were easily anticipated, and are now well known. The lack of intent, however, is important for thinking about the prospects for reversing these trends.

If the decline in the position of human rights in American foreign policy has been largely relative, then any revival—much like the initial post–cold war increase in the prominence of international human rights concerns—will depend on space being opened by the retreat of competing security objectives. A return to a more active, assertive, and consistent international human rights policy must wait for the re-opening of the political space currently pre-empted by the war on terrorism.

3. HUMAN RIGHTS, SECURITY, AND FOREIGN POLICY

A defender of the war on terrorism might argue that the story I have told so far is a simple one of competing foreign policy objectives: Major security interests have appropriately pushed human rights and democracy promotion to the sidelines. I suggest, however, that the actual dynamic has been rather different. In this section I focus on qualitative substantive changes in the understanding of security, that is, the American tendency to conceive new threats in moralized terms and to respond with an irrational exuberance for a militarized crusade.

Up to this point I have talked of "security" as if its meaning was obvious and constant. Protecting the national territory from invasion may fit this description. However, most other security interests are more thoroughly constructed and variable (see also §8.9).

Consider a simple three-variable model. What is to be secured—the state (national security) or citizens (personal security)? Where does the threat lie—externally or internally? And what is the nature of the threat—material or moral/ideological?

The relatively constant and uncontroversial dimensions of "security" address external material threats to the state. Security thus understood is indeed plausibly seen as an appropriately overriding concern of foreign policy. Without national security from external material threats, all other interests and values are at risk. As we move away from this relatively simple case, however, "security" becomes more obscure and its priority more contentious. In addition, its conceptual and normative relationships to human rights may vary considerably.

The security of individual citizens has strong connections with human rights. In fact, internationally recognized human rights can be seen as measures to secure individuals from the threats posed by modern states and modern markets. However, state security is not necessarily connected to individual human rights; it depends on the character of the state being protected and the means used to secure it.

To oversimplify, human rights are about protecting citizens from the state (see, however, §§9.2, 9.6 on states and human rights). National security is about protecting the state from its (perceived) enemies. Those enemies may themselves be citizens. And even when the enemies are primarily external, the rights of citizens may need to be sacrificed in order to carry out defensive measures.

An antagonistic relationship between (national) security and human rights is especially likely when security is seen in moral rather than material terms and to the extent that threats are perceived to lie in internal subversion. This was a common perception during the cold war. With "security" understood almost exclusively as a matter of *national* security (which was understood to have a significant ideological dimension), U.S. foreign policy was extremely tolerant of regimes that systematically sacrificed the human rights of their citizens to the (alleged) imperatives of protecting the nation from communist attack and subversion. Central America (§6.2) and the Southern Cone (§6.3) provide perhaps the most striking examples, but there were many instances in Asia (for example, South Korea and Vietnam) and Africa (for example, South Africa and Zaire) as well.

The end of the cold war led to a redefinition of American security interests in less ideological terms. This eliminated the American incentive to court repressive regimes in order to keep them out of the communist camp. At the same time, it undermined the principal rationale for repression by rightist dictatorships. Taken together, they greatly reduced the antagonism between human rights and security in American foreign policy.

In other words, not only were security concerns reduced in number, but the concept of "security" changed after the end of the cold war. Russia still posed most of the same material threats in 1995 that it did in 1985; the end of the cold war, and the dramatic decline in the Russian threat, did not coincide with a substantial reduction in Soviet military power. Rather, the ideological threat posed by communism disappeared with glasnost and new thinking, the collapse of the Soviet bloc, and the dissolution of the Soviet Union.

In addition, there was a partial move toward a conception of security with more of a personal dimension—or in the language that became popular in the 1990s, "human security." The roots of this change, as noted in §8.10, can be traced to the Conference on Security and Co-operation in Europe. Certainly human security never displaced national security on the American foreign policy agenda. However, it did acquire a significant place. This is perhaps most evident in the rise of armed humanitarian operations that received strong American support, from Somalia and Bosnia through Kosovo and East Timor (see Chapter 8). More broadly, the concept of peacebuilding was added to the international security lexicon, and a human rights dimension was incorporated into a number of post-conflict peacekeeping operations.

Terrorism has modestly increased the material threat to the United States, but the big change has been in the expansion of the other dimensions of security. The war on terrorism has led to a significantly more ideological vision of security—a theme pursued in greater detail in the next section. The focus on personal security has receded in favor of a renewed emphasis on national security. And the internal dimensions of security have moved to the forefront, as expressed in the language of homeland security. As during the cold war, security and human rights are again increasingly coming to be seen as competing rather than reinforcing concerns.

4. IRRATIONAL EXUBERANCE:
THE CASE OF THE AXIS OF EVIL

The implication of the preceding section is that human rights and democracy promotion have lost out less as a result of carefully considered trade-offs of competing interests and more due to a decision to reorient American policy around an ideological crusade. In this section I suggest, by examining the case of the "axis of evil," that this has introduced a substantially irrational element into American policy. I also argue that the new crusade against terrorism has facilitated dangerous new trends in American foreign policy, particularly the demonization of enemies and a tendency to act unilaterally.

A. *The Axis of Evil*

One striking consequence of the post-9/11 environment has been the rhetorical creation of the Iraq–Iran–North Korea "axis of evil." In fact, there are no policy connections among these three countries that would plausibly make them an axis. Quite the contrary, Iran and Iraq have been bitter enemies, and North Korea is not closely linked to either of the other two regimes. This new enemy has been constructed out of a hodgepodge of very different (and largely unrelated) concerns—most notably terrorism, proliferation, regional security, and general anti-Americanism.

The glue that holds together this disparate set of issues and countries is the general antiterrorist hysteria in American policy. No rational assessment of American interests would suggest that American policy ought to focus on these three regimes. This is true even in the narrow case of a well-designed war on terrorism.

Terrorists sponsored by these three regimes have not directed their activities against the United States or the U.S. military. In fact, nationals of these countries—in sharp contrast to those of Saudi Arabia, for example—were not even involved in the terrorist attacks on Americans. The global role of these three countries makes them no more deserving of special attention. Other states, including American allies, are equally culpable. Syria, for example, has been as active in the Middle East as Iran. The devastation wreaked by Pakistani-supported Kashmiri terrorists has been at least as significant as anything caused by terrorists supported by the axis of evil—not to mention the long-standing Pakistani support for the Taliban, prior to its post-9/11 about-face.

Much the same is true of the other "crimes" of these regimes. Consider proliferation. North Korea has indeed been guilty of breaching international nonproliferation norms, as well as particular agreements with the United States. But our "ally" Pakistan is the most flagrant proliferator of the past decade, in a regional security context at least as unstable as that of the Korean peninsula. (There is also evidence suggesting that Pakistan has contributed to North Korea's nuclear program.) Iraq's nuclear ambitions seem, by the evidence of the recent war, to have been thwarted by international sanctions and monitoring. And Iran, although a legitimate proliferation concern, does not appear to be an imminent threat and has been less than entirely clear in its expression of its intentions.

B. *Human Rights: The Case of Iran*

From a human rights perspective, these problems might be forgivable if these "evil" states were the world's leading human rights violators. A strong case can be made that North Korea and Saddam Hussein's Iraq belonged on any "top ten" list. But the inclusion of Iran in such company is absurd. Revolutionary Iran is in many regards an extremely unappealing regime, but respect for human rights and democracy are far more advanced in Iran than in America's leading ally in the region, Saudi Arabia.

Iran is is one of the few countries in the region with a vibrant opposition and real possibilities for reform. Relatively free elections are held regularly for a legislature and government that have considerable influence over policy. Despite substantial censorship and a serious problem of legal and political attacks on opposition journalists, Iran is one of the few countries in the region with a substantial cadre of opposition journalists. State-supported vigilante violence is a recurrent problem, but opposition political figures face far fewer threats to their personal security than in most of the rest of the region. And women's rights are further advanced in Iran than in most Arab countries; certainly compared to Saudi Arabia, Iran, especially Tehran, is a paradise for women's rights.

U.S. policy, however, has largely sacrificed the chance to facilitate the ongoing process of reform in Iran. Quite the contrary, the bellicose words and actions of the United States have made life more difficult for reformers. Rather than recognize the positive (if limited) changes in Iran over the past decade, the United States has chosen to single out Iran for special attack. It has even sacrificed opportunities to pursue convergent interests cooperatively, most notably in Afghanistan and Iraq.

There has been, in effect, a choice to keep Iran as an enemy rather than either help to reform it or try to settle outstanding issues. And the Bush administration has chosen to make Iran not just an ordinary enemy, but a demonized one. This certainly has been facilitated by the earlier demonization of revolutionary Iran following the hostage crisis. But that was more than two decades ago. The re-demonization of Iran, as part of the axis of evil, has been largely driven by the hysteria of the war on terror. (The Iranian government, for its own political reasons, seems at least equally intent on casting the United States as a demonized enemy—further suggesting that none of this is conducive to reform or the expansion of human rights.)

5. THE WAR AGAINST IRAQ

One might describe the focus on the axis of evil as silly. Certainly the idea that these three second- or third-rate powers are the appropriate focal point for the foreign policy of "the world's only superpower" is patently ludicrous. This silliness has had serious negative consequences, most directly for reformers and human rights in Iran, and more generally in the turn of American attention away from human rights and other concerns. But the consequences pale before those associated with the war on Iraq.

Like the axis of evil itself, the justification for the invasion of Iraq was cobbled together out of a variety of disparate concerns, including weapons of mass destruction, terrorism, "regime change," a history of animosity, and regional security. Like the general charge against the axis of evil, the particular elements of the charge against Iraq are problematic. And the combination was held together with a lot of post-9/11 hysteria.

The threat of weapons of mass destruction was largely imaginary. Iraq's contribution to international terrorism (before the U.S. invasion and occupation) was not especially notable. There is no hint elsewhere in American foreign policy that even the most vicious behavior of a government is legitimate grounds for a military invasion. And Iraq was no serious threat to its neighbors, having been effectively hobbled by the first Gulf war and a decade of international sanctions.

In addition to the disorder, death, and destruction that have characterized "liberated" Iraq, the United States has embarked on a series of direct violations of human rights and humanitarian law. Abu Ghraib has entered the popular lexicon as a symbol of sadistic political brutality. Clearly such excesses are not part of official American policy. But many have argued that they have been facilitated, even encouraged, by American policies and practices that suggest that human rights and the rule of law often must be sacrificed to the fight against terror.

Guantánamo has been carved out as a nether world where neither American nor international (nor Cuban) law applies and where issues of innocence, proof, responsibility, and proportionality are deemed irrelevant. "Extraordinary renditions"—kidnapping suspected terrorists, transporting them across international boundaries, and delivering them into the hands of "friendly" security services that regularly practice torture—reflect a cynical evasion of even the most rudimentary principles of the rule of law. President Bush insisted, with apparent sincerity, that the United States neither practices nor tolerates torture, while Vice President Cheney and his staff campaigned for months against legislation that codified this claim and existing American legal obligations under the torture convention. And the list goes on, with the consequence that even America's closest Western allies have strongly, with increasing vigor, condemned American lawlessness and violations of human rights.

I do not mean to suggest that the war on terrorism directly caused the invasion of Iraq. Rather, it enabled a shift in policy, most notably toward unilateralism and the demonization of enemies. It also helped to hold together the various justifications that were used to build the political coalitions that backed the war. Without the paranoia over terrorism, it is hard to imagine the Bush administration marshaling the national and international support needed to launch the war against Iraq.

6. CONCLUSION

The world has become a less secure place, and one less hospitable to human rights, since September 11, 2001. Sadly, the United States bears some responsibility for this deterioration. Although there has not been a conscious decision to downgrade human rights, democracy, and broader humanitarian concerns, this has nonetheless occurred.

In the 1990s, the United States, with surprising frequency, used its immense power on behalf of humanitarian concerns. Security and economic interests remained at the core of American foreign policy, but American power was used, repeatedly and very prominently, on behalf of the victims of repression. No less importantly, the number of reprehensible American "friends" declined dramatically.

Although the war on terrorism has not produced a dramatic reversal, today the United States much more frequently embraces repression. It seems less willing to expend its resources on behalf of human rights and humanitarian concerns. When the United States does assert itself—in an increasingly unilateral way—it is on behalf of a vision of security that has little human dimension. As a result, American interests garner much less international support.

From a human rights point of view, this represents a terrible waste of the opportunities provided by the post–cold war "unipolar moment." As the insurgency drags on in Iraq, and American practices of illegal detention, torture, and cruel and inhuman treatment of detainees continue to receive increased publicity, whatever moral high ground the United States achieved at the end of the cold war is being squandered, if not sacrificed.

If my analysis is correct, though, recovery may not be as difficult as it might appear. If the absolute place of human rights in American foreign policy has not declined, and if the Bush vision of the war on terror continues to be supported by only a narrow segment of the American electorate, then a gradual reassertion of a more central place for human rights is possible, perhaps even probable.

DISCUSSION QUESTIONS

1. How much *has* the world changed since 9/11? For Americans? Europeans? Muslims? Arabs? Israelis? Palestinians? Iraqis? Pakistanis? Afghanis? Africans? Latin Americans? East Asians?

2. *Is* it true that human rights became permanently entrenched in American and broader Western foreign policies in the 1990s? If the war on terrorism drags on, is it not likely to undercut further the progress of the 1980s and 1990s? What if dramatic acts of terrorism become an annual event in the United States? A monthly event? Just how deep does the commitment to international human rights really go?

3. Is there any evidence that human rights are making a comeback in foreign policy as the initial shock of 9/11 wears off? Is there a difference between the United States and other Western countries?

4. In the last months of 2005, as I was completing revisions of this chapter, the issue of U.S. complicity in the torture of suspects in the war on terror became a major national and international political issue. Should we really care all that much about the treatment of terror suspects? Or those who are reliably known to be terrorists? Why should terrorists be entitled to the protections of the rules they seek to overthrow?

5. Are terrorists really forcing us to conceptualize human rights and security as competing concerns? Can a war on terror be effective while respecting the full range of internationally recognized human rights for all? If not, what is the problem with limited, targeted infringements of internationally recognized human rights? Isn't this precisely the sort of emergency that justifies overriding the prima facie priority of human rights?

6. What about the *domestic* human rights impact of the war on terror? How significant are the restrictions on human rights that have been imposed since 9/11 in places like the United States and Britain? Aren't they actually very modest, and probably justifiable (even if controversial)? Certainly they shouldn't be seen in the same light as the cynical abuses of the language of antiterrorism by, say, the Russians in Chechnya, should they?

7. Let us agree that the world has become a worse place for human rights since 9/11. Isn't blaming the United States tantamount to blaming the victim?

SUGGESTED READINGS

As with globalization, the immense literature on the war on terrorism includes relatively little with a primary focus on human rights. Two important exceptions are Thomas G. Weiss, Margaret E. Crahan, and John Goering, eds., *Wars on Terrorism and Iraq: Human Rights, Unilateralism, and U.S. Foreign Policy* (New York: Routledge, 2004), and Richard Ashby Wilson, ed., *Human Rights in the 'War on Terror'* (Cambridge: Cambridge University Press, 2005). Also interesting is Thomas Cushman, ed., *A Matter of Principle: Humanitarian Arguments for War in Iraq* (Berkeley: University of California Press, 2005). See also several of the chapters in David P. Forsythe, Patrice C. McMahon, and Andrew Wedeman, *American Foreign Policy in a Globalized World* (New York: Routledge, 2006).

On the broad issue of trade-offs between human rights and security in the context of combating terrorism, see Christian Walter, ed., *Terrorism as a Challenge for National and International Law: Security versus Liberty?* (Berlin: Springer, 2004), M. Katherine B. Darmer, Robert M. Baird, and Stuart E. Rosenbaum, eds., *Civil Liberties vs. National Security in a Post-9/11 World* (Amherst, Mass.: Prometheus Books, 2004), Wolfgang Benedek and Alice Yotopoulos-Marangopoulos, eds., *Anti-Terrorist Measures and Human Rights* (Leiden: Martinus Nijhoff, 2004), and Michael Freeman, *Freedom or Security: The Consequences for Democracies Using Emergency Powers to Fight Terror* (Westport, Conn.: Praeger, 2003).

Good recent books with an American focus include Karen J. Greenberg, ed., *The Torture Debate in America* (Cambridge: Cambridge University Press, 2006), Karen J. Greenberg and Joshua L. Dratel, eds., *The Torture Papers: The Road to Abu Ghraib* (Cambridge: Cambridge University Press, 2005), and Rachel Meeropol, ed., *America's Disappeared: Detainees, Secret Imprisonment, and the 'War on Terror'* (New York: Seven Stories Press, 2005). See also William F. Schulz, *Tainted Legacy: 9/11 and the Ruin of Human Rights* (New York: Thunder's Mouth Press/Nation Books, 2003) and Ann Fagan Ginger, ed., *Challenging U.S. Human Rights Violations Since 9/11* (Amherst, Mass.: Prometheus, 2005).

Notes

Chapter One

1. Participation in the League's Minorities System, however, was forced upon a defeated Germany and the new states of Central and Eastern Europe as the price of international recognition. The victorious powers refused to be covered, even in their European territories, let alone in their colonial empires. The countries of Latin America also refused to join. And the United States was not a member of the League.

2. Although no negative votes were cast, the Soviet Union and its allies abstained, claiming that insufficient emphasis was given to economic and social rights. South Africa abstained, because of the provisions on racial equality. So did Saudi Arabia, because of the provisions on gender equality and the right of Muslims to renounce their religion (see also §3.9.A).

Chapter Two

1. This is not exactly correct. Although children are human beings, they usually are not thought to have, for example, a right to vote, on the grounds that they are not fully developed. But once they reach a certain age, they must be recognized to hold all human rights equally. Similarly, those who suffer from severe mental illness are often denied the exercise of many rights—but only until they regain full use and control of their faculties. Furthermore, both children and those with severe mental disabilities are denied the protection or exercise of only those rights for which they are held to lack the necessary requisites. They still have, and must be allowed to enjoy equally, all other human rights. And in the case of children, the 1989 Convention on the Rights of the Child seeks to clarify this special status, including rights to special protections.

2. Some other languages stress a different multiplicity of meaning in their parallel terms. For example, Spanish, French, and German all use terms—*derechos humanos, droits de l'homme, Menschenrechte*—that contain words meaning both law and rights. Were we working in one of these languages, our discussion at this point might take a slightly different route.

3. Alan Gewirth, *Human Rights: Essays on Justification and Application* (Chicago: University of Chicago Press, 1984).

4. The common argument that some internationally recognized human rights (especially civil and political rights) cannot be implemented because of the demands of economic development advocates only a temporary, and regrettable, strategic sacrifice. The arguments I am

interested in here claim that certain (more or less) permanent divergences from the norms of the Universal Declaration are intrinsically desirable.

5. Maurice Cranston, *What Are Human Rights?* (London: Bodley Head, 1973), pp. 66–67.

6. Henry Shue, *Basic Rights: Subsistence and Affluence in U.S. Foreign Policy* (Princeton: Princeton University Press, 1980, 1996), pp. 51–64.

7. In what follows, I focus on the "external" dimensions of sovereignty, that is, sovereignty as it appears in the relations of states. Here the emphasis is on the absence of any superior (sovereign) above the state and thus on the sovereign equality of states. The "internal" dimensions of sovereignty concern the supreme authority of the state within its territory. Here the focus is on the legal and political superiority of the state over other actors. In the contemporary world, internal sovereignty is usually seen to rest on the state acting in the name and interests of the people: "popular sovereignty."

8. For an extended discussion of this idea, see Hedley Bull, *The Anarchical Society* (New York: Columbia University Press, 1977).

9. Robert Gilpin, "The Richness of the Tradition of Political Realism," in *Neo-Realism and Its Critics,* ed. Robert O. Keohane (New York: Columbia University Press, 1986), p. 305.

10. Hans Morgenthau, *Politics Among Nations,* 2nd ed. (New York: Alfred A. Knopf, 1954), p. 9.

11. George F. Kennan, "Morality and Foreign Policy," *Foreign Affairs* 64 (Winter 1985–1986): 206; and *Realities of American Foreign Policy* (Princeton: Princeton University Press, 1954), p. 48.

12. George F. Kennan, *The Cloud of Danger: Current Realities of American Foreign Policy* (Boston: Little, Brown, 1977), p. 45.

13. Herbert Butterfield, *Christianity, Diplomacy, and War* (London: Epworth Press, 1953), p. 11.

14. Robert J. Art and Kenneth N. Waltz, "Technology, Strategy, and the Uses of Force," in *The Use of Force,* ed. Robert J. Art and Kenneth N. Waltz (Lanham, Md.: University Press of America, 1983), p. 6.

Chapter Three

1. Rhoda Howard has labeled this perspective "cultural absolutism." See "Cultural Absolutism and the Nostalgia for Community," *Human Rights Quarterly* 15 (May 1993): 315–318.

2. The Torture Convention provides a limited and partial system of universal jurisdiction. See §5.3.B.

3. This section draws on and summarizes the argument in Jack Donnelly, *Universal Human Rights in Theory and Practice,* 2nd ed. (Ithaca: Cornell University Press, 2003), Chapter 5.

4. Adamantia Pollis and Peter Schwab, "Introduction," in *Human Rights: Cultural and Ideological Perspectives,* ed. Adamantia Pollis and Peter Schwab (New York: Praeger, 1980), p. xiv; Yougindra Khushalani, "Human Rights in Asia and Africa," *Human Rights Law Journal* 4 (no. 4, 1983): 404.

5. It is easy, though, to overstate the significance of even this kind of universality, which is usually at such a high level of generality that it allows practices that many adherents of this "shared" value would consider savage and inhuman. For example, virtually all societies agree that it is wrong to inflict arbitrary violence on the innocent. Their conceptions of arbitrary

and innocent, however, are so varied as to render this universality (almost) empty in concrete legal and political contexts.

6. Fouad Zakaria, "Human Rights in the Arab World: The Islamic Context," in *Philosophical Foundations of Human Rights*, ed. UNESCO (Paris: UNESCO, 1986), p. 228; Abul A'la Mawdudi, *Human Rights in Islam* (Leicester: Islamic Foundation, 1976), p. 10.

7. Khalid M. Ishaque, "Human Rights in Islamic Law," *Review of the International Commission of Jurists* 12 (1974): 32–38.

8. Dunstan M. Wai, "Human Rights in Sub-Saharan Africa," in *Human Rights: Cultural and Ideological Perspectives*, ed. Adamantia Pollis and Peter Schwab (New York: Praeger, 1980), p. 116.

9. Timothy Fernyhough, "Human Rights and Precolonial Africa," in *Human Rights and Governance in Africa*, ed. Ronald Cohen, Goran Hyden, and Winston P. Nagan (Gainesville: University Press of Florida, 1993), p. 61.

10. Ibrahim Anwar, "Luncheon Address," paper presented at the JUST International Conference, "Rethinking Human Rights," Kuala Lumpur, 1994, p. 2; Radhika Coomaraswamy, "Human Rights Research and Education: An Asian Perspective," in *International Congress on the Teaching of Human Rights: Working Documents and Recommendations* (Paris: UNESCO, 1980), p. 224; Hung-Chao Tai, "Human Rights in Taiwan: Convergence of Two Political Cultures?" in *Human Rights in an East Asian Perspective*, ed. James C. Hsiung (New York: Paragon House, 1985), p. 88.

11. Tai, "Human Rights in Taiwan," p. 79.

12. Andrew J. Nathan, "Sources of Chinese Rights Thinking," in *Human Rights in Contemporary China*, ed. R. Randle Edwards, Louis Henkin, and Andrew J. Nathan (New York: Columbia University Press, 1986), p. 148.

13. Manwoo Lee, "North Korea and the Western Notion of Human Rights," in *Human Rights in an East Asian Perspective*, ed. James C. Hsiung (New York: Paragon House, 1985), p. 131.

14. Henry Shue, *Basic Rights: Subsistence, Affluence, and U.S. Foreign Policy* (Princeton: Princeton University Press, 1980, 1996), pp. 29–34.

15. Only Somalia and the United States are not parties to the Convention on the Rights of the Child. See also §5.3 and Tables 5.1 and 5.2.

16. John Rawls, *The Law of Peoples* (Cambridge: Harvard University Press, 1999), pp. 31–32, 172–173 and *Political Liberalism* (New York: Columbia University Press, 1996), pp. xliii–xlv, 11–15, 133–172, 174–176, 385–396.

17. Rawls, *Political Liberalism*, p. 133.

18. Jeremy Bentham, *Rights, Representation, and Reform: Nonsense upon Stilts and Other Writings on the French Revolution* (Oxford: Clarendon Press, 2002).

19. See, for example, John Finnis, *Natural Law and Natural Rights* (Oxford: Clarendon Press, 1980); Jacques Maritain, *The Rights of Man and Natural Law* (New York: C. Scribner's Sons, 1943).

20. The burden of proof, it seems to me, lies with those who hold otherwise. Some states may be unusually vulnerable to external pressure and thus may formally endorse international norms advocated by leading powers. (Even that seems to me not obviously correct. I read

hypocrisy more as evidence of the substantive attractions of the norms that are hypocritically endorsed.) I can see little evidence, however, that societies feel similarly compelled.

21. Donnelly, *Universal Human Rights,* §6.4.

22. Robert E. Goodin et al., *The Real Worlds of Welfare Capitalism* (Cambridge: Cambridge University Press, 1999).

23. For the purposes of the discussion here I remain agnostic as to the "we" making such judgments—although I am implicitly speaking from the perspective of an engaged participant in international society.

Chapter Four

1. Marcelo Cavarozzi, "Political Cycles in Argentina since 1955," in *Transitions from Authoritarian Rule: Latin America,* ed. Guillermo O'Donnell, Philippe C. Schmitter, and Laurence Whitehead (Baltimore: Johns Hopkins University Press, 1986).

2. Quoted in Amnesty International USA, *Disappearances: A Workbook* (New York, 1981), p. 9.

3. Guatemala was the first country to use disappearances systematically as a means of repression, in the 1960s. The practice seems to have been introduced into South America through the example of the Brazilian military in the late 1960s. For a good general introduction, see ibid.

4. Americas Watch, *Truth and Partial Justice in Argentina: An Update* (New York, 1991), p. 6. In Uruguay, however, as we will see, most of the disappeared reappeared. Chile fell somewhere in between. But the basic strategy was similar in the three countries.

5. Ian Guest, *Behind the Disappearances: Argentina's Dirty War Against Human Rights and the United Nations* (Philadelphia: University of Pennsylvania Press, 1990), p. 41.

6. V. S. Naipaul, *The Return of Eva Perón* (New York: Vintage Books, 1981), pp. 170, 162.

7. Lawrence Weschler, *A Miracle, a Universe: Settling Accounts with Torturers* (New York: Pantheon Books, 1990), p. 145.

8. John Simpson and Jana Bennett, *The Disappeared: Voices from a Secret War* (London: Robson Books, 1985), p. 225.

9. Ibid.

10. Quoted in ibid., p. 66.

11. In fact, one of the tragic ironies in Uruguay was that the Tupamaros had already been destroyed before the coup. In Chile there was no guerrilla threat at all.

12. Lawyers' Committee for International Human Rights, *The Generals Give Back Uruguay* (New York, 1985), p. 57; Weschler, *A Miracle, a Universe,* p. 112; Inter-Church Committee on Human Rights in Latin America, *Violations of Human Rights in Uruguay* (Toronto, 1978), p. 7; Martin Weinstein, *Uruguay: Democracy at the Crossroads* (Boulder: Westview Press, 1988), pp. 44, 52; David Pion-Berlin, *The Ideology of State Terror: Economic Doctrine and Political Repression in Argentina and Peru* (Boulder: Lynne Rienner, 1989), p. 101.

13. Simpson and Bennett, *The Disappeared,* p. 110.

14. See Americas Watch, *The Vicaria de la Solidaridad in Chile* (New York, 1987).

15. Lawyers' Committee for International Human Rights, *The Generals Give Back Uruguay,* pp. 32–35.

16. See Weschler, *A Miracle, a Universe,* pp. 173–236.

17. Hannah Arendt, *The Human Condition* (Chicago: University of Chicago Press, 1958), p. 241.

18. From Zbigniew Herbert, "Mr. Cogito on the Need for Precision," quoted in Weschler, *A Miracle, a Universe,* p. 191.

Chapter Five

1. Stephen D. Krasner, "Structural Causes and Regime Consequences: Regimes as Intervening Variables," in *International Regimes,* ed. Stephen D. Krasner (Ithaca: Cornell University Press, 1982), p. 2.

2. See http://www.unhr.ch/html/menu2/8/1503.htm.

3. For a complete list of countries considered, see http://www.unhchr.ch/html/menu2/8/stat1.htm.

4. See http://hrw.org/english/docs/2003/04/25/global5796.htm.

5. Optional procedures for complaints by one state against another have never been used.

6. Those interested in a sampling of the kinds of decisions taken by the HRC probably should begin with http://www.ohchr.org/english/about/publications/docs/sdecisions-vol6.pdf, the most recent compilation of decisions currently available online, covering the years 1996–1999.

7. The possibilities for evolving interpretations are suggested by the fact that the HRC has issued a second set of general comments on four articles on which it previously commented more than a decade earlier.

8. The 1990 International Convention on the Protection of the Rights of Migrant Workers and Members of Their Families envisions a similar procedure. The convention, however, did not enter into force until 2003 and at the end of 2005 had only 34 parties.

9. See http://www.unhchr.ch/tbs/doc.nsf/newhvoverduebytreaty?OpenView&Collapse-View. Only the Convention on the Rights of the Child has fewer late reports than parties. Comprehensive state-by-state data is presented at http://www.ohchr.org/english/bodies/docs/RRH.pdf.

10. This was no coincidence. In fact, one could largely plot economically worthless land by looking at a map of the Homelands. For example, Bophuthatswana was made up of nineteen separate pieces. KwaZulu contained twenty-nine major and forty-one minor pieces of unconnected territory. And mineral rights were not even formally placed under the control of the Homeland governments.

11. Work is also under way on a treaty on the rights of persons with disabilities, finally building on the 1975 Declaration on the Rights of Disabled Persons. If a new treaty-based single-issue regime emerges in the next few years, it is likely to be here.

12. A two-tier system, involving a separate commission that considered complaints before they went to the Court, was revamped in the late 1990s, in part because of an increased post–cold war caseload, to provide direct access to an expanded system of regional judicial enforcement. In addition, jurisdiction of the Court was made compulsory (previously states had the option to participate only in the Commission, not the Court).

13. Cecilia Medina Quiroga, *The Battle of Human Rights: Gross, Systematic Violations and the Inter-American System* (Dordrecht: Martinus Nijhoff, 1988), p. 312.

14. For a discussion of national human rights NGOs in Chile, see §4.4.

15. For a detailed account of Argentina's efforts in the United Nations, see Ian Guest, *Behind the Disappearances: Argentina's Dirty War Against Human Rights and the United Nations* (Philadelphia: University of Pennsylvania Press, 1990), pt. 2.

16. See Robert Pastor, *Condemned to Repetition: The United States and Nicaragua* (Princeton: Princeton University Press, 1987), pp. 149–151.

17. Quoted in Helsinki Watch Committee, *The Moscow Helsinki Monitors: Their Vision, Their Achievement, the Price They Paid, May 12, 1976–May 12, 1986* (New York, 1986), p. 5.

18. For up-to-date information, see OSCE's excellent Web site: http://www.osce.org/.

Chapter Six

1. The domestic and international sides of this arrogance come together in the reluctance of the United States to ratify international human rights treaties. Only in 1992, more than a quarter century after it was adopted, did the United States ratify the International Covenant on Civil and Political Rights. No serious consideration has been given to ratification of the International Covenant on Economic, Social, and Cultural Rights.

2. Liisa Lukkari North, "El Salvador," in *International Handbook of Human Rights,* ed. Jack Donnelly and Rhoda E. Howard (Westport, Conn.: Greenwood Press, 1987), pp. 125–126.

3. Lars Schoultz, *National Security and United States Policy Toward Latin America* (Princeton: Princeton University Press, 1987), p. xi.

4. Jeane J. Kirkpatrick, "Dictatorships and Double Standards," *Commentary* 68 (November 1979).

5. The Committee of Santa Fe, *A New Inter-American Policy for the Eighties* (Washington, D.C.: Council for Inter-American Security, 1980), p. 37.

6. See, for example, Americas Watch Committee and the American Civil Liberties Union, *As BAD as Ever: A Report on Human Rights in El Salvador* (New York, 1984).

7. Americas Watch, *Annual Report, June 1984–June 1985* (New York, 1985), p. 4.

8. Cynthia Brown, ed., *With Friends like These: The Americas Watch Report on Human Rights and U.S. Policy in Latin America* (New York: Pantheon Books, 1985), p. 20. Compare with the Watch Committees and Lawyers' Committee for Human Rights, *The Reagan Administration's Record on Human Rights in 1986* (New York, 1987), pp. 49, 92–99, and *The Reagan Administration's Record on Human Rights in 1987* (New York, 1988), p. 106. On the Reagan administration's systematic misrepresentation of the facts, see Americas Watch, *Managing the Facts: How the Administration Deals with Reports of Human Rights Abuses in El Salvador* (New York, 1985).

9. This is not to suggest that human rights ought to have been at the top (or even necessarily that they ought not to be at the bottom). My purpose here is simply to describe the place of human rights concerns in the policies of the two administrations.

10. Christopher Coker, *The United States and South Africa, 1968–1985: Constructive Engagement and Its Critics* (Durham, N.C.: Duke University Press, 1986), p. 105.

11. The two quoted passages were taken from Olav Stokke, "Norwegian Aid: Policy and Performance," in *European Development Assistance,* ed. Olav Stokke (Oslo: Norwegian Institute of International Affairs, 1984), pp. 328–329; and Olav Stokke, "The Determinants of Norwegian Aid Policy," in Stokke, *European Development Assistance,* p. 170.

12. Quoted in Charles Cooper and Joan Verloren van Themaat, "Dutch Aid Determinants, 1973–85: Continuity and Change," in *Western Middle Powers and Global Poverty: The Determi-*

nants of the Aid Policies of Canada, Denmark, the Netherlands, Norway, and Sweden, ed. Olav Stokke (Uppsala: Almquist and Wiksell International, 1989), p. 119.

13. Peter Baehr, Hilde Selbervik, and Arne Tostensen, "Responses to Human Rights Criticism: Kenya-Norway and Indonesia-the Netherlands," in *Human Rights in Developing Countries: 1995* (The Hague: Kluwer Law International, 1995), p. 79. The discussion in this paragraph and the next draws heavily on this article.

14. Jan Egeland, *Impotent Superpower—Potent Small State: Potentialities and Limitations of Human Rights Objectives in the Foreign Policies of the United States and Norway* (Oslo: Norwegian University Press, 1988), pp. 3, 5.

15. Ibid., p. 15.

16. *Statements and Speeches* 82/12 (Ottawa: Bureau of Information, Department of External Affairs). Quoted in Rhoda E. Howard and Jack Donnelly, *Confronting Revolution in Nicaragua: U.S. and Canadian Responses* (New York: Carnegie Council on Ethics and International Affairs, 1990).

17. Egeland, *Impotent Superpower,* p. 23.

18. Norway and the Netherlands are usually the world's two leading aid providers on a per capita basis, for most of the past thirty years contributing eight to ten times more per capita than the United States.

19. Students of comparative politics usually refer to this as a "corporatist" system. Each well-defined segment of society—each "corporate" group—is seen as entitled to have its interests taken into account, even if it is at the moment politically out of power. The United States, by contrast, tends to operate with a "winner-take-all" approach, as the early years of the Reagan revolution demonstrated clearly.

Chapter Seven

1. Fang Lizhi, "Declaration to Support Democratic Reform in Mainland China," *World Affairs* 152, 3 (Winter 1989–1990): 136–137.

2. *World Affairs* 152 (3) (Winter 1989–1990): 138.

3. Jonathan D. Spence, *The Search for Modern China* (New York: W. W. Norton, 1990), p. 742.

4. The statue, however, was a late and rather desperate gesture calculated to appeal to the United States more than to the Chinese people. Any Chinese who would have responded positively to this ostentatiously foreign symbol certainly were already mobilized behind the students.

5. Assuming a growth rate of one-third raises the cost to over $15 billion. China also lost access to about $1 billion in World Bank loans for the better part of a year. Assessing the impact on private funding is more complex. Commercial borrowing was stagnant from 1987 through 1992. Direct foreign investment stagnated from 1988 through 1990, grew some in 1991, and then took off dramatically in 1992 (Nicholas R. Landy, *China in the World Economy* [Washington, D.C.: Institute for International Economics, 1994], tables 3.6 and 3.7). Structural economic and legal factors lie at the root of these lulls, which predate Tiananmen. Nonetheless, most observers had expected a surge in foreign investment in late 1989 and 1990. This seems to have been delayed until 1991–1992, at a cost to China of another few billion dollars.

6. The discussion of Japanese policy here draws heavily on K. V. Kesavan, "Japan and the Tiananmen Square Incident," *Asian Survey* 30 (July 1990): 669–681, and David Arase, "Japanese Policy Toward Democracy and Human Rights in Asia," *Asian Survey* 33 (October 1993): 935–952.

7. Actual Japanese loan disbursements to China, however, did drop from a high of $670 million in 1989 to $539 million in 1990 and to $424 million in 1991 (almost exactly the 1987 level), in contrast to the large increases anticipated when the new five-year aid plan was approved in August 1988. See Landy, *China in the World Economy*, table 3.5b. Thus, even Japan's most reluctant sanctions had immediate and direct economic costs to China of perhaps $2 billion.

8. Peter Van Ness, "Australia's Human Rights Delegation to China, 1991: A Case Study," in *Australia's Human Rights Diplomacy*, by Ian Russell, Peter Van Ness, and Beng-Huat Chua (Canberra: Australian National University, Australian Foreign Policy Papers, 1992), p. 83.

9. China considers Tibet an integral part of its territory. Others consider it an occupied country. In either case, Tibetan culture and religion have been under sustained and often violent attack for more than half a century.

10. David M. Lampton, "America's China Policy in the Age of the Finance Minister: Clinton Ends Linkage," *China Quarterly* 139 (September 1994): 615.

11. Quoted in Bruce Stokes, "Playing Favorites," *National Journal*, March 26, 1994, p. 714.

12. Thomas Friedman, in the next day's *New York Times*, quoted in Lampton, "America's China Policy," p. 597.

13. Ann Kent, "China and the International Human Rights Regime: A Case Study of Multilateral Monitoring, 1989–1994," *Human Rights Quarterly* 17 (February 1995): 17.

14. Nihal Jayawikcrama, "Human Rights Exception No Longer," in *The Broken Mirror: China After Tiananmen*, ed. George Hicks (Farmington Hills, Mich.: St. James Press, 1990), p. 362, quoted in Kent, "Multilateral Monitoring," p. 15.

15. Quoted in Kent, "Multilateral Monitoring," p. 13.

16. Kent, "Multilateral Monitoring," p. 21.

17. Ibid., p. 12.

18. "U.S. Interference Protested," *Beijing Review* 32 (June 12–25, 1989): 10. Note that the scheduled June 12–18 issue did not appear.

19. Ding Xinghao, "Managing Sino-American Relations in a Changing World," *Asian Survey* 31 (December 1991): 1168.

20. Kent, "Multilateral Monitoring," p. 21.

21. *Economist*, October 26, 1996. For the curious, the firm was Mobil.

22. Quoted in Stokes, "Playing Favorites," p. 713.

23. Bilahari Kausikan, "Asia's Different Standard," *Foreign Policy* 92 (1993): 37.

Chapter Eight

1. Lawrence Freeman, "Why the West Failed," *Foreign Policy* 97 (Winter 1994–1995): 59, quoted in Thomas G. Weiss and Cindy Collins, *Humanitarian Challenges and Intervention* (Boulder: Westview Press, 1996), p. 84.

2. I use the term bilateral rather than unilateral to emphasize the fact that the "unilateral" intervener operates within a bilateral relationship with the target country. In evaluating the in-

tervention, the internal and external behavior of the target is essential. One judges the bilateral interaction, not a unilateral act.

3. In such cases, it may be difficult to distinguish between bilateral and multilateral regional action. Consider, for example, the use of the Organization of Eastern Caribbean States as a cover for U.S. intervention in Grenada.

4. The case of Kosovo also raises the specter of what might be called coercive regionalism, in which the target of action is not a member of the intervening "regional" community. In partial rebuttal, however, one might argue that the NATO intervention was in pursuance of emerging OSCE norms; that is, NATO was remedying a legal/institutional defect in the emerging European security regime and thus acting with considerable moral and even political authority.

5. Almost all interventions are likely to be contested in the sense that someone other than the target objects on some ground. Here I am interested only in contested justifications that arise from conflicting principles that have wide and deep endorsement within international society.

6. Peter R. Baehr, "Controversies in the Current International Human Rights Debate," *Human Rights Review* 2, no. 1 (2000): 32, note 75.

7. As we saw in Chapter 4, the juntas that ruled Argentina during the Dirty War could, with apparent seriousness, justify the arbitrary murder of more than 10,000 Argentinians, and probably as many as 20,000, as a matter of (national) security. Even more importantly, such claims resonated with a significant proportion of the governments of the world, including the United States. Even making such a claim today would be difficult. And the number of governments that would give serious consideration to such arguments is today more like a few handfuls, in contrast to the several dozen of thirty years ago.

Chapter Nine

1. Alison Brysk, *From Tribal Village to Global Village: Indian Rights and International Relations in Latin America* (Stanford: Stanford University Press, 2000).

2. Margaret E. Keck and Kathryn Sikkink, *Activists Beyond Borders: Advocacy Networks in International Politics* (Ithaca: Cornell University Press, 1998).

3. John Gerard Ruggie, "International Regimes, Transactions, and Change: Embedded Liberalism in the Postwar Economic Order," *International Organization* 36 (Spring 1982): 397–415.

Chapter Ten

1. For a good general overview of the work of the 1990s, see Marina Ottaway and Thomas Carothers, eds., *Funding Virtue: Civil Society Aid and Democracy Promotion* (Washington, D.C.: Carnegie Endowment for International Peace, 2000).

2. Bureaucratically, it was reflected in the change from the Bureau of Human Rights and Humanitarian Affairs to the Bureau of Democracy, Human Rights, and Labor.

3. Human Rights Watch, *In the Name of Counter-Terrorism: Human Rights Abuses Worldwide,* http://hrw.org/un/chr59/counter-terrorism-bck4.htm#P286_64797.

4. For an overview of the human rights situation in Chechnya, see Human Rights Watch, *Russia: Abuses in Chechnya Continue to Cause Human Suffering* (January 29, 2003), http://www.hrw.org/press/2003/01/russia012903.htm; and *Human Rights Situation in Chechnya* (April 2003) http://www.hrw.org/backgrounder/eca/chechnya/index.htm. For current (although in some cases not entirely nonpartisan) information, see http://www.watchdog.cz/.

5. "Since it launched a military operation in Chechnya in 1999, Russia's leaders have described the armed conflict there as a counter-terrorism operation and have attempted to fend off international scrutiny of Russian forces' abusive conduct by invoking the imperative of fighting terrorism. This pattern has become more pronounced since the September 11 attacks, as Russia sought to convince the international community that its operation in Chechnya was its contribution to the international campaign against terrorism. . . . World leaders, until then critical of Russia's conduct in Chechnya, did little to challenge these claims." *Human Rights Situation in Chechnya* (April 2003), http://www.hrw.org/backgrounder/eca/chechnya/index.htm.

6. Information on Israeli human rights violations is highly politicized. B'Tselem, the Israeli Information Center for Human Rights in the Occupied Territories, is perhaps the best neutral source. See www.betselem.org.

7. For a powerful illustration of this phenomenon in microcosm, see *Al-Mawazi, Gaza Strip: Intolerable Life in an Isolated Enclave* (B'Tselem, March 2003), http://www.betselem.org/Download/2003_Al_Mwassy_Eng.pdf.

8. Political assassinations—if not terrorism, then extra-judicial executions—have become a regular part of the Israeli response to terrorism. In Chechnya, torture has become so pervasive that in the summer of 2003 the European Committee for the Prevention of Torture issued a rare public statement (http://www.cpt.coe.int/documents/rus/2003–33-inf-eng.htm), following strongly worded criticism by the Parliamentary Assembly of the Council of Europe in the spring.

9. For appeals by human rights NGOs calling on Western states to be more vocal on the issue of Chechnya, see http://www.hrw.org/press/2003/06/russia062003.htm, http://www.hrw.org/press/2003/05/russia053003.htm, and http://www.reliefweb.int/w/rwb.nsf/0/5404f2f0528bc31949256cb6000da38f?OpenDocument.

Appendix:
Universal Declaration of Human Rights

GENERAL ASSEMBLY
RESOLUTION 217A (III), 10 DECEMBER 1948

Whereas recognition of the inherent dignity and of the equal and inalienable rights of all members of the human family is the foundation of freedom, justice and peace in the world,

Whereas disregard and contempt for human rights have resulted in barbarous acts which have outraged the conscience of mankind, and the advent of a world in which human beings shall enjoy freedom of speech and belief and freedom from fear and want has been proclaimed as the highest aspiration of the common people,

Whereas it is essential, if man is not to be compelled to have recourse, as a last resort, to rebellion against tyranny and oppression, that human rights should be protected by the rule of law,

Whereas it is essential, to promote the development of friendly relations between nations,

Whereas the peoples of the United Nations have in the Charter reaffirmed their faith in fundamental human rights, in the dignity and worth of the human person and in the equal rights of men and women and have determined to promote social progress and better standards of life in larger freedom,

Whereas Member States have pledged themselves to achieve, in co-operation with the United Nations, the promotion of universal respect for and observance of human rights and fundamental freedoms,

Whereas a common understanding of these rights and freedoms is of the greatest importance for the full realization of this pledge,

Now, therefore,

The General Assembly

Proclaims this Universal Declaration of Human Rights as a common standard of achievement for all peoples and all nations, to the end that every individual and every organ of society, keeping this Declaration constantly in mind, shall strive by teaching and education to promote respect for these rights and freedoms and by progressive measures, national and international, to secure their universal and effective recognition and observance, both among the peoples of Member States themselves and among the peoples of territories under their jurisdiction.

Article 1.   All human beings are born free and equal in dignity and rights. They are endowed with reason and conscience and should act towards one another in a spirit of brotherhood.

Article 2.   Everyone is entitled to all the rights and freedoms set forth in this Declaration, without distinction of any kind, such as race, colour, sex, language, religion, political or other opinion, national or social origin, property, birth or other status.

Furthermore, no distinction shall be made on the basis of the political, jurisdictional or international status of the country or territory to which a person belongs, whether it be independent, trust, non-self-governing or under any other limitation of sovereignty.

Article 3.   Everyone has the right to life, liberty and the security of person.

Article 4.   No one shall be held in slavery or servitude; slavery and the slave trade shall be prohibited in all their forms.

Article 5.   No one shall be subjected to torture or to cruel, inhuman or degrading treatment or punishment.

Article 6.   Everyone has the right to recognition everywhere as a person before the law.

Article 7.   All are equal before the law and are entitled without any discrimination to equal protection of the law. All are entitled to equal protection against any discrimination in violation of this Declaration and against any incitement to such discrimination.

Article 8.   Everyone has the right to an effective remedy by the competent national tribunals for acts violating the fundamental rights granted him by the constitution or by law.

Article 9.   No one shall be subjected to arbitrary arrest, detention or exile.

Article 10.   Everyone is entitled to full equality to a fair and public hearing by an independent and impartial tribunal in the determination of his rights and obligations and of any criminal charge against him.

Article 11.   1. Everyone charged with a penal offence has the right to be presumed innocent until proved guilty according to law in a public trial at which he has had all the guarantees necessary for his defence.

2. No one shall be held guilty of any penal offence on account of any act or omission which did not constitute a penal offence, under national or international law, at the time when it was committed. Nor shall a heavier penalty be imposed than the one that was applicable at the time the penal offence was committed.

Article 12.   No one shall be subjected to arbitrary interference with his privacy, family, home or correspondence, nor to attacks upon his honour and reputation. Everyone has the right to the protection of the law against such interference or attacks.

Article 13.   1. Everyone has the right to freedom of movement and residence within the borders of each state.

2. Everyone has the right to leave any country, including his own, and to return to his country.

Article 14.   1. Everyone has the right to seek and to enjoy in other countries asylum from persecution.

2. This right may not be invoked in the case of prosecutions genuinely arising from non-political crimes or from acts contrary to the purposes and principles of the United Nations.

Article 15.   1. Everyone has the right to a nationality.

2. No one shall be arbitrarily deprived of his nationality nor denied the right to change his nationality.

Article 16.   1. Men and women of full age, without any limitation due to race, nationality or religion, have the right to marry and to found a family. They are entitled to equal rights as to marriage, during marriage and at its dissolution.

2. Marriage shall be entered into only with the free and full consent of the intending spouses.

3. The family is the natural and fundamental group unit of society and is entitled to protection by society and the State.

Article 17.   1. Everyone has the right to own property alone as well as in association with others.

2. No one shall be arbitrarily deprived of his property.

Article 18.   Everyone has the right to freedom of thought, conscience and religion; this right includes freedom to change his religion or belief, and freedom, either alone or in community with others and in public or private, to manifest his religion or belief in teaching, practice, worship and observance.

Article 19.   Everyone has the right to freedom of opinion and expression; this right includes freedom to hold opinions without interference and to seek, receive and impart information and ideas through any media and regardless of frontiers.

Article 20.   1. Everyone has the right to freedom of peaceful assembly and association.

2. No one may be compelled to belong to an association.

Article 21.   1. Everyone has the right to take part in the Government of his country, directly or through freely chosen representatives.

2. Everyone has the right of equal access to public service in his country.

3. The will of the people shall be the basis of the authority of government; this will shall be expressed in periodic and genuine elections which shall be by universal and equal suffrage and shall be held by secret vote or by equivalent free voting procedures.

Article 22.   Everyone, as a member of society, has the right to social security and is entitled to realization through national effort and international co-operation and in accordance with the organization and resources of each State, of the economic, social and cultural rights indispensable for his dignity and the free development of his personality.

Article 23.   1. Everyone has the right to work, to free choice of employment, to just and favourable conditions of work and to protection against unemployment.

2. Everyone, without any discrimination, has the right to equal pay for equal work.

3. Everyone who works has the right to just and favourable remuneration insuring for himself and his family an existence worthy of human dignity, and supplemented, if necessary, by other means of social protection.

4. Everyone has the right to form and to join trade unions for the protection of his interests.

Article 24.   Everyone has the right to rest and leisure, including reasonable limitation of working hours and periodic holidays with pay.

Article 25.   1. Everyone has the right to a standard of living adequate for the health and well-being of himself and of his family, including food, clothing, housing and medical care and necessary social services, and the right to security in the event of unemployment, sickness, disability, widowhood, old age or other lack of livelihood in circumstances beyond his control.

2. Motherhood and childhood are entitled to special care and assistance. All children, whether born in or out of wedlock, shall enjoy the same social protection.

Article 26.   1. Everyone has the right to education. Education shall be free, at least in the elementary and fundamental stages. Elementary education shall be compulsory. Technical and professional education shall be made generally available and higher education shall be equally accessible to all on the basis of merit.

2. Education shall be directed to the full development of the human personality and to the strengthening of respect for human rights and fundamental freedoms. It shall promote understanding, tolerance and friendship among all nations, racial or religious groups, and shall further the activities of the United Nations for the maintenance of peace.

3. Parents have a prior right to choose the kind of education that shall be given to their children.

Article 27.   1. Everyone has the right freely to participate in the cultural life of the community, to enjoy the arts and share in scientific advancement and its benefits.

2. Everyone has the right to the protection of the moral and material interests resulting from any scientific, literary or artistic production of which he is the author.

Article 28.   Everyone is entitled to a social and international order in which the rights and freedoms set forth in this Declaration can be fully realized.

Article 29.   1. Everyone has duties to the community in which alone the free and full development of his personality is possible.

2. In the exercise of his rights and freedoms, everyone shall be subject only to such limitations as are determined by law solely for the purpose of securing due recognition and respect for the rights and freedoms of others and of meeting the just requirements of morality, public order and the general welfare in a democratic society.

3. These rights and freedoms may in no case be exercised contrary to the purposes and principles of the United Nations.

Article 30.   Nothing in this Declaration may be interpreted as implying for any State, group or person any right to engage in any activity or to perform any act aimed at the destruction of any of the rights and freedoms set forth herein.

Glossary

American exceptionalism is the belief that the United States is culturally and politically different from, and usually superior to, other countries. It can be traced to the colonial period and the biblical image of the city on the hill. In the area of human rights, it tends to be expressed in the common American view that the United States in some important sense defines international human rights standards.

Anarchy, the absence of political rule, is characterized by the lack of authoritative hierarchical relationships of superiority and subordination. In international relations, anarchy refers to the fact that there is no higher authority above states. Anarchy, however, need not involve chaos (absence of order). Thus, international relations has been called an anarchical society, a society in which order emerges from the interactions of formally equally sovereign states.

Apartheid, an Afrikaans term meaning "separateness," was the policy of systematic, official racial classification and discrimination in South Africa. Building on a long tradition of racial discrimination, white South African governments in the 1950s and 1960s developed an unusually extensive, highly integrated system of official discrimination touching virtually all aspects of public life and many aspects of private life as well. The policy was officially renounced following a (whites only) plebiscite in March 1992.

The **categorical imperative** is Kant's fundamental principle of morality. Kant argues that there is one and only one fundamental moral principle: Act so that you always treat other people as ends, never as means only. This principle is an imperative (a command), and it is categorical (it applies without exception, in all times, places, and circumstances). It is a classic example of deontological ethics, moral systems that focus on the inherent character of an act (and the intentions of the actor) rather than on the consequences of acts.

Civil and political rights are one of two principal classes of internationally recognized human rights. They provide protections against the state (such as rights to due process, habeas corpus, and freedom of speech) and require that the state provide certain substantive legal and political opportunities (such as the rights to vote and to trial by a jury of one's peers). They are codified in the International Covenant on Civil and Political Rights and in Articles 1–15, 18–21 of the Universal Declaration of Human Rights (see Table 1.1).

Cold war is the term used for the geopolitical and ideological struggle between the Soviet Union and the United States following World War II. It began in earnest roughly in 1948, waxed and waned over the following forty years, and finally ended with the collapse of the Soviet bloc in 1989.

Cosmopolitan and **cosmopolitanism** refer to a conception of international relations that views people first and foremost as individual members of a global political community ("cosmopolis") rather than as citizens of states.

Disappearances are a form of human rights violation that became popular in the 1970s. Victims, rather than being officially detained or even murdered by the authorities or semiofficial death squads, are "disappeared," taken to state-run but clandestine detention centers. Torture typically accompanies disappearance, and in some countries the disappeared have also been regularly killed.

Economic, social, and cultural rights are one of two classes of internationally recognized human rights. They guarantee individuals socially provided goods and services (such as food, health care, social insurance, and education) and certain protections against the state (especially in family matters). They are codified in the International Covenant on Economic, Social, and Cultural Rights and in Articles 16–17, and 22–27 of the Universal Declaration of Human Rights (see Table 1.1).

Ethnic cleansing is the genocidal "purification" of the population of a territory through murder and forced migration. The term entered international political vocabularies to describe the strategy and practices of Serbian separatists in the former Yugoslavian republic of Bosnia-Herzegovina during the civil war of 1992–1995.

The **1503 procedure** is an investigatory procedure (established by ECOSOC Resolution 1503) of the United Nations Commission on Human Rights that deals with situations of gross, persistent, and systematic violations of human rights.

Genocide, in the narrow technical sense of the term, involves systematic killing and similar methods aimed at destroying, in whole or in part, a people *(genos)* or ethnic or religious group. In a looser sense of the term, it involves targeted mass political killing—"politicide"—directed against a group that may not be defined by common descent.

The **Helsinki process** is an informal description of the human rights activities undertaken within the Conference on Security and Co-operation in Europe (CSCE). The term derives from the Helsinki Final Act of 1975, which defined the terms of reference of the CSCE.

Human rights, the rights that one has simply because one is a human being, are held equally and inalienably by all human beings. They are the social and political guarantees necessary to protect individuals from the standard threats to human dignity posed by the modern state and modern markets.

The **Human Rights Committee** is a body of 18 independent experts created by the International Covenant on Civil and Political Rights. Its principal activities are reviewing periodic state reports on compliance with the Covenant and reviewing individual complaints of violations. Compare **treaty bodies.**

Humanitarian intervention is **intervention** (see below), almost always involving the use of force, for humanitarian purposes, typically in situations of genocide, armed conflict, or severe humanitarian crisis (especially massive famine).

An **intergovernmental organization**—often referred to as an international organization—is a treaty-based organization of states. Prominent global examples include the United Nations and the World Health Organization. The European Union is the most prominent regional example. Compare nongovernmental organization.

The **International Bill of Human Rights** is the informal name for the Universal Declaration of Human Rights and the International Human Rights Covenants, considered collectively as a set of authoritative international human rights standards. This title underscores the substantive interrelations of these three documents.

The **International Human Rights Covenants** comprise the International Covenant on Economic, Social, and Cultural Rights and the International Covenant on Civil and Political Rights, which were opened for signature in 1966 and entered into force in 1976. Along with the Universal Declaration of Human Rights, these are the central normative documents in the field of international human rights.

An **international regime** is a set of principles, norms, rules, and decision-making procedures accepted by states (and other relevant international actors) as binding in an issue area. The notion of a regime points to patterns of international governance that are not necessarily limited to a single treaty or organization.

Internationalist and **internationalism** refer to a conception of international relations that stresses both the centrality of the state and the existence of social relations among those states. See also **society of states**.

Intervention, as the term is used in international law and relations, means coercive interference, usually involving the threat or use of force, against the sovereignty, territorial integrity or political independence, or any matters essentially within the domestic jurisdiction, of a state.

The **like-minded countries** are a group of about a dozen small and medium-sized Western countries, including Canada, the Netherlands, and the Nordic countries. They often act in concert in international organizations and generally pursue foreign policies that are more "liberal" than those of the United States, Japan, or the larger Western European countries. The like-minded countries particularly emphasize development issues, and they have tried to play an intermediary role between the countries of the South and the larger northern countries.

A **nongovernmental organization (NGO)** is a private association of individuals or groups that engages in political activity. International NGOs (INGOs) carry on their activities across state boundaries. The most prominent human rights INGOs include Amnesty International, Human Rights Watch, and the Minority Rights Group. In some areas, especially international relief, NGOs are frequently referred to as private voluntary organizations (PVOs).

Nonintervention is the international obligation not to interfere in matters that are essentially within the domestic jurisdiction of a sovereign state. This duty is correlative to the right of sovereignty and expresses the principal practical implications of sovereignty, viewed from the perspective of other states.

Peacekeeping involves the use of lightly armed multilateral forces to separate previously warring parties. Peacekeeping is distinguished from collective security enforcement by a limited mandate, an effort to maintain neutrality, and reliance on the consent of the parties in whose territory peacekeepers are placed.

Quiet diplomacy is the pursuit of foreign policy objectives through official channels, without recourse to public statements or actions. A standard mechanism for pursuing virtually all foreign policy goals, it became a political issue in the United States in the late 1970s and 1980s, when conservative critics of the policy of the Carter administration and defenders of the policy of the Reagan administration argued that U.S. international human rights policy toward "friendly" (anticommunist) regimes should in most cases be restricted *solely* to quiet diplomacy.

Realism (Realpolitik) is a theory of international relations that stresses the absence of international government (that is, the presence of international **anarchy**) and the centrality of egoism in human motivation, thus requiring states to give priority to power and security in international relations and to exclude considerations of morality from foreign policy.

A **relativist** believes that values are not universal but are a function of contingent circumstances. **Cultural relativism** holds that morality is significantly determined by culture and history. Marxism is another form of **ethical relativism**, holding that values are reflections of the interests of the ruling class. **Radical relativism** sees culture as the source of all values.

The **society of states** conceptualizes "the international community" as a largely contractual community whose principal members are states. See also **internationalism**.

To be **sovereign** is to be subject to no higher authority. International relations over the past three centuries have been structured around the principle of the **sovereignty** of territorial states.

Statist and **statism** refer to a theory of international relations that stresses the centrality of sovereign states. Realism is usually associated with a statist theory of international relations.

A **treaty** is an agreement between states that creates obligations on those states. Treaties are one of the two principal sources of international law, along with custom (regularized patterns of action that through repeated practice have created expectations and thus acquired an obligatory character). The two most important international human rights treaties are the International Covenant on Economic, Social, and Cultural Rights and the International Covenant on Civil and Political Rights.

Treaty bodies is the term of art used for the various committees created under the International Human Rights Covenants and other international human rights treaties to monitor state compliance. Compare **Human Rights Committee**.

The **Universal Declaration of Human Rights** is a 1948 General Assembly resolution that provides the most authoritative statement of international human rights norms. Together with the International Human Rights Covenants, it is sometimes referred to as the **International Bill of Human Rights.**

Universalism is the belief that moral values such as human rights are fundamentally the same at all times and in all places. It is the opposite of **relativism.**

Utilitarianism is a moral theory (most closely associated with Bentham and Mill) that holds that the right course of action is that which maximizes the balance of pleasure over pain. This is the most common form of consequentialist ethics, which focus on the consequences of acts rather than their inherent character.

Index